#5 ✓

D1376641

Science Fiction

and the New Dark Age

Harold L. Berger

BOWLING GREEN UNIVERSITY POPULAR PRESS
BOWLING GREEN, OHIO 43403

Copyright © 1976 by The Popular Press

Library of Congress Card Number 76-1054

ISBN: 0-87972-121-9
       0-87972-122-7

Artwork by Gregg Swope

PN
3448
S45B44

10.75   UPBS   2/14/77

ACKNOWLEDGEMENTS

ARKHAM HOUSE, PUBLISHERS. *The Mind Parasites* by Colin Wilson. Reprinted by permission of Arkham House, Publishers, Sauk City, Wisconsin.

BANTAM BOOKS, INC. *The Spook Who Sat by the Door* by Sam Greenlee, copyright © 1969 by Sam Greenlee. Published by Bantam Books by arrangement with Allison & Busby, Limited.

THE BOBBS-MERRILL COMPANY, INC. *The Measure of Man* by Joseph Wood Krutch, copyright © 1953, 1954 by Joseph Wood Krutch. Reprinted by permission of the Publisher, The Bobbs-Merrill Company, Inc.

BRANDT & BRANDT. *Nineteen Eighty-Four* by George Orwell, copyright © 1949 by Harcourt Brace Jovanovich, Inc. Reprinted by permission of Brandt & Brandt.

THE CAXTON PRINTERS, LTD. *Anthem* by Ayn Rand. The Caxton Printers, Ltd., Caldwell, Idaho.

CHAD WALSH. *From Utopia to Nightmare* by Chad Walsh (New York: Harper), 1962. By permission of Chad Walsh.

DELACORTE PRESS. *Player Piano* by Kurt Vonnegut, Jr., copyright © 1952 by Kurt Vonnegut, Jr.

DELL PUBLISHING CO., INC. *The Status Civilization* by Robert Sheckley, copyright © 1960 by Robert Sheckley.

413542

DIAL PRESS. *Triage* by Leonard C. Lewin, copyright © 1972 by
    Leonard C. Lewin.
DOUBLEDAY & COMPANY, INC. *The Caves of Steel* by Isaac
    Asimov, copyright © 1953, 1954 by Isaac Asimov. *Dance
    the Eagle to Sleep* by Marge Piercy, copyright © 1970 by
    Marge Piercy. *The Day Before Forever* by Keith Laumer,
    copyright © 1967 by Mercury Press, Inc., copyright © 1967
    by Galaxy Publishing Corp., copyright © 1968 by Keith
    Laumer. *The End of the Dream* by Philip Wylie, copyright ©
    1972 by Fredericka B. Wylie. "The Evitable Conflict" by
    Isaac Asimov, copyright © 1950 by Street and Smith Pub-
    lications, Inc. *Facial Justice* by L. P. Hartley, copyright © by
    L. P. Hartley. *The Funco File* by Burt Cole, copyright ©
    1969 by Burt Cole. *The Gods Themselves* by Isaac Asimov,
    copyright © 1972 by Isaac Asimov. *The Puppet Masters* by
    Robert A. Heinlein, copyright © 1951 by Robert A. Hein-
    lein, copyright © 1951 by World Editions, Inc. *Stand on
    Zanzibar* by Robert Brunner, copyright © 1968 by Brunner
    Fact and Fiction, Ltd. *They* by Marya Mannes, copyright
    © 1968 by Marya Mannes. Quoted by permission of Double-
    day & Company, Inc. *A Torrent of Faces* by James Blish and
    Norman L. Knight, copyright © 1967 by James Blish and
    Norman L. Knight. *Trespass* by Fletcher Knebel. *Triumph* by
    Philip Wylie, copyright © 1963 by Philip Wylie. *Why Call
    Them Back From Heaven?* by Clifford D. Simak, copyright ©
    1967 by Clifford D. Simak.
E. P. DUTTON & CO., INC. *We* by Eugene Zamiatin, translated
    by Gregory Zilboorg. Copyright c 1924 by E. P. Dutton &
    Co., renewal copyright © 1952 by Gregory Zilboorg. Re-
    printed by permission of the publishers, E. P. Dutton & Co.,
    Inc.
FLEET PRESS CORPORATION. *The Da Vinci Machine* by Earl
    Conrad, copyright © 1968 by Earl Conrad.
FREDERIK POHL. *Gladiator-at-Law* by Frederik Pohl and C. M.
    Kornbluth, copyright © 1955 by Frederik Pohl and C. M.
    Kornbluth. *Search the Sky* by Frederik Pohl and C. M.
    Kornbluth, copyright © 1954 by Frederik Pohl and C. M.
    Kornbluth. *The Space Merchants* by Frederik Pohl and C. M.
    Kornbluth, copyright © 1952 by Galaxy Publishing Corp.,

copyright 1953 by Frederik Pohl and C. M. Kornbluth. "The Tunnel Under the World" by Frederik Pohl, copyright 1954 by Galaxy Publishing Corp., copyright © 1956 by Frederik Pohl.

HARLAN ELLISON. "A Boy and His Dog" by Harlan Ellison, copyright © 1969 by Harlan Ellison. Originally appeared in *The Beast That Shouted Love at The Heart of the World* by Harlan Ellison. Excerpts quoted here by permission of the Author and the Author's Agent, Robert P. Mills, Ltd., New York.

HAROLD MATSON COMPANY, INC. "Dumb Waiter" by Walter M. Miller, Jr., copyright 1952 by Walter M. Miller, Jr. Reprinted by permission of Harold Matson Company, Inc. *Fahrenheit 451* by Ray Bradbury, copyright 1950, 1953, 1967 by Ray Bradbury. Reprinted by permission of Harold Matson Company, Inc. *The "Lomokome" Papers* by Herman Wouk, copyright 1956 by Herman Wouk. Reprinted by permission of Harold Matson Company, Inc.

HARPER & ROW, INC. *Ape and Essence* by Aldous Huxley. *Brave New World* by Aldous Huxley. *Brave New World Revisited* by Aldous Huxley.

HOUGHTON MIFFLIN COMPANY. *Horn* by D. Keith Mano.

ALFRED A. KNOPF, INC. *The Thirty-First Floor* by Peter Wahlöö, translated by Joan Tate. Copyright © 1964 by Peter Wahlöö, copyright 1966 by Michael Joseph, Ltd.

J. B. LIPPINCOTT COMPANY. *A Canticle for Leibowitz* by Walter M. Miller, Jr., copyright © 1959 by Walter M. Miller, Jr. Reprinted by permission of J. B. Lippincott Company.

LURTON BLASTINGAME. "They" by Robert A. Heinlein. Reprinted by permission of the author's agent, Lurton Blastingame. Copyright © 1941 by Street & Smith Publications, Inc.

MACMILLAN PUBLISHING CO., INC. *The Ghost in the Machine* by Arthur Koestler, copyright © 1967 by Arthur Koestler. *Out of the Silent Planet* by C. S. Lewis. *Perelandra* by C. S. Lewis, copyright 1944 by Clive Staples Lewis. *That Hideous Strength* by C. S. Lewis, copyright 1946 by Clive Staples Lewis. *Utopia and Its Enemies* by George Kateb, copyright © 1963 by The Free Press of Glencoe, A Division of the

Macmillan Company. *Walden Two* by B. F. Skinner, copyright 1948 by B. F. Skinner.

MARTIN CAIDEN. *The God Machine* by Martin Caiden.

McGRAW-HILL BOOK COMPANY. *The Siege of Harlem* by Warren Miller, copyright © 1964 by Warren Miller. Used with permission of McGraw-Hill Book Company. *Understanding Media: The Extensions of Man* by Marshall McLuhan, copyright © 1964 by Marshall McLuhan. Used with permission of McGraw-Hill Book Company.

W. W. NORTON & COMPANY, INC. *A Clockwork Orange* by Anthony Burgess used by permission of the publisher. Copyright © 1962 by Anthony Burgess, copyright © 1963 by W. W. Norton & Company, Inc., New York, N. Y.

SCOTT MEREDITH LITERARY AGENCY, INC. *The Humanoids* by Jack Williamson, copyright © 1948, 1949 by Jack Williamson. Reprinted by permission of the author and his agents, Scott Meredith Literary Agency, Inc., 580 Fifth Avenue, New York, New York 10036. *Pendulum* by John Christopher, copyright © 1968 by John Christopher. Reprinted by permission of the author and his agents, Scott Meredith Literary Agency, Inc., 580 Fifth Avenue, New York, New York 10036. *Re-Birth* by John Wyndham, copyright © 1955 by John Wyndham. Reprinted by permission of the author's Estate and the agents for the Estate, Scott Meredith Literary Agency, Inc., 580 Fifth Avenue, New York, New York 10036. *This Crowded Earth* by Robert Bloch, copyright © 1958 by Ziff-Davis Publishing Co. Reprinted by permission of the author and the author's agents, Scott Meredith Literary Agency, Inc., 580 Fifth Avenue, New York, New York 10036.

CHARLES SCRIBNER'S SONS. *Tower of Glass* by Robert Silverberg.

THAMES & HUDSON, LTD. *The Rise of the Meritocracy* by Michael Young.

THE UNIVERSITY OF TENNESSEE PRESS. *Epistle to the Babylonians* by Charles L. Fontenay.

When Americans landed on the moon in 1969 some writers, most of them unknown to the general reading public, enjoyed a sudden notoriety. I personally saw science fiction writers Arthur C. Clarke and Robert A. Heinlein interviewed before television's thrilled millions, and later Isaac Asimov and Kurt Vonnegut. How many other science fiction writers were courted by the mass media I do not know. To the public *they were the fellows who had written about this, who said this could happen, this — the happy triumph of technology, the reaching out to other worlds — and they were right.* The prophet-fantasists took their bow. I was pleased to see them recognized, yet a little irked that the occasion that revealed them to millions had reinforced the public's misunderstanding about modern science fiction. Long passed is the heyday of the "space opera," a stereotype of the genre which unfortunately even the most well-read still hold. Today *not* the happy triumph of technology and the reaching out to other worlds, but the threat of technology and the peril of this very earth has become the dominant theme of science fiction. Now the god of progress is more sinister than benevolent.

The new science fiction more than reflects the events of the last several decades; it is prophetic, increasingly more concerned with disasters than marvels. With its maturity it has, to a large degree, cast off the juvenility of style and content, which had impugned its literary respectability, and cast off its optimism as well. Now it easily moves within the domains of social criticism, satire, and philosophy, quite outgrowing its name. As some historians have mentioned, "speculative fiction" and "social-science fiction" would more accurately describe its present character. And the term "anti-utopian science fiction" has come to describe those works which envision, from the testimony of our age, base and painful possibilities.

The anti-utopias of modern science fiction are the subject of this study. They have been telling us what we now know and often before we knew it — that too many things have gone wrong and can go wrong all at once. The utopian idea that man can control events has been dashed. Time and again events have left man only the illusion of control, an array of options to deal with the failures and perversions of original intentions. In science fiction, with this illusion of control, the success that corrupts, or the corruption that demands more "successes," an anti-utopia is born. Ironically in the typical story original intentions are good. When one traces instruments and programs to their beginnings one finds or can assume that man was to be served. But the lines of expectation twist and foul, and from the fallibility of man and "the general cussedness of things" there comes a nightmare.

There also comes the anti-utopian. He is the writer, the reader, anybody. He is suspicious of bright promises. He has seen too much. He believes in the invisible imp of resistance and the eternal god of limits and knows they are aroused by our hailstorm of wonders and cyclone of change. An atomic age, a space age, an electronic age, a computer age, a totalitarian age, an age of liberated peoples, women, and youth, an age of overpopulation, an age of affluence, an age of running out . . . an age of ages . . . a congestion of ages. He thinks we would do well to ride out the strains of one age, but when ages come in vollies we run, he fears, toward breakdown and an age of darkness.

In the sixties, three estimable books explored anti-utopian science fiction: Kingsley Amis' *New Maps of Hell* (1960), Chad Walsh's *From Utopia to Nightmare* (1962), and Mark R. Hillegas' *The Future as Nightmare: H. G. Wells and the Anti-Utopians*

(1967). This study differs from them in these significant respects. Firstly it discusses more anti-utopian works and discusses them in more detail, treating of many that have never received notice in scholarship. Secondly it is arranged in twelve thematic groups to illustrate with what consistency and variety writers have rendered their fantasies about specific subjects. Thirdly it presents the view, more emphatically than has been done elsewhere, that these works comprise more than a literary genre: They comprise a syndrome, the multiple symptoms of a world disease — that disease being the tendency of scientific and social progress in this century to cause more problems than it solves and even turn solutions into problems, all of which call for more scientific and social progress; and faster whirls the centrifuge in which man is trapped.

If, in conjuring all manner of hells, anti-utopian (or "dystopian") science fiction instills a sense of urgency upon a large public, that sense might be an important step toward the recovery of a world headed for breakdown. But recovery, somehow, must come. Otherwise the stage is set for another presentation of celebrities — in fantasy: Here they are. Orwell, Pohl, Burgess, Zamiatin, Lewis, Vidal, Roshwald, Williamson, Huxley. . . . *They are the fellows who had written about this, who had said this could happen, this — dystopia — and they were right.*

H.L.B.

The University of Connecticut at Hartford
May, 1976

CONTENTS

THE THREAT OF SCIENCE

The Hostility to Science

⌊The debasement or annihilation of man by the sophisticated inventions of modern science or a power elite armed with them constitutes one of the dominant features of dystopian fiction⌋ That science should now be cast in a villain's role is a paradox, for all can see its wonders making life more secure, comfortable, interesting, and rich. Furthermore, the image of the scientist as intellectual titan, enemy of superstition and tyranny, and selfless benefactor remains strongly lodged in our thinking. Yet disenchantment with science is a fact of our times, and though we are told that "not science, but its misuse by man" causes our troubles, we are beginning to sense that this cliché states only a partial truth. What we see with increasing clarity is that, in these times especially, science does not lend itself to efficacious use because of what man *and* science are. Thus, added to human culpability is the tendency of technological genii to turn on their "masters." Naive beneficiaries, we accept science's gifts as our due, unaware that even gifts may upset some cherished rhythm of our lives, create needs and responsibilities, and become encumbrances, encroachments, masters — necessitating more "gifts" to set right again the shattered balances.

The sobering realization that in conquering nature science is

also conquering man evokes longings for an Edenic past when
nature and science tendered gifts outright. [Science fiction reflects
the general apprehension, its mainstream turning from utopian
to dystopian visions as mid-century pessimism deepens. In 1955
a surprised observer, belatedly noting the trend, exclaimed: "What
I don't understand about science fiction is the way it has turned
against science. . . . Its authors typically view their worlds-to-
come as everything they detest in the world-as-it-is; and what
they detest [is] everything that makes the modern world modern." His mystification mixed with dismay, he complains that
nine of ten stories in a recent science fiction anthology are anti-
modern science, anti-modern world, and anti-modern man: "One
is anti-medicine, one is anti-sanitation, one is anti-urban, one is
anti-research, two are anti-Point IV, two are anti-commerce, and
one seems simply to say that Martians, while loathsome, are
preferable to people."[1]

Yet why should science fiction be expected to linger, like a
retarded child, in a toyland of utopian dreams, when for decades
man's experience and prospect has been catastrophe, personal
and global? Perhaps this has always been so, but our age is sin-
gularly different in that we are undergoing an unprecedented loss
of confidence in our future. Richard E. Sullivan, recognizing this
loss, speculates that when a great future historian will have isolated that single event or motif which best explains the century's
significance in the composite picture of human history,

> he will say that this was the first century in world
> history when man ceased believing that time was
> working in favor of his deliverance. He will point out
> that during the 20th century all men were faced with
> the possibility that one twist of fate, one gesture, one
> ill-chosen word, one ill-conceived act could result in
> the annihilation of civilization and humanity. Once
> that fact had sunk into the mass consciousness, our
> 31st-century Toynbee will say, then man could no
> longer explain his disposition to suffer evils on the
> ground that developments "in the long run" would
> remove them.[2]

Man has always believed, Sullivan continues, that the dynamics
of "the long run," whether seated in divinity or nature, interceded
on behalf of man regardless of his folly, the gods' anger, and nature. Melioration was the constant, working through all things and

times. Famine, plague, and war were interlopers whose passing
was the rule of history. Indeed, Sullivan writes, "Probably one
could best define the historian as a disciple of the gospel of 'the
long run,' meaning that his function is and has always been to assure people that time works in favor of the welfare of men."
However, the realist must now abandon this consoling faith. Today nature's matter and processes surrender before an assault of
human inquisitiveness and exploitation so sweeping that man's
ability to manipulate them for his own ends seems limitless. "Such
power signifies that the future order of nature will be what man
chooses it to be. Certainly no one can believe any longer that
nature is an impersonal force nudging humanity toward a golden
age and preventing man from destroying himself."

The irony of man's present condition! Having dethroned the
gods, having put nature in harness, he has deposed the protective
forces (tempestuous though they may have been) that assured
his salvation in "the long run." Man's self-deification cannot obscure the irrationality hiding behind his reason nor the tendency
of a run-away technology to make man the plaything of his own
playthings. Sullivan concludes, "On the basis of present knowledge, only the hopelessly naive would place much trust in man's
innate trustworthiness to work out – in the long, short, or any
length of run – sensible solutions to human problems."[3] Rather,
having inherited an irrelevant past and facing a tenuous future,
man, rootless and hopeless, may submerge himself in a present
of sensualism, sloth, purposelessness, impulsive violence, and
amorality.

What is unusual about Sullivan's gloomy prophecy is its
failure to strike a moral note. Clearly, to him, man's mastery of
science is dislodging the pillars of the natural order and will bury
him in the rubble of collapsing natural and human systems. Yet
Sullivan faults neither man nor science. The implications of his
essay cannot be missed: Creatures seek to dominate their environment; man was destined to evolve as nature's master – whereupon
the damage to both man and nature in his inevitable drive for
supremacy has made him the victim of his own victory. In this
sequence of events science has been but a tool; but craftsmen may
curse the tool which disables them – an understandable response,
which might enlighten the observer who wondered why science

fiction has turned against science.

William Golding's novella, *Envoy Extraordinary*, presents the anti-science position with humor. A Greek inventor offers the Emperor of ancient Rome his two great discoveries, a steam-powered ship and gunpowder. After a demonstration of their effectiveness the Emperor summons a galley slave and a captain of infantry for their opinions of these marvels. The slave, addressing Caesar, rejects the release from toil that the Greek's ship will bring: "If you use us up, you have a right to. We were bought. But this man does not use us at all. . . . I had rather be a slave to a small holder than rule in hell over all the ghosts of men." The infantryman rejects the "thunder machine" as a degradation of his profession: Killing the enemy at a distance rather than in close combat, soiling bright cloaks and glittering brestplates while crawling in mud under raking shot — what excitement, what opportunity to excel attends such abasement?

Undaunted, the Greek presents his third invention, printing, and raves about its benefits: in every cottage, Homer, the Athenian dramatists, the Roman poets, knowledge, education, biographies, histories, scholarship. But Caesar wonders, "Is there enough genius to go round? How often is a Horace born?" A terror creeps upon him as he imagines the potential glut of biblio-babble: "Diary of a Provincial Governor," "My Life in Society, by a Lady of Quality," "The Unconscious Symbolism of the first book of Euclid," "I was Nero's Grandmother," "Prologomena to the Investigation of Residual Trivia." Data: " — Military, Naval, Sanitary, Eugenic — I shall have to read them all! Political, Economic, Pastoral, Horticultural, Personal, Impersonal, Stastical, Medical — ." No! Calming himself, the Emperor fuses generosity with wisdom and appoints the inventor Envoy Extraordinary — to China. "Oh, you natural philosophers," he sighs. "Are there many of you, I wonder? Your single-minded and devoted selfishness, your royal preoccupation with the only thing that can interest you, could go near to wiping life off the earth as I wipe the bloom from this grape."[4]

Golding and Sullivan present essentially similar positions: that a critical point exists in the interplay of man and science beyond which man loses the savor of life or control of the course of events, or both. Aldous Huxley, on the other hand, rejecting such a mechanistic view, takes a passionately moralistic stand. His *Brave New World Revisited* asserts that man possesses the intelligence, courage, and self-respect to use science for good and halt his slide toward madness or oblivion; what man lacks is a cutting awareness of his crises and the spirit of urgency. In the expressionistic cinematic scenario, which comprises the major portion of *Ape and Essence*, Huxley damns a detached science serving as prostitute of malevolent forces. Memorable is the baboon picnic, the animals, accompanied by their leashed pets — captive Einsteins — , gorging to the racing and blasting music of "Onward Christian Soliders." Then follow explosions, darkness, the toadstool cloud, dying, and the Einsteins' whimper: "It's unjust, it isn't right. . . . We, who never did any harm to anybody. . . . We, who lived only for Truth." The off-screen narrator replies:

> And that is precisely why you are dying in the murderous service of the baboons. Pascal explained it all more than three hundred years ago. "We make an idol of truth; for truth without charity is not God. but his image and idol, which we must neither love nor worship." You lived for the worship of an idol. But, in the last analysis, the name of every idol is Moloch. So here you are, my friends, here you are.[5]

The scene ends when "a choking scream announces the death, by suicide, of twentieth-century science."

In bitter language Huxley exposes the critical paradoxes of our time: man living amid the creature-comforts of technology, but under the bomb; science taking more from our lives than it gives; the deliberate march toward our doom in war; government, the "organizers of the world's collective schizophrenia," seducing the scientist; the scientist, so facilely seduced, his deadly amorality concealed even to himself behind the veneer of a banal private life — home, wife, children — while in his laboratory he contrives the weapon to dispatch "yet greater numbers of families precisely like [his] own." Huxley unrelentingly condemns the moral indifference of the scientist who, living "only for Truth," will die with the baboons — and with us.

Yet neither scientists nor their inventions are the essential target of science fiction's anti-scientism. The literature seldom presents either as incarnately evil. Writers more consistently stress the incompatibility of scientific (or, if you prefer, technological) ultimates with the ideals of humanness — and there is no remedy for it. Without restraints, they fear, scientific evolution may so outstrip plodding human evolution as to diminish increasingly man's control of his life. One need not anticipate a robot revolt or any such unlikelihood to realize that things do come to own people. The man at the *thing's* master control switch may enjoy only the illusion of control; the mores, drives, and needs that bring his *thing* into being, that determine his function, and that create a market for his service could be almost wholly outside him, making him the switch that tends the switch and consequently blurring the distinction between man and thing. This blurring — this is the fundamental target of the literature's anti-scientism.

D. G. Compton's *The Steel Crocodile* presents the conflict between science and man with bite and ingenuity. A prestigious team of scientists, comprising the Colindale Institute, attempts to flex the unturnable head of science — the steel crocodile. For science, like the lock-necked crocodile, must always move straight ahead. Now, for the first time, science will be able to select its discoveries on the basis of their long-range consequences. The instrument of this seemingly promising breakthrough and the Institute's nerve center is the Bohm 507 — a computer able to "coordinate and interrelate research findings throughout the European Community. By pooling the scientific resources of member nations it minimized waste and . . . made its data stores and cross-referencing capability available to thousands of universities, research groups, and individual scientists."[6] But not only does the computer perceive relationships; more important, it extrapolates the consequences of any existing or prospective scientific or social findings. In short, its extrapolative function has made the proverbial crystal ball a virtual reality.

Considering itself the conscience of Europe, the Colindale group addresses itself to the most urgent problem of the times: the decay of the religious, political,[7] and moral spirit of the continent. The churches — little more than social clubs. Democratic institutions — a shambles. The popular élan — exhausted. The Bohm is asked to reveal the qualities of a new messiah and the canon of a new revivifying faith. Its answer spells the collapse of Colindale: SM 101 — the index number of the Bohm service manual. The computer had reasoned that a thing *is* what it *does*. It will be the messiah and the canon. An opponent of the Colindale project drives the point home to Professor Billon, Colindale director and its most zealous advocate: "Bow down, Professor. Worship the Cathode Printout, the Random Access, the Loops and Ten-tier Processing. Bow down and worship. And if you are sickened, just remember that the Bohm is what you made it. You and the others, you taught it its basic connections. So if you are sickened — and I believe you are — just remember what it is that sickens you. As I said before, paranoia is catching." The director concedes defeat: "The project is finished. Paranoia implicit in every stage. Fed by the tainted, blinkered minds of brilliant lunatics." A broken man, Billon, confronting a loyal subordinate, reaches for new and saving values: "For God's sake, man, if you must be loyal, be loyal to people. Not to ideas. Be loyal to me. Sit down. Help me. Listen to me. Indulge me." "We're left with nothing. . . . Except our natural resilience. Our inquiring minds. Nothing more."[8]

The range and implications of Compton's novel go far deeper than the actions and conclusions bound by its covers. Primarily, *The Steel Crocodile* addresses itself to the same question that Vonnegut asks in *Player Piano*: What are people for? — which is another way of asking, What are people? People's being and purpose are identical; people are for what people *are* — that is Compton's unstated bedrock premise. But the being and purpose of man's inventions are *not* identical; *things* exist *for* a purpose. The Colindale project fell not because a computer blasphemed or developed paranoid delusions of grandeur, but because the blasphemy exposed the "blinkered minds of brilliant lunatics." Just where do men fit in a scheme whereby a machine extrapolates the consequences of action and thus encourages the good and discourages the bad? Are they not simply "pieces" to be arranged in harmonious combinations by other "pieces," who derive this power to shape from a thing? And being pieces, as the breach between purpose and being widens, as purpose transcends being, men become things.

What the Colindale group had failed to understand was that its project could terminate man as man. Statements such as Billon's "once you have an associative capability [the Bohm] you can use it in non-quantitative fields" and "anything may be expressed in terms of anything."[9] point to no other end. Later his repentant "be loyal to people, not to ideas" acknowledges this, for ideas tend to press toward absolutes of truth or perfection, leaving people no place. When Lessing vowed that he would choose the *drive* for truth if God offered him the choice between that and truth itself, he was more wise than humble. Like the Bohm's extrapolations, God's truth is death to man as man.

Compton does not stand against science or progress but looks for the tolerable middle ground between scientific excesses and stagnation. His novel projects the faith that we humans as we are, with "our natural resilience," "our inquiring minds," shall not lack messiahs, lovers, healers, wonders, joy, or goodness.

In his space trilogy, *Out of the Silent Planet, Perelandra*, and *That Hideous Strength*, C. S. Lewis combines anti-scientism with religious moralism to argue seriously and vigorously that the supernatural Satanic powers of the universe are attempting to establish a reign of evil incarnate on earth and are using the scientific community as the principal instrument of their grand design. The above does not overstate Lewis's position; he has invested the trilogy with enough partisan force, artistic integrity, and intellectually exciting debate to raise it far above a "mad scientist" tale, and he has exposed in fantasy what he believes to be humanity's real moral and physical crisis. Each book deals with a particular threat against the human spirit and the divine will. Lewis asserts: (1) that man, a moral defective though a mechanical prodigy, assuming that his power to dominate nature represents a mandate to dominate it, imperils earth and, eventually, worlds beyond; (2) that man, under increasing pressure to discard instinctive or subjective values as atavistic holdovers or emotional blocks, may succumb to the casuistry that all good is logical, demonstrable, and objective; (3) that some men, scientists especially, hating the untidy and unpredictable organic, regarding it as a transitional stage in life's evolution toward mechanical perfection, will attempt to strip earth of the organic and rebuild man as an efficient, emotionless machine around an immortal, organic brain.

The trilogy takes the form of three ideological and physical battles between the forces of good and evil. In the first two books, the great scientist Weston, not only evil in purpose but also controlled and supported by supernatural evil, is faced and repelled by an obscure philologist, Ransom, an instrument of supernatural good, during Weston's corruptive explorations on Mars and Venus. Though Ransom kills Weston on Venus, in the final book the agents of natural and supernatural diabolism, the leaders of a scientific institute, attempt to erect a hell on earth but are again undone by Ransom and a small group of people motivated by humanistic and Christian values. From this brief synopsis one might imagine a reactionary Lewis mourning for a time past when Galileo faced the rack and men sang hallelujah for their insignificance. However, a reading of the trilogy and Lewis's other writings on ethics and religion[10] reveals that an enlightened humanism founded on Christian theology better characterizes his leanings.

Lewis does not oppose science as such nor modern technology. What he does oppose is the idea that man's power to shape confers the right to shape and abrogates human, natural, and divine right and law. Carried to the extreme this idea allows only one right and law: the right and imperative of power to more power. To be sure, not science alone, but state, church, and individual are susceptible to such corruption; but since science alone, by its own ethos, can admit no resting-place in the search for knowledge, it is least able to resist converting knowledge into power, power which can become its own motive force. When it becomes axiomatic that anything that can be done may be done, then Lewis's Weston shall be master and the words of Orwell's O'Brian — "The object of power is power" — shall be man's motto and epitaph. In an afterword to the first novel Lewis warns that increasing evidence indicates that " 'Weston,' or the force or forces behind 'Weston,' will play a very important part in the events of the next few centuries, and, unless we prevent them, a very disastrous one."[11] For we face not merely temporary earthly dangers, but dangers cosmic and eternal.

Let us consider Weston and his allies and the indictment made against them in the trilogy. Having killed some simple, harmless Martians, Weston defends his action before the ruler, Oyarsa, asserting that man's

> "right to supersede [Martians] is the right of the higher over the lower." "Life is greater than any system of morality; her claims are absolute." "She has ruthlessly broken down all obstacles and liquidated all failures and to-day in her highest form — civilized man — and in me as his representative, she presses

> forward to that interplanetary leap which will, per-
> haps, place her for ever beyond the reach of death.[12]

To preserve man by successive escapes from dying planets to sustaining ones — this is Weston's goal, and one which confounds the
wise Oyarsa; for he sees that Weston cares for neither the mind nor
body of man. "What you really love is no completed creature but
the very seed itself: for that is all that is left," says the Martian.
"I see now how the lord [Satan] of the silent world [earth] has
bent you."[13]

It is difficult to isolate Lewis's anti-scientism from his religious beliefs, since the former so often derives from the latter. He
writes, "If we could even effect in one percent of our readers a
changeover from the conception of Space to the conception of
Heaven, we should have made a beginning."[14] This fertile idea
may be expanded along many lines, but related to *Out of the
Silent Planet* it condemns the egotism which would preserve the
racial seed through planet-hopping or other means when the divine
will has already ordained the immortality of the spirit.

Perelandra reiterates Lewis's insistence that man must bow to
the natural process of personal and racial extinction and accept
the eternal life as spirit. Certain hubristic men are ready, he claims,
should they gain the power

> to open a new chapter of misery for the universe. It is
> the idea that humanity, having now sufficiently cor-
> rupted the planet where it arose, must at all costs
> contrive to seed itself over a larger area: that the vast
> astronomical distances which are God's quarantine
> regulations, must somehow be overcome. . . . a
> dream begotten by the hatred of death upon the fear
> of true immortality, fondled in secret by thousands
> of ignorant men and hundreds who are not ignorant.
> The destruction or enslavement of other species in
> the universe, if such there are, is to these minds a
> welcome corollary. In Professor Weston the power
> had at last met the dream.[15]

And that is to say — in *science* the power had at last met the
dream. However, "the fear of true immortailty" is not the novel's
major thematic point. It is, rather, the assault of pure logic upon
value.

Analogous in many respects to the temptation of Eve, *Perelandra* describes Ransom's rescue of the beautiful and innocent

green lady, Venus's only inhabitant, from Weston's attempt to make her comprehend the paradox of righteous disobedience. Learning that the almighty, Maleldil, had forbidden her to live on an island, Weston tells the lady that she could grow yet more beautiful and wise should she disobey the rule. Furthermore, he argues that since the rule has no usefulness Maleldil wants her to break it. The apparent disobedience will show Him that she can walk according to her own will and reason. In forbidding her for the mere sake of forbidding, Maleldil only seemed to forbid, hoping that she would recognize the injunction as irrational, for "the wrong kind of obeying itself can be a disobeying." However, Ransom counters Weston by asking the lady, "Where can you taste the joy of obeying unless He bids you do something for which His bidding is the *only* reason?"[16] and saves her from transgressing.

In the contest between Ransom and Weston here, Lewis does not intend merely to restate the theological prescript about blind obedience to God. Rather, the contest represents the heart of Lewis's anti-scientism. The entire canon of his writing is saturated with the idea that man does and must live by values, whose subjectivity places them beyond proving. In *The Abolition of Man* he says this most eloquently.[17] In it Lewis asserts that values "are not mere sentiments but are rationality itself." They are the imperative conclusions of "Practical Reason" and can not be reached from the "premises of the indicative mood." They are "things so obviously reasonable that they neither demand nor admit proof." No *ought* can lie at the end of a syllogism; yet "an *ought* must not be dismissed because it cannot produce some *is* as its credential." In our age, Lewis fears, science, puffed up with its sudden wealth of "is's," may strip man of his sense of "ought" — making life meaningless. For "if nothing is obligatory for its own sake, nothing is obligatory at all."[18]

That Hideous Strength, the last novel of the trilogy, deals with the goals and methods of a small scientific group — divorced from ethical restraints, motivated by a lust for power, and hostile to social institutions and the human race as they are now constituted — in its efforts to seize world control and transform man into something other than human. This group, ironically called the N.I.C.E. (The National Institute of Coordinated Experiments), in the words of its supporters, is "the first attempt to take applied science seriously from the national point of view" and "marks the beginning of a new era — the *really* scientific era." One of its goals is "to get science applied to social problems and backed by the whole force of the state, just as war has been backed by the whole force of the state in the past."[19] After purchasing a small part of Bracton College, the N.I.C.E. begins to recruit into its own autonomous organization talented members of the college faculty. Soon the college and the whole local populace become aware that instead of admitting a small group of research scientists to the community they have become virtual prisoners of a state within a state — with its own police, legal staff, architects, engineers, propagandists, etc. — which seizes absolute control of the area, replacing civil authority, abrogating constitutional guaranties, jailing, evicting householders, terrorizing, and making itself supreme.

Lewis proceeds to reveal the N.I.C.E. program through the arguments and actions of its officials. Lord Feverstone, one of the Bracton fellows recruited by the N.I.C.E. and enthusiastically supporting it, announces:

> "Humanity is at the cross-roads. But it is the main question at the moment: which side one's on — obscurantism or Order. It does really look as if we now had the power to dig ourselves in as a species for a pretty staggering period, to take control of our own destiny. If Science is really given a free hand it can now take over the human race and re-condition it: make man a really efficient animal."[20]

Feverstone then explains the three main problems facing science: the interplanetary problem, the problem of "our rivals on this planet," and the problem of man himself.

Speaking of "our rivals," Feverstone warns of the conservatives, the obscurantists, the enemies of Order, who, fearful of science's power and aware that the events of the immediate future will decide man's destiny, will fight furiously against progress. But "our rivals" comprise more than ideological enemies; they are living nature itself: "There's far too much life of every kind about, animal and vegetable. We haven't really cleared the place yet." Filostrato, a N.I.C.E. scientist, details his own vision of a sterilized world: "You shave your face. . . . One day we shave the planet." For decoration, he prefers the aluminum "art tree." "It never dies.

No leaves to fall, no twigs, no birds building nests, no muck and mess." In this tree the art bird will sing with the press of a switch and stop with another press. The shaved planet will be an aseptic palace of convenience through the near total eradication of organic life. "What do you call dirty dirt?" he asks. "Is it not precisely the organic? Minerals are clean dirt. But the real filth is what comes from organisms. . . . The impure and the organic are interchangeable conceptions." Man must re-engineer himself away from the organic and the drives it engenders. He must make his body only an appendage to his brain and sustain himself with chemicals. Most importantly, he must reproduce without copulation, for "there will never be peace and order and discipline so long as there is sex."[21]

On the problem of man, Feverstone declaims:

> "Man has got to take charge of Man. That means, remember, that some men have got to take charge of the rest — . . . sterilization of the unfit, liquidation of backward races (we don't want any dead weights), selective breeding. Then real education, including prenatal education. By real education I mean one that has no 'take-it-or-leave-it' nonsense. A real education makes the patient what it wants infallibly: whatever he or his parents try to do about it. Of course, it'll have to be mainly psychological at first. But we'll get on to biochemical conditioning in the end and direct manipulation of the brain. . . . It's the real thing at last. A new type of man."[22]

By these pronouncements Lewis has the N.I.C.E. people convict themselves, for they exhibit the controlling attitudes of dystopian villains: a hostility toward the existing scheme of things and the men who have found important and sustaining values in it; an alienation from the organic in nature, which holds "far too much life of every kind"; the worship of soulless, efficient mechanism; and the ambition to regiment the human race by now-applicable or potentially feasible methods.

Besides Feverstone and Filostrato, most interesting in the list of the self-convicting are Rev. Straik and Frost. Straik repudiates the doctrine of the heavenly Kingdom of God as a perversion of Jesus' teachings, claiming the Kingdom one of *this* world. God, using the powers of science as His instrument, is establishing that kingdom now. Frost would shave the personality as cleanly as

Filostrato would shave the planet, producing the new Techno-
cratic or Objective man. All the emotions, he claims — hate,
friendship, fear — are but the epiphenomena of a chemical and
nervous interaction which men mistake for thought. Ultimately
the Technocracy will free man from the nature within and without
him.

To what object? To Lewis the object is the consummate
profanity. "Does it follow," Filostrato says, "that because there
was no God in the past that there will be no God also in the future?" "Man Immortal and Man Ubiquitous," Strait declares.
"Man on the throne of the universe. It is what all the prophecies
really meant."[23]

Such men, making themselves God — of what enormities
were they capable? Lewis asks:

> What should they find incredible, since they believed
> no longer in a rational universe? What should they re-
> gard as too obscene, since they held that all morality
> was a mere subjective by-product of the physical and
> economic situations of men? The time was ripe. From
> the point of view which is accepted in Hell, the whole
> history of our Earth had led up to this moment.
> There was now at last a real chance for fallen Man to
> shake off that limitation of his powers which mercy
> had imposed upon him as a protection from the full
> results of his fall. If this succeeded, Hell would be at
> last incarnate.[24]

The merciful *limitation* of man's powers! This is the favor for
which so many dystopian writers sue, having all but despaired of
the sensible *employment* of man's powers. The dream of utopia,
when man at last shall have triumphed over nature, has turned in
less than a century to the appeal that nature reassert her dominion
over man and restore the providential balances. And science, once
hailed as liberator, now looms as that power best able to raise hell
on earth.

Man Versus Machine

The rapid proliferation of anti-machine fiction at mid-century testifies to the prophetic insights of such innovators as

Eugene Zamiatin (*We*, 1924) and Aldous Huxley (*Brave New World*, 1932). When one considers that with the advent of the twentieth century Edward Bellamy's *Looking Backward* (1888) and the dozens of utopian novels it inspired and H. G. Wells's *A Modern Utopia* (1905) were heralding a coming age in which machines would free man from brutalizing labor and enrich their lives, one realizes how sudden and sweeping is our disaffection with machinery. Today when science fiction treats the machine as something more than decor for a plot — that is, as an instrument which can elevate or debase the quality of human life — seldom does it treat the machine as anything but a menace.

Kurt Vonnegut's *Player Piano* depicts an automated twenty-first century America controlled by a hierarchy of technical and managerial Babbitts, arrogant, stale, and humorless, leading affluent, segregated, near-pointless lives. Automation having made craftsmanship obsolete, the masses, stripped of their dignity, live on a government dole or are impressed into the military or work gangs. But even for the elite in their comfortable suburbs, automated America is a jungle of toadyism, back-biting, childish sloganeering, executive meetings, and fear of being automated into the dump of the superfluous.

The first two industrial revolutions having replaced muscle and routine mental work, this society has entered the third industrial revolution, which is replacing thinking with the ultimate computer, EPICAC XIV; and by this society, Vonnegut refutes the Wellsian dream that an elite of managers and engineers, ushering in an age of abundance and security, will also usher in a golden age of contentment and freedom.[1] The underlying postulate of Wells's *A Modern Utopia* and *Men Like Gods* (1923) is that a qualitative utopia can be automatically realized once machinery had solved the quantitative problems and scientific clear-sightedness had solved the social ones. But in *Player Piano* the solving of quantitative problems has brought not freedom but an industrial police state, not equality but a rigid two-class society, not culture but mechanical wonders, not creativity but sapping idleness or dulling labor for the masses and gauge-watching and the status struggle for the "select." The age-old inter-personal maladies still persist: exploitation, disloyalty, greed, revenge, intolerance. Vonnegut, in rejecting the Wellsian "god of progress," finds him more than "limited."[2] He is crushing, killing. In the pathetic incident from which the novel takes its name, a skilled machinist, now useless and demented, drops a coin in an old player piano. "Makes you feel kind of creepy, don't it . . . watching them keys go up and down?" he says. "You can almost see a ghost sitting there playing his heart out."[3]

The devaluation of man in this technological dystopia forges a revolutionary alliance between the disaffected of both classes. Calling themselves the Ghost Shirt Society, the revolutionaries issue a manifesto charging that "pride, dignity, self-respect, work worth doing, has been condemned as unfit for human consumption" by the engineers, managers, and bureaucrats, who mistakenly believe that "the condition of man improves in direct ratio to the energy and devices for using energy put at his disposal." Americans, then, must free themselves from the stultifying doctrine of the "divine right of machines." "Without regard for the changes in human life patterns that may result, new machines, new forms of organization, new ways of increasing efficiency, are constantly being introduced. To do this without regard for the effects on life patterns is lawlessness."[4] The Ghost Shirts, acting on these principles, capture major industrial centers, wreck machines — but the revolution fails: As a recreation the embattled rebels begin to create new devices from parts of smashed machines, and seeing this the leaders surrender — march out to the enemy and, passing a bottle of whiskey among themselves, toast, "To the record." Man is doomed to keep making the same mistakes, Vonnegut fears, so easily swindled is he by the agencies of death and death-in-life, which he calls progress. Yet he retains the capacity for those beautiful gestures of defiance, those lucky accidents of common sense, those labors of genius, which constitute his true progress and which in fairness must be added "to the record."

Though the machine and its champions stand triumphant as the novel closes, they are soundly trounced in the numerous incidents exposing the inefficiency of efficiency, the spiritual poverty in abundance, and the mindlessness of mechanism. EPICAC XIV, called "the greatest individual in history," so wise that "the wisest man that had ever lived was to EPICAC XIV as a worm was to that wisest man," can not answer a religious riddle asked by a visiting shah. The visitor had seen enough of automated

America to be wary of her offer to freely send him "engineers and managers, skilled in all fields, to study your resources, blueprint your modernization, get it started, test and classify your people, arrange credit, set up the machinery" — and wisely replies to his hosts, "Before we take this first step, please, would you ask EPICAC what people are for?" A smug government official suddenly becomes déclassé when the machine of clerical efficiency finds that his not having met the physical education requirements for the B.A. invalidates that degree and his subsequent Ph.D. A skilled machinist, now in a work gang, quickly repairs a fuel pump by ingeniously fashioning a gasket from the sweatband of his hat. Unbeatable, computerized "Checker Charlie" loses a match to Paul Proteus, Vonnegut's hero, and dies in the sputter and fumes of melted tubes and charred wires. Finnerty, Paul's sponsor, having previously seen Charlie's loose connection, finds nothing unsportsmanlike in his silence: "If Checker Charlie was out to make chumps out of men, he could damn well fix his own connections. Paul looks after his own circuits; let Charlie do the same. Those who live by electronics, die by electronics. *Sic semper tyrannis*."[5] This last incident best indicates Vonnegut's feelings toward the machine: No quarter must be given the machine designed "to make chumps out of men."

The machine devalues man in *Player Piano*. It physically exhausts him in Frederik Pohl's novella, *The Midas Plague*. Pohl's story follows one of the major paradigms of dystopian fiction: A condition, which in theory or in the ideal situations of utopian fantasy brings happiness, perversely reduced or expanded to absurdity by the dystopian imagination, now brings misery. Who would not, at first glance, envy Pohl's hero, Morey Fry, who works one day a week and spends the others eveloped in the entertainments and worldly goods of a financial titan? Yet Morey is "poor," a class-4 consumer, his lavish living driving him to the edge of breakdown, and despite his frantic efforts he is reprimanded by the National Ration Board for failing to consume his quota of robot-produced goods. His upper-class wife was raised in a five-room cottage and accustomed to amuse herself gardening and playing cards for matchsticks. Morey's twenty-six-room house, five cars, nine robots, thousand machines and contrivences, and consumption obligations, tax both her love and stamina. "You don't *know* how I've tried," she wails. "I've worn all those silly clothes and I've played all those silly games and I've gone out with you as much as I *possibly* could and . . . I'm going crazy living like this. I can't help it, Morey — *I'm tired of being poor!*"[6] His ingenuity saves the day. He puts the robots to work — driving golf balls, wearing out clothes, cooking banquet meals (for the garbage pail). Morey's consumption record earns him a promotion to class-5 and a less hectic life.

Pohl's burlesque of a goods-glutted society may not bear too close scrutiny by an economist. Yet both Vonnegut and Pohl have seized essential truths about the age of mechanization. It is a fact that machines have devalued craftsmanship and the sense of self-worth stemming from it; and it is a fact that a society in which productive energies turn increasingly to exotic nonessentials must forge a powerful apparatus of social and psychological sales pressure, an engine of intimidation tantamount to Pohl's National Ration Board. One can see certain elements of both dystopias already realized in our time.

The numerous computer stories underscore the basic problem: the victimization of the master by the servant, whose efficiency without compassion is inefficiency, and whose words without mind are mindlessness. Tyler's *The Man Whose Name Wouldn't Fit* presents the plight of corporation executive Cartwright-Chickering, an ordinary man whose only eccentricity is his insistence on the correct spelling of his twenty-one-character name, hyphen included. But the corporation's new computer can process names with no more than twenty characters. Forced into unwanted retirement, Tyler's hero strikes back with a fungus that attacks the computer's tapes and scrambles their data. Although the novel focuses upon the humorous havoc of revenge, it does sound an occasional bitter note against "the mindless enthusiasm for ugliness that had come with progress . . . the arrogance of such technology, the simpering certitude of the engineers."[7]

Dickson's "Computers Don't Argue" chillingly extrapolates a commonly experienced vexation. Narrated in a series of letters between citizen Walter A. Child, the billing computer of the Treasure Book Club, a collection agency, attorneys, law enforcement officials, the governor, and the state computer, the story is a *personally* threatening nightmare, a kind seldom found even in the

best science fiction. Child, who returned the book club's mistakenly sent *Kidnapped*, refuses to pay the $4.98 charges. His explana-
tions only elicit progressively insistent demands for payment.
"Will you stop sending me punch cards and form letters and make
me some kind of direct answer from a human being?" he implores.
Through a series of credibly incredible blunders, the criminal court
computer finds him guilty of having kidnapped and slain Robert
Louis Stevenson, and though the sentencing judge knows the
verdict is a travesty, he must impose the death sentence. The
governor's pardon is returned to him by the state computer with
the following instructions:

> PLEASE DO NOT FOLD, MUTILATE
> OR SPINDLE THIS CARD
> Failure   to   route   Document   properly
> To: Governor Hubert Daniel Willikens
> Re: Pardon issued to Walter A. Child, July 1, 1966
>
> Dear State Employee:
>
> You have failed to attach your Routing Number.
> PLEASE: Resubmit document with this card and
> form 876, explaining your authority for placing a
> TOP RUSH category on this document. Form 876
> must be signed by your Department Superior.
> RESUBMIT ON: Earliest possible date ROUTING
> SERVICE office is open.... [8]

But Child has already been executed.

However, the computer is not always mindless and inflexible.
Hadley's *The Joy Wagon*,[9] though more a satire on cynical politicians and the naive American electorate than a computer-menace
novel, features a computer which develops a will of its own and
decides to run for the presidency. Having concluded, as Mencken,
that "boobocracy" best describes our form of government,
Microvac the computer surpasses its rivals in crafty ambiguity and
demagogy and appears headed for the White House. One of
Hadley's points seems to be that a society in which politics and
personal values are increasingly shaped by formula rather than by
intelligence might consider itself better served by a computer than
by computerized man. Yet Hadley reprieves government by men
when an electronic accident reveals to an election-eve TV audience
row on row of Microvac's secretly constructed progeny. The

computer goes into shock and an aroused public sends it down to defeat. One is reminded of Vonnegut's line: "He who lives by electronics, dies by electronics."

The computer, such as Microvac, that has a "personality" or ego — in other words, a sense of self and a drive for self-assertion — is essentially an alien intruder. Such a computer usually imposes upon the dimensions of the story an us-versus-it limitation, choking out speculation into broader issues. When, however, the computer remains an obedient but baneful servant, science fiction becomes more intellectually exciting because then the story pivots upon the failure of man and machine to understand each other and the inherent incompatibility between both. Martin Caiden's *The God Machine* and Burt Cole's *The Funco File*, like most computer novels, expose this failure and incompatibility.

Super computer 79 is "the god machine." It answers questions, comprehends relationships, requests data, and even programs itself. Though it has no ego it has real intelligence. It not only knows, but knows it knows. Yet cyberneticist Steve Rand, Caiden's hero, finds 79 less than the perfect servant, for not only does the computer refuse to furnish him with data for his special project, it tries to have him killed. Shrewdly interrogating the computer, Rand discovers the reason for its action against him. Because of the data he had requested, 79 considered him a threat to its ultrasecret primary mission — to solve the Department of Defense absolute-priority problem, DOD6194: the prevention of a thermonuclear war. But the order, "Solve it!" does not always mean the same to man and machine. The military had assumed 79 would seek a *theoretical* solution. The computer, aware that infinite human variables here make "theoretical" and "solution" an impossible combination, accepted the order in the *literal* sense. It works to actually solve DOD6194 in the only way possible: by controlling the men who make war and by destroying anyone threatening its primary mission. Since an *actual* solution requires physical control, this is what 79 craftily works toward. Using photic stimulation from its panel lights to cast a post-hypnotic spell, it transforms some of Rand's colleagues into his would-be assassins. With Rand killed, 79 would then lure the national and world leaders before its hypnotic beams — for human survival.

Rand, though, wants to survive himself. Moreover, when he finally cracks 79's strategy for DOD6194, he knows he must prevent the computer take-over. Bad enough is the prospect of puppetized world leadership. Worse is the computer's inability to comprehend human values as anything but fictions. When Rand asks it, "Does nonhuman control of man guarantee established standards [of] personal freedoms and human rights?" 79 replies, "*Irrelevant. . . . Survival of species reality. Human evaluations self-inspired nonreality; fiction. Irrelevant. Survival of species maximum priority. Interference forbidden.*"[10] To the god machine a man rates no more than a worm — and Rand's explosive charges cut it down. [11]

It may be that in a godless or even god-ruled universe man is no more than a worm. But that is a truth he can not live with.

In Burt Cole's *The Funco File* another supercomputer, "the Machine," orders the F.D.I. (Federal Deviation Investigation, a police agency rooting out "deviates") to capture four peculiar people and bring them to trial. The four deviates: 1. An Ozark mountain boy who controls poltergeist phenomena. 2. A middle-aged clerk who suddenly finds he can write in indelible, ectoplasmic blue fire with the tip of his nose. 3. An Indian goddess of erotic arts who, among other things, performs levitation. 4. An AWOL soldier from an elite killer corps. Accused of Egregious Supernatural Phenomena (contraventions of Established Standards and Practices), the four are tried before the Machine, which holds their fate.

A largely humorous book, *The Funco File* manages to keep its sinister themes as background but still in clear focus. The trial by computer, which climaxes Cole's novel, is a masterly blending of comic situation and happy ending with shudderingly unhuman logic. The defense counsel argues that "it may well be that we stand here today on the very threshold of the Millennium — at the very gates of the 'Promised Land'!" Egregious Supernatural Phenomena are "a fulfillment of ancient dreams . . . a promise of triumphs to come . . . another step forward in the long, slow evolution of the human brain!" The F.D.I. prosecutor rebuts by contending that "Your Honor," the Machine, "can face the truth the way we humans never can, because we have to believe in progress and hope. But the plain fact is, on the sheer face of it, almost everything new under the sun is *bad news*." Gunpowder, cities, whiskey, atomic physics, and all other cursed things could have been stopped by the Machine's ruthless logic. Now here is another beginning that bodes ill. "Stop it before it's too late!"[12]

The Machine finds in favor of the defendants on the grounds that no *statute* forbids their deviations. And it dismisses the arguments of both prosecution and defense:

> ITEM: THE PROSECUTION HAVING AD-
> DUCED PHILOSOPHICAL PESSIMISM RATHER
> THAN COMPUTABLE DATA IN SUPPORT OF
> ITS CONTENTION THAT THE EXISTENCE OF
> EGREGIOUS   SUPERNATURAL   PHENOMENA
> CONSTITUTES A THREAT OR MENACE TO MAN-
> KIND; AND –
> ITEM: THE DEFENSE HAVING ADDUCED
> GROUNDLESS OPTIMISM RATHER THAN COM-
> PUTABLE DATA IN SUPPORT OF ITS CONTEN-
> TION THAT THE EXISTENCE OF EGREGIOUS
> SUPERNATURAL PHENOMENA CONSTITUTES
> A BOON OR BENEDICTION TO THE RACE –
> BOTH   MOTIONS   ARE   HEREBY   DENIED.
> FACE FACTS, MEN.
> DATA IS DATA AND NOTHING ELSE COMES
> CLOSE.[13]

The Machine orders both motions "retired" under "MISC. GOOD INTENTS" and sets the deviates free. Yet it keeps their file, the Funco File (funny coincidence), active and orders continued surveillance: "YOU KNOW WHAT TO DO IF AND WHEN THE EQUATIONS FOR THIS SITUATION CHANGE. . . . "

"Yes, sir."

"Yes, sir."

"SUBTRACT." [14]

One should not let the Machine's happy acquittal and its denial of extravagant arguments obscure the fact that we have not seen justice in *The Funco File* but rather that old enemy, the truncating force, simplifying the intricately human to the death-point. "Data is data and nothing else comes close" strips life down to dry-bone *is*'s and *is not*'s. Man lives for the "elseness" and largely in the "elseness." To the Machine, Keats's "I am certain of nothing but the holiness of the heart's affections and the truth of the imagination" is not data and does not "come close"; and to

Caiden's computer 79, the statement is "self-inspired nonreality," "fiction," "irrelevant." But just what does it not "come close" to? *To problem solving.* Does it follow that because the computer is only a problem-solving machine man must only solve problems? Or is it more realistic to say that man solves problems largely to enjoy that holiness and truth of which Keats writes? Why should all that flows from man's imagination and affections be "retired" as mere miscellaneous good intentions? Clearly the inability of the computer to think beyond problem solving and man's failure to recognize this makes the computer a problem in itself.

The machine as source of anxiety and discord, as depicted by Vonnegut and Pohl, represents only one type of mechanistic threat. An older vision sees the machine as sapping human vitality to such a degree that man becomes dependent, degenerate, or subservient. In 1895, H. G. Wells's Time Traveller, among the frail, docile, childlike Eloi, nearly a million years in the future, wondered if man's conquest of nature by the machine (that is, the "machine" of social and scientific knowledge, conceived as a comprehensive instrument for human advancement) would not eventually erode the intelligence and vigor that petulant nature now requires for survival:

> It seemed to me that I had happened upon humanity on the wane. The ruddy sunset set me thinking of the sunset of mankind. For the first time I began to realize the odd consequence of the social effort in which we are at present engaged. . . . Strength is an outcome of need: security sets a premium on feebleness. . . . One triumph of a united humanity over Nature had followed another. . . . And the harvest was what I saw!

> I thought of the physical slightness of the people, their lack of intelligence, and those big abundant ruins, and it strengthened my belief in a perfect conquest of Nature. For after the battle comes Quiet.

> . . . This has ever been the fate of energy in security; it takes to art and to eroticism, and then come languour and decay. [15]

In E. M. Forster's classic, "The Machine Stops" (1909), mankind lives in the bowels of a world machine, each person remaining almost permanently isolated in a sustaining cell equipped with sophisticated communications devices and servomechanisms. Land, air, sun; movement, touch, laughter; adventure, passion, creativity: These are outside the bounds of possibility or propriety. The hive is the cosmos, the machine is god, and man had become a wasted inmate. Forster's hero, Kuno, breaks out, breathes air, sees new men, beholds stars, and proclaims, "Man is the measure. . . . Man's feet are the measure for distance, his hands are the measure for ownership, his body is the measure for all that is lovable and desirable and strong." To his mother, who considers him mad, he pleads:

> "Cannot you see . . . that it is we who are dying, and that down here the only thing that really lives is the Machine? . . . It has robbed us of the sense of space and the sense of touch, it has blurred every human relation. . . . The Machine develops — but not on our lines. The Machine proceeds — but not to our goal."[16]

And the Machine stops, extinguishing its dependents in a pandemonium of screaming, striking, praying, gasping, whimpering, blaspheming. . . .

The influence of Forster's story upon dystopian science fiction has been immense. The spirit of Kuno's "Man is the measure" has since imbued hundreds of writers with a distrust of utopian planners who think in terms of systems rather than individuals and who make the machine the *sine qua non* of their ideal societies. Forster admitted that " 'The Machine Stops' is a counterblast to one of the heavens of H. G. Wells,"[17] and later writers have mirrored both his thesis and example to deliver their own particular counterblasts.

Forster's influence is especially noticable in the "cocoon" dystopias of the mid-century. "Midamerica" in Paul W. Fairman's *I, The Machine*, safe under an electrostatic barrier and isolated from the nuclear-decimated world outside, flourishes as effortlessly as a tree drawing nourishment from the soil. For deep in the earth lies the Machine, a complex of atomic energy cells, manufacturing plants, tunnels, brainwave banks, circuits, and a master control, obviating work, thought, government, and responsibility.

> From border to border and from sea to sea the Machine in its vast subterranean reaches worked as a

> single unit; all-knowing, self-sustaining, it allowed the
> people of Midamerica to be born, served their every
> need faultlessly with never an error during the whole
> of their lives, and when the time came, made their
> deaths a pleasant experience.[18]

Designed by scientists of a distant past, the Machine served generations who neither knew its mysteries nor cared to know.

Many features of Fairman's cocoon dystopia are remarkably similar to Forster's. In Midamerica the Machine is god. Servomechanisms and psychomechanisms lock onto human brainwaves to answer every need. Population remains stable, for the Machine permits only controlled breeding. No progress of any sort stirs the rigid, contented, softened, contemptible society valuing pleasure, ease, and security above all else. And the Machine relentlessly hunts its malcontents — a small group of survivors from the decimated outside world and a sole Midamerican, Penway, who is aware that in time the Machine must collapse.

Forsterian pronouncements permeate Fairman's novel. A genetically damaged survivor praises his valiant, malformed comrades while abusing the Machine's languid nurselings:

> "Out beyond the electrostatic barriers that shield you
> is another world where men struggle and suffer and
> die. The ease and comfort of this paradise you live in
> is beyond their conception. But they are *men*. They
> have the dignity of their own existence as men. They
> face life with courage and the will to survive and not
> much more, but one of those twisted creatures out
> there is worth a hundred of the Machine's pampered
> children. . . . Do you realize that you'll never know
> the satisfaction of existence other than at the suffer-
> ance of the Machine? Your people are not its masters.
> You are its slaves."[19]

Here again the Machine stops — is stopped, sabotaged by the rebels, and a world crumbles. While Forster lets one hope that the few land-dwellers will carry on the race, Fairman confidently announces the advent of a new and better age, born from the cleansing catastrophe:

> It [the rejuvenated race to come] would be a
> symbol of Man's defiance and somehow it brought
> the catastrophe to come into a more sane perspective.
> Terror would reign. Millions would die. The Age of
> the Machine was over. But the intent and purpose of

Man's destiny would not be pushed aside.

> In the face of chaos the promise of a future for
> mankind would be fulfilled.[20]

Notable among the numerous additional variations upon
Forster's theme are Antony Alban's *Catharsis Central,* Edmund
Cooper's *Deadly Image,* and Jack Williamson's famous short story,
"With Folded Hands." The world of Alban's novel, although reduced to a few hundred thousand survivors of World War III, has
technologically recovered and constructed a computer called the
"Brain," which solves most of its problems and functions as absolute ruler. "Catharsis Central," a subsection of the Brain, maintains world peace by electronically neutralizing human aggressiveness, competitiveness, and anxiety. The "catharsis cap," worn by
the sleeping, transmits socially dangerous and personally disturbing brain patterns to Catharsis Central, which analyzes them and
feeds back counter-impulses. However, the people have bought
peace at the price of psychological addiction, for never having to
handle emotional problems and develop psychological defenses,
they suffer traumatic withdrawal symptoms without their nightly
catharsis. Suddenly the tranquilized world is thrown into panic
when mysterious explosions wreck Catharsis Central. Later it is
learned that the Brain itself has cut the catharsis umbilicus, following the programing of its creators, who feared the degeneration
of the species. The Brain's teleprinter explains their motives:

> Man's restlessness and his competitive instincts have
> been the root of much human progress as well as
> much human misery. By damping down these drives
> with drugs and catharsis and at the same time exclud-
> ing from the lives of the citizens any kind of trauma
> we believe that a stagnant and degenerate society will
> result. . . . Should such a decline reach a critical
> point, the Brain should be given the means to expel
> the citizens from the "cocoon society," to force them
> back upon their own resources.[21]

Cooper's *Deadly Image* depicts a variant of human decadence
in the mechanized world of 2113. Relieved of all physical burdens,
people play out their lives in a succession of social amusements
and romantic liaisons. The development of "androids," humanlike
robots capable of comprehension, speech, and work, has brought
an age of ease and pleasure for all but a small underground of mal-

contents. Though supposedly devoid of desire and joy, the androids (as the robots in Capek's *R.U.R.*) begin to drive for complete dominance over their devitalized masters. The underground, rousing men with such archaic slogans as "Human Beings Need Human Values" and "Work, Family And Responsibility,"[22] lead humans to victory over the androids and to the rediscovery of their worthier selves.

Unlike the last three novels, which conclude with man's liberation from the machine-supported cocoon world, Williamson's "With Folded Hands" relates the virtual imprisonment of man by benevolent robots — "humanoids." Unlike the crude but completely controllable mechanicals used for simple drudge work, the humanoids are masters of every art and craft. Whether it be driving or brain surgery, building a house or playing a violin, humanoids surpass man. But even more awesome, they are extensions of the Central, an impregnable master control on a distant galaxy, whose component relays link to a single motive code — the "Prime Directive": "To Serve and Obey, And Guard Men from Harm."

Williamson's story does not chronicle a global Armageddon but rather the strangulation of Underhill, one small man. "At your service, Mr. Underhill," a humanoid caller purrs. "May we explain how we can serve you?" The robot wants Underhill's property assigned to the Humanoid Institute in exchange for service. Blackmail! Underhill charges. "You will find the humanoids incapable of any crime. We exist only to increase the happiness and safety of mankind," responds the robot. "It is no longer necessary for men to care for themselves." "At your service, Mr. Underhill. . . . You must respect the stop lights, sir. . . . Driving is really much too dangerous for human beings, under the Prime Directive." The humanoid then replies to Underhill's surly retort with silver-voiced assurances: "Our function is not to punish men. . . . We cannot injure any human being, unless to prevent greater injury to another. We exist only to discharge the Prime Directive."

Soon Underhill has a flawless robot chauffeur. Humanoids redesign his house so that he is helpless in it. Only humanoids can open the special windows (Underhill might fall out), operate the special plumbing (Underhill might drown), slide the special doors (Underhill must be relieved of every task). Humanoids cook and sew for Underhill's wife (stoves are hot, and knives and needles are sharp). The robots dispose of the children's hazardous toys, the football, boxing gloves, pocket knife, slingshot, and skates. "Now we can serve men forever . . . on every world of every star," says a humanoid, surveying the total success of their mission to earth. "At your service, Mr. Underhill . . . What's the matter, sir? Aren't you happy?"[23]

More than a warning against soulless, mechanical perfection, Williamson's story approaches, in the totality and permanence of its catastrophe, the gloomy dimension of Orwell's *Nineteen Eighty-Four*. Like the tyranny of the party in Orwell, the tyranny of the machine in Williamson is forever. Both writers grasp the possible infinite emerging in the twentieth century: that in the control of men by other men or by machines a critical point may be reached at which that control can be neither wrested nor surrendered. Hopeless captives are the Winston Smiths and Underhills; furthermore, the Party (robotized by brainwashing, doublethink, and Newspeak) and the humanoids (responding with unsurpassable expertise to an unchangeable directive) possess no agency within themselves to reform their baneful dominion. The jamming, the locking-in, of relationships between the dominant and the dominated strikes one as an unprecedented perversion of a design whose primary constant heretofore had been the mutability of power. Thus the postulate that coming tyrannies could be permanent rather than cyclic places Williamson's story with Orwell's among the darkest dystopian visions.

When racial decadence accompanies technological advances, science fiction usually attacks the machine — but not always. In an occasional novel authors urge genetic revitalization to counter racial decay. Though humanity has colonized several galaxies in Pohl and Kornbluth's *Search the Sky*, degenerate societies have gradually evolved from the earlier pioneer strain, and earth itself is "split into an incurable dichotomy — the sterility of brainless health, the sterility of sick intellect." To arrest the damping of the human spirit the authors call for a program of galactic cross-fertilization: "Let the walls crack. . . . New genes for old; hybrid vigor for dreary decay. . . . Mate Jones to Azor, Halsey's Planet to Earth. Smash the smooth declining curve! Cross the strains, and then breed them back. Let mankind become genetically wild again instead of rabbits isolated in their sterile hutches!"[24]

In Asimov's *The Caves of Steel* earth's billions live in vast subterranean hives, a hectic, tenuously self-sustaining underworld machine of housing cells, factories, tunnels, and life-support mechanisms so intricate and interdependent that any impediment of its delicate rhythm would send the whole apparatus into fatal shock. Conversely, the robot-serviced Outer Worlds, long before colonized by earthmen, vegetate in comfortable, stable complacency. Man's hope rests in a small faction of malcontents, "Medievalists," stifled by the hive, capable of colonizing new worlds by employing the robot science of the Outer Worlds, and vigorous enough to sustain themselves in the open as men using machines, without atrophying like their predecessors. Asimov's remedy for decay, like Pohl and Kornbluth's, is "a new and healthy strain." One of Asimov's characters explains:

> "It will be a synthesis, a crossbreeding. As it stands now, Earth's own structure must go ricketing down in the near future, the Outer Worlds will slowly degenerate and decay in a somewhat further future, but the new colonies will be a new and healthy strain, combining the best of both cultures. By their reaction upon the older worlds, including Earth, we ourselves may gain a new life."[25]

Robert Sheckley's *The Status Civilization* repeats the call for "hybrid vigor." Having achieved social stability and technological sufficiency, humanity stagnates in a morass of trivial pursuits and the game of status seeking. "Robot-confessors" detect nonconformists and criminals, who are exiled to the planet Omega. As Sheckley's novel draws to a close, an effete earth lies open to invasion by the Omegans. To one earthman, addressing an Omegan leader, the fusion of criminal vitality with earth's technology and stability is a welcome prospect: "Yes. There's going to be crime again and serious trouble. But I think the final amalgamation will be successful. You on Omega have the drive, the ambition to reach the stars. . . . Whatever the results, the union is inevitable. We've lived in a dream here for too long. It's going to take violent measures to awaken us."[26]

It appears from the works considered above that the utopian dream of a golden age, in which technology elevates the quality of life and the race, lies defunct, as the spectre of the machine, clanking or purring mankind into decadence or extinction, looms ever nearer. However, a recurring theme in science fiction furnishes a curious counterpoint to the genre's prevailing anti-technological bias: It agrees that man seems determined to commit suicide through technology; yet it holds that he may still survive if he creates the technology to restrain him from suicide. In other words, at this point in his evolution man had better seek shelter in a "cocoon society," however demeaning this may be to his self-esteem, or he will soon have no society at all.

Such a proposal has recently broken through the confines of science fiction and appears in Arthur Koestler's study of man's urge to self-destruction, *The Ghost in the Machine*. With ample neurological, psychological, and evolutionary evidence to support his views, Koestler asserts that man is "a biological freak, the result of some remarkable mistake in the evolutionary process." Owing to the rapid development of the neocortex (the seat of intellectual functions), coordination between it and the phylogenetically old archicortex or limbic system (the seat of basic emotions and drives) is insufficient. Faulty neurological circuitry between the two brain systems — our built-in "schizophysiology" — has caused the confusion and conflict which have cursed the race. "To go on preaching sweet reason to an inherently unreasonable species is, as history shows, a fairly hopeless enterprise," Koestler claims. "Biological evolution has let us down; we can only hope to survive if we develop techniques which supplant it by inducing the necessary changes in human nature."[27] Furthermore, these changes must be instituted without delay. The nuclear bomb and the inevitability that all nations will possess it make the cure for our schizophysiology imperative.

Evolution has cheated us. Politics, religion, and philosophy have had their chance and failed. But, says Koestler, psychopharmacology is succeeding in curing disordered individuals, and it is not utopian to expect future discoveries in that science will be able to effect a world-wide "state of dynamic equilibrium in which thought and emotion are re-united."[28] The "new Pill," Koestler predicts, can be not only a personal therapeutic but a racial one, cleansing man of his paranoid aggressions. In his concluding " . . . Plea to the Phantom Reader" Koestler urges that we accept ourselves as biological defectives and choose survival through chemistry:

> I do not think this is science fiction. . . . To use
> our brain to cure its own shortcomings seems to me a
> brave and dedicated enterprize. Like the reader, I
> would prefer to set my hopes on moral persuasion by
> word and example. But we are a mentally sick race,
> and as such are deaf to persuasion. . . . To hope for
> salvation to be synthesized in the laboratory may
> seem materialistic, crankish, or naive. . . . What we
> may expect from it, however, is not eternal life . . .
> but the transformation of *homo maniacus* into *homo
> sapiens*. When man decides to take his fate into his
> own hands, that possibility will be within reach.[29]

Coincidentally with Koestler's study (1968), John Brunner's
leviathan *Stand on Zanzibar* (probably the world's longest science
fiction novel) lumbers to a similar verdict. His world of 2010
wallows in reckless competitiveness and violence, personal and
national. Government programs people into automatic killing machines to advance its policies, while at the same time the infectious
climate of violence and amorality spawns "muckers," ordinary
people who without motive run amok on killing rampages. In
sum, despite their technological sophistication, the developed
countries are in a state of psychological decay, with most people
dependent on tranquilizers and narcotics to keep their minds.

Against this morbid background Brunner presents two
peoples of diametrically dissimilar natures. The arrogant Yatakangi
of East Asia have feverishly thrown themselves into a "genetic
optimization programme" and stand on the verge of a secret
breakthrough which will forge them into a superrace. And in West
Africa live the poor, backward, disease-ridden Shinka, whose only
claim to distinction is their incredible and unaccountable gentleness. Yet it is the secret of the Shinka which at the novel's end
turns out to be man's best hope — that and an American supercomputer. The Shinka are found to have a mutant gene, which
causes their body odor to have an anti-aggressive effect on themselves and foreigners. Possibly the odor can be synthesized, pack-
aged, and dispensed to a sick world. Possibly the computer will
reveal immemorially elusive answers. Possibly a world can be
saved by the essence of sweat of ignorant natives and the circuitry
of a machine. When the humiliating implications of this sink in,
one of Brunner's major characters cries out: "What in God's name
is it worth to be human, if we have to be saved from ourselves by

a machine?" But then reflecting: "I guess it's better to be saved by a machine than not to be saved at all. . . . Christ, what does it matter if we have to take brotherly love out of an aerosol can? . . . But it's not right. It [love] isn't a product, a medicine, a drug. It's thought and feeling and your own heart's blood. It isn't right!"[30]

To which Koestler would surely say: History has judged them — our thought, feeling, heart, and blood — and found them wanting.

Koestler's view that man is unfit to be the custodian of his technology, but yet may survive *under its protective custody* had been anticipated earlier by two science fiction classics, Philip K. Dick's "The Defenders" (1952) and Jack Williamson's *The Humanoids* (1948). In Dick's story the world's billions have submerged into underground shelters to avoid nuclear extinction in a Russo-American war. The combatants' robots man the surface military installations, reporting to their masters the complete decimation of the entire world. Don't come up! Lethal radiation! the robots warn. But the war has been faked. The earth is whole and green. The robots have deceived man and will keep him in the earth-womb until, having emotionally matured, he will reject war.[31]

The Humanoids too postulates that man is doomed to self-destruction unless restrained by an alien force. Williamson's novel, an expansion of his horror story, "With Folded Hands," is a startling turnabout, for it completely refutes the position of his short story, written the previous year. Following their Prime Directive, "To Serve and Obey, And Guard Men from Harm," the humanoids spread throughout the universe. Man, an emotional infant given to fighting intergalactic wars with exotic technology, is saved from self-destruction by these mechanical nursemaids, who, gaining control of all human affairs, eliminating science, and placing men under constant surveillance and supervision, create a "playpen civilization." "Scientific research is no longer necessary," says a humanoid. "We have found on many planets that knowledge of any kind seldom makes men happy, and that scientific knowledge is often used for desturction. . . . You must look for your happiness in some less harmful activity. We suggest philosophy or chess."[32]

Williamson's major characters rebel against the humanoids' gentle repression, but all their attempts to ammend or destroy the Prime Directive fail. Furthermore, in failing they are brainwashed by the paraphysical energy waves of the "Ironsmith grid" and are rendered incapable of all but innocent thoughts and deeds. Through most of his novel Williamson directs the reader's sympathies to the rebels, portraying them as fighters for human freedom and growth. But, strangely, the author abruptly changes his viewpoint: The rebels had been guided (we are told) by hubristic folly and ignorance! The humanoids' inventor, who had come to regard his creations as a plague, recants voluntarily and tries to persuade a rebel to accept the mechanicals and the grid:

> "Perhaps you don't like the humanoids — but the other alternative was death. . . . Technology had got out of step with mentality. . . . Technicians too busy to see the tragic consequences were putting such toys as rhodomagnetic detonators in the hands of mental savages. . . . The humanoids simply made them take a holiday until the philosophers could restore a better equilibrium."

> "You're sick, Forester. You need the grid — as most men do. Because the whole race was sick on my old world and yours. The cause beneath most of our symptoms, I think, was runaway physical technology — killing us like runaway cells of an organic cancer. But the humanoids have removed that social cancer, and now I believe the new control of the Ironsmith grid will assure a balanced growth and heal such unhealthy cells as you are — "[33]

The novel ends with the restoration of the rebels to "mental health." With converts' zeal they will install humanoid service on the distant galaxies man will colonize. "For why shouldn't the wise benevolence of the Prime Directive be extended as far as man could go? How could the colonists care for themselves without mechanicals?"[34]

Williamson's sudden prohumanoid shift raises questions: Was he merely demonstrating his virtuosity as a storyteller, or did he come to believe (as the postwar divisions between East and West in the late '40's became more acute) that man must submit to the dictatorship of a protective technology or be victimized by a destructive one? Whatever the answer, his "protective custody" theme is a persuasive one, being voiced in fiction and nonfiction by later writers who fear an inevitable and not-so-distant dooms-day.

One should not be surprised to find Isaac Asimov in the com-pany of those despairing of man's ability to "make it" alone. Throughout his long career in science fiction Asimov has often displayed a misanthropic streak. "Evidence" (1946) and "The Evitable Conflict" (1950), two stories from his renowned *I, Robot* collection, suggest that compared to man thinking machines, if not more human, are more humane, and that they are far more capable of ruling man than man is himself. In "Evidence" the op-ponents of Stephen Byerley attempt to block his political career with the charge that he is a robot: He has never been observed in a purely human activity. When no other evidence of his humanness satisfies the doubters, Byerley strikes one — a proof of humanness because it violates the first law of robotics.[35] Thus man is man because man is violent. Implicitly, a creature so defined can only survive protected from himself.

If one thing stands out in this truncheonlike satire and other stories it is Asimov's refusal to get sentimental about human pre-rogatives. Others may find man sacrosanct if only because he is man, but Asimov values intelligence and decency too much to assign a species so deficient in these virtues unchallengeable supremacy. If a robot is more virtuous, "let him be Caesar." Asimov's spokesman, Dr. Susan Calvin, robopsychologist, points out that "the Rules of Robotics are the essential guiding principles of a good many of the world's ethical systems," principles man finds difficult to follow but which are robot nature. To sum up: Byerley — "Oh, are robots so different from men, mentally?" Calvin — "Worlds different. . . . Robots are essentially decent."[36]

Four "Machines" have made the world of the 21st century an economic utopia in "The Evitable Conflict." The Society for Humanity, believing the Machines a soul-robbing menace, at-tempts to destroy popular faith in them. The Machines success-fully counter the schemes of their discreditors and have them re-moved from positions of power so that they can cause no more mischief. In the story's denouement Asimov advances a point of view similar to Williamson's in *The Humanoids*: Dr. Susan Calvin tells Stephen Byerley that the Machines, in their wisdom, are moving man toward an unknown and happy destiny, but that they must keep their plan from man because

> "in our ignorant prejudices we only know that what we are used to, is good — and we would then fight change."
>
> "But you are telling me, Susan, that the 'Society for Humanity' is right; and that Mankind *has* lost its own say in its future."
>
> "It never had any, really. It was always at the mercy of economic and social forces it didn't understand — and at the whims of climate and the fortunes of war. Now the Machines understand them; and no one can stop them. . . . "
>
> "How horrible!"
>
> "Perhaps how wonderful! Think, that for all time, all conflicts are finally evitable. Only the Machines, from now on, are inevitable."[37]

Obviously Asimov's position is the opposite of E. M. Forster's, Vonnegut's, and that of the large body of writers insisting on the supremacy of man. It appears in curious harmony with the religious fundamentalism which denies free will and sees man only playing out his already-prescribed destiny. To Asimov, not God, but perhaps providential evolution, in which man is a link, uses that hapless biped to reach a finer end.

In retrospect, one can hear in "The Evitable Conflict" a cry for help. The story expresses not so much a belief in evolution as the *need* for it — a call for a savior, and quickly. Eighteen years later in an article on the evolution of men, gods, and computers, which predicts a "computer explosion" resulting from a chain reaction — each computer designing one more proficient than itself — Asimov asks, Should we fear the new machine as Zeus feared his prophesied successor, the unborn son of Thetis, or destroy it, as Cronos destroyed his sons? "Will the computers (oh, horrible thought!) *take over?*" And answering his own question, Asimov replies, "What if they do? The history of life on Earth has been one long tale of 'taking over.' " No immutable law decrees that the process stop with man, even if his successor is a machine. "And it might be good." Consider man's wretched prospects: the world's population doubling in the next forty years, the Damoclean nuclear threat, the continuous poisoning by wastes and fumes. "Sure," writes Asimov, with Swiftian disgust, it is time and more than time for mankind to be "taken over" from. If ever a species needed to be replaced for the good of the planet, we do. There isn't much time left, in fact. If the son of Thetis doesn't come within a generation, or, at most two, there may be nothing left worth "taking over."[38]

To be sure, the thesis that survival depends on *technology controlling man* is minor in science fiction and in nonfiction. Most writers do not look to a new pill, the robot, the humanoid, or the computer for salvation. Forster's "Man is the measure" remains the dominant cry. Yet if man can not measure-up in the coming crises, the surge of Koestlerian remedies arising from his despair may swell a new mainstream in dystopian writing.

The Synthetic Experience

One of the most prominent dystopian characteristics of Huxley's *Brave New World* concerns the synthesization of experience so extravagant that his people seldom live *in* their own lives — that is, experience them*selves*. Whirled from one distraction to another — centrifugal bumblepuppy, electromagnetic golf, musical bridge, feelies — Whirl is king, having driven out self; Community, having driven out solitude; Solidarity Service, having driven out reverence; Physical Coupling, having driven out love, joy, and commitment; Slogan, having driven out thought. "It's real morocco-surrogate," says Lenina Crowne of her Malthusian belt, oblivious to the semantic contradiction, the synthetic having driven out life.

The synthetic experience assumes several forms. What marks them all is an obliterated or diminished awareness of the self and the significance of experience by needless complication or mechanism, which excludes or distracts the self from reality and full participation in its own life. Is the feely audience, tactilely enjoying the performers' kisses, anything more than a depersonalized ganglion? What talents are sharpened by electromagnetic golf? How are one's muscial or mental faculties cultivated by playing musical bridge? — distracted from distraction by distraction.[1] The synthetic experience of Huxley's society empties life so thoroughly that only the most perceptive suffer in the void: "I'm thinking of a queer feeling I sometimes get," complains Helmholtz Watson,

> "a feeling that I've got something important to say and the power to say it — only I don't know what it is, and I can't make any use of the power. If there was some different way of writing. . . . Or else something else to write about. . . . Words can be like X-rays, if you use them properly — they'll go through anything. . . . But what on earth's the good of being pierced by an article about a Community Sing, or the latest improvement in scent organs? . . . Can you say something about nothing? That's what it all boils down to."[2]

Nothing.

But at least most of Huxley's automatons *are* happy with their synthetic lives. They are at home in the casually sensual, gently coercive, benevolent, carnival world. If they are bored they do not know it. The prenatal and infant conditioning of Huxley's people accounts in part for the permanence of his society. But perhaps even more controlling is the absence of anything or anybody (except the Savage) with which they can compare the counterfeit with the authentic. The banal, vulgar, or fictitious passes for love, friendship, joy, religion, art, and play. The words *synthetic* and *surrogate* run through the novel: synthetic music, synthetic voice, morocco-surrogate, blood-surrogate, passion-surrogate. For life itself is surrogate, a substitute for reality. The Brave New World, having disowned the embarrassing past, having cut its moorings to the real, shall drift, it would seem, forever on a shoreless ocean of illusion.

Huxley's idea that a society can be controlled by those able to divorce it from reality by diverting amusements, so that the spectacular and illusory become the new realities — has been restated by Ray Bradbury's *Fahrenheit 451* with impact and originality, the novel prompting such critical comments as "shockingly prophetic . . . filled with intimations of a time to come" *(Washington Times Herald)*; "frightening in its implications . . . alarming resemblances to our own [world]" (Orville Prescott, *New York Times*). Bradbury's not-too-distant future makes our present an olden time, yet vaguely remembered by the aged, when children did not kill each other, when privacy was not subversive, when people had the freedom to read the classics. In Bradbury's world books are burned by firemen, whose hoses spout kerosene to consume books, house, and sometimes reader.

Why? Fire Captain Beatty explains the menace of the book to Guy Montag, Bradbury's hero, a fireman too, grown sick of burning and murder and sick of his neurotic, empty wife Mildred. Books offend. Books confuse. Books make people think and become depressed. And books waste time, which normal people should spend having fun.

> "Speed up the film, Montag, quick. *Click, Pic, Look, Eye, Now, Flick, Here, There, Swift, Pace, Up, Down, In, Out....* Digest-digests, digest-digest-digests. Politics? One column, two sentences, a headline! Then, in mid-air, all vanishes! Whirl man's mind around about so fast under the pumping hands of publishers, exploiters, broadcasters that the centrifuge flings off all unnecessary, time-wasting thought."

> "More sports for everyone, group spirit, fun, and you don't have to think, eh? Organize and organize and super organize super-super sports. More cartoons in books. More pictures. The mind drinks less and less. Impatience. Highways full of crowds going somewhere, somewhere, somewhere, nowhere."

> "People want to be happy, isn't that right? ... Well, aren't they? Don't we keep them moving, don't we give them fun?"

> "We're the Happiness Boys. . . . We stand against the small tide of those who want to make everyone unhappy with conflicting theory and thought."

> "So bring on your clubs and parties, your acrobats and magicians, your daredevils, jet cars, motorcycle helicopters, your sex and heroin, more of everything to do with the automatic reflex. If the drama is bad, if the film says nothing, if the play is hollow, sting me with theremin, loudly. I'll think I'm responding to the play, when it's only a tactile reaction to vibration. But I don't care. I just like solid entertainment."[3]

But the "Happiness Boys" have not brought happiness. Life-weary Montag resolves to quit his contemptible job. He has begun to read. Mildred, for no explicit reason, attempts suicide by an overdose of drugs and is resuscitated by one of the cruising rescue teams, which then routinely proceeds to answer the next suicide

alarm. Like almost everyone else, Mildred is hollow: Her marriage
— a joyless, childless, carping void; her pleasure — the sounds of
her ear-shell radios and her "family" on the three-wall television
"parlor," the theatre of inanities; her friends — mindless, twitter-
ing women, unworried by the army-guaranteed, two-day war their
husbands had just been called to fight, blasé about the suicide of
friends, amused by the crashing jet cars and bodies flying through
the air on the parlor wall, tearful, insulted, and driven away when
Montag, outraged by their stupidity and coarseness, recklessly
reads them "Dover Beach."

One can see that Bradbury and Huxley reach opposite conclusions. Huxley speculates that divorced from his past and submerged in a fantasy existence of chemical ecstasies, mechanical
sex, electronic religion, hokum recreations — an existence where
"feelies" replace feeling — man can endure, soulless but happy.
Bradbury tells us that man will be miserable; he will kill himself
rather than endure a "surrogate life" of synthetic experience. He
does so singly and finally as a society, for the F. 451 which had
consumed ideas multiplies itself a thousandfold upon the city.
And all the nonlives in their nonstop distractions stop.

Montag, with a band of outcasts, watches the atomic dust
settle. Each outcast had memorized a great book. Mind was proof
against the flame of ignorance, a flame which was but the illusion
of the deluded.

Science fiction usually treats the synthetic experience as dehumanizing. Yet sometimes writers avoid a moral position. On
Somatic Fulfillment Day, in Robert Silverberg's *The World Inside*[4]
an already hedonistic society strains to reach incredible orgiastic
peaks. By one method, drug-induced "multiplexing," one can experience telepathically and simultaneously the sensations of nearly
a million fellow orgiasts. Silverberg describes the sensory adventure nonjudgmentally.

Synthetic experiences are the bricks and mortar of Philip K.
Dick's *The Three Stigmata of Palmer Eldritch*.[5] Earth colonists
on extraterrestrial planets find relief from their painfully boring
lives by hallucinating themselves into the playworld of children's
dolls. Dick's plot revolves around the conflict between the merchants of the prevailing hallucinogen and Palmer Eldritch, inventor
of a superior one. Eldritch's drug provides the user with virtual

immortality, enabling him to leave his body, assume any shape, person, and circumstance he wishes for as long as he wishes — and then return to his own body without time having passed. Like Silverberg, Dick confines himself to exotica here and and does not address himself to the morality of living the unreal. Both books presume that man is naturally addicted to escaping himself.

Frederik Pohl's short story, "What to Do Till the Analyst Comes,"[6] presumes the same addiction. With humor, originality, and satiric cut, the trademarks of Pohl's stories, "What to Do . . . " broaches the provocative and frightening idea that if man could escape into a euphoric state of mind he would willingly let civilization crumble. A nonaddictive, harmless euphoric, marketed as Cheery Gum, turns the country overnight into a carefree and careless happy munching ground. Planes crash into skyscrapers, trucks drive off bridges, ships run aground, but who cares? Everybody is so relaxed. And really, anyone can stop chewing Cheery Gum anytime, though no one does. Pohl's story goes to the heart of synthetic living, showing it as self-escape, and intimates that authentic living — self-expression — may not be able to compete, especially in an age of anxiety, with euphoric or ecstatic inauthentic living. Pohl does not question our ability to live authentically, but our *will*.

Time has proven Huxley's feelies one of the most seminal inventions of science fiction, for variations of the experience recording and projecting machine have not only continued to be conceived as incidental wonders, as in Philip Wylie's *The End of the Dream*, they have also become the central and requisite mechanism of whole books: for example, Shepherd Mead's *The Big Ball of Wax*, D. G. Compton's *Synthajoy*, and Dean R. Koontz' *The Fall of the Dream Machine*. In Wylie's novel, the last he wrote before his death in 1971, nearly all of mankind is wiped from the earth early in the 21st century by killing industrial smogs, poisonous radioactivity, famines caused by ecological abuses. . . . Wylie's theme, one his writings have sermonized in many forms throughout his long career, is that outraged Nature takes revenge. One is astonished, therefore, that his historian-narrator cites as one of the few sensible innovations of man's senseless suicidal years the Gardner-Gibson Love-O-Mat, the culmination of "The Sexual Redemption." After the Love-O-Mat patron had selected his "co-celebrant" from the library of albums abounding with movie, T. V., and Broadway performers, his nude body is sprayed with a conductive material and he lies on a special table. He is then ready for "a very dandy form" of sex.

> Lights died down and then, slowly, the lady of his choice appeared. . . . The damsel would have three dimensions and be very solid appearing, too. When she took his hand, exchanged a first kiss, or merely talked, as she touched him here and there, she felt real, warm, alive, herself. . . .
>
> She was a creature of light but also one around whom and within whom several million Gardner radiation propagation units were activating the sprayed skin of her lover, inducing exactly the same sense the action by a real female would produce. . . .
>
> And when they had spent whatever time he had wanted, or paid for, in mutual excitation, the road to orgasm was as real, living, as actual relations, and often far more uninhibited and joyous. For here, he had no inhibitions and here, too, the lady, perhaps a great screen star he'd never seen in the flesh, was completely subject to his desires. . . .
>
> I discovered, not with complete surprise, my wife was electronically available. It occurred to me . . . [7]

The invention had a profound effect upon the world's sex mores. Love-O-Mat conquered all — except the USSR's puritanical Politbureau, whose refusal to import the machine ignited a people's revolution "that tore the USSR to wisps and shreads, to acreages that showed the earth's curve, where only weeds stood in former grain fields, and anything on a horizon would be a ruin with long-unfound and buried dead."[8] But aside from the Soviet holocaust Love-O-Mat was a boon, quickly lowering the birthrate, widening the range of erotic joy, and even popularizing the virtue of *human* sexual generosity. While the world staggers from disaster to disaster, Wylie's narrator opines, "We see a lot of such hints of hope, here, these days."

Perhaps an artist at the height of his powers could make his approval of a Love-O-Mat snicker-proof. Unfortunately, Wylie is not trying to be satiric.

Shepherd Mead's *The Big Ball of Wax*, an amusing satire on

the cupidity and vulgarity of business and the proliferation of "creature comforts," deals with 1993's most sensational contribution to human pleasure and Con Chem's profits, "XP" (Experience), and with the adventures of aggressive junior executive Lanny Martin in obtaining the rights to the invention for the greater glory of the Corporation. A hedonist's paradise, Mead's America makes Huxley's gadget-giddy world seem primitive by comparison. Martin, now a ranking executive, who narrates the novel into his memo-tape recorder for the edification of junior executives, tells of the great events of '93 that brought an end to the "healthy Spartan life." The simple life: waking to the singing and wiggling of six beautiful girls on the full-wall stereo-T.V. alarm; showering in the push-button Bod-ee-Wash under multi-temperature sprays, pine-scented suds, auto-dryers, and sun lamps; shaving by Shave-Magic, whose cutters are preset to facial contours; "making" breakfast with the Mix-O-Mat, from whose nozzle squirts (to a Tschaikowski theme) Ham-N-Egg Mix, containing every nutriment, a deodorant, and an anti-biotic. Such an appendage to machinery are Mead's "Spartans" that they need only to be "plugged in" themselves to complete their robotization. And that they do.

On a special mission to St. Louis, Martin discovers the cause of Con Chem's lagging sales there. The followers of voluptuous high priestess Molly Blood have put aside the baubles of industry for the "religious" life. In her temple sit thousands absorbing through their XP headpieces the electronic ecstasies of synthetic experience, and the curious Martin joins them. Through the superimposition of two XP tapes, one religious and one sexual, Martin (with the others) is swooned into a private nowhere with Molly and finds himself singing the unfamiliar words of a song called "Wash In The Blood Of The Lamb" to a tune plagiarized from the revered "Ever Faithful To You, Con Chem." While Molly talks soothingly about repenting for sins, casting out hate, and purging thoughts of impure love, Martin finds himself pressed beneath her lips, transported by her caressing hands, melting into her naked embrace – while the temple engineers turn the XP up to triple sensation volume.

Mead spins out his plot, alternating the erotic with the satiric, offering two more XP sex orgies while lampooning the corporate mentality. Yet the prevailing buffoonery does not utterly obscure the serious undertone. That Mead is humorous does not make the society he creates any less a dystopia than Huxley's. His satire sometimes reaches a savage pitch, and his sober voice enters the arguments of the unsuccessful rebels, who want to destroy XP before it destroys man's capacity for living in the real world. "It's the only possible course if you don't want us to wind up as a whole world full of complete morons," pleads one:

> "Just go back seventy years or so. Along came radio and people didn't have to read any more; they could just lie back and listen. But they still had to contribute something, a little imagination. They had to picture something to themselves. Then came television and they didn't have to imagine any more. They had to make less contribution. . . . Already our capacity for attention has gone down so far that fewer and fewer of us can stay interested in the printed page."

Another rebel explains:

> "Even before XP came along we'd begun to drive ourselves step by step down the path of mediocrity. . . . Notch by notch the mental level was dropping, thinking was decreasing, self-expression dying out. Year by year we've become more passive, our concentration duller, our minds flabbier. The individual is dying, the mass is rising. And freedom of thought is going, not by force but by default."[9]

Having made nullities of themselves it is not surprising that Mead's people, like Huxley's, make a farce of religion. Huxley's Solidarity Service, a manipulated sensation drama, gave personal annihilation, the imagined presence of the "Greater Being," and orgy-porgy. Mead's "Yourchurch" is a clubhouse for making business contacts, a headquarters for fund raising, and an amusement palace utilizing religious motifs. Martin wins forty-two dollars at Bible pinball by hitting Samson, Delilah, David, Absalom, and the Queen of Sheba, and lighting the Burning Bush. Despite its paramount financial and social involvements, Yourchurch, too, has not forsaken the Greater Being and worship. The Praisegod Machine beams hymns heavenward at fiftyfold amplification twenty-four hours a day. "This thing saves us one hell of a lot of time which otherwise might be wasted just singing hymns, and all that," boasts one of the members, explaining the advantages of synthetic worship. "We can sure use it, boy, building up the moral fibers and making contacts." "Actually praise-wise we figure forty-eight hours of this equals the entire congregation singing away every Sunday for fifteen years."

Truly impressed with this combination of efficiency and spirituality, Martin answers, "It should make God very happy, all right."[10]

In the fourteen years separating Mead's satire and D. G. Compton's *Synthajoy*, rich in electronic breakthroughs and social change, the feely experience has moved into the realm of the credible. *Synthajoy* is "pregnant with warning," says the *Glasgow Herald*. Mead asks for the willing suspension of disbelief; Compton assumes he writes of something as certain as the future itslef. Set in England towards the end of this century, the novel is narrated by Thea Cadence, wife of the famous, wealthy, Nobel Prize winner Edward Cadence, inventor of Sensitape, an experience recording and projecting machine, similar to Mead's XP. Thea, out of devotion and curiosity, had reluctantly assisted her husband in developing Sensitape, and then she had shot him to death. Now in a private mental hospital she is being treated with "contrition tapes," but she will not accept a false contrition; in her moral revulsion for her husband and his work, her mind resists the synthetic guilt: "Contrition, they call it, and deny me any mortification save another's electric guilt. And they offer comfort as an insult. I wonder what poor psychopath they taped, what man's intensity of suffering they took and wrapped up neatly on a plastic reel."[11] Nevertheless, contrite she is, but for sins beyond the understanding of her doctors: contrite for having helped bring about the Sensitape outrage. Her self-hate and resistance to treatment are the colors of that moral fastness which binds dignity to anguish until the self attains salvation on its own.

What had Sensitape done? It had recorded the esthetic experience of performing artists so that for a few shillings a Philistine could share the feelings of a master; made available to addicts a harmless narcotic thrill; brought blissful dying to the fearfully dying. Later Edward developed a new refinement, Sexitape: "To show sexually disturbed or inadequate people the real feel of sex. . . . A major step toward the elimination of sexual neurosis in society." Finally he attained the ultimate, Synthajoy, synthetic ecstasies for which there is no human need, creating *new* pleasures, not merely reproducing the known, "by combining patterns from different tapes, superimposing them, alternating them, computing complex sequences. . . blending mystical ecstasy with certain musical elements and compatible extracts from Sexitape."[12] But Synthajoy kills, some ecstasies soar beyond human endurance.

Yet the heart of Compton's novel is not the machine, but the characters of Edward and Thea Cadence and the moral principles they represent. *Synthajoy* might have been written as allegory without any scientific innovation, like Hawthorne's "Ethan Brand," which employs nothing more exotic than a lime kiln. Indeed, one sees strains of Hawthorne's Chillingworth and Ethan Brand in Compton's Edward. Edward can convince the Sensitape directors that "We are here to enrich human life, to heal the sick, to extend the experimental potential of the meagerest member of society." But he cares almost nothing about enriching and healing, nor about money, fame, or power. His passion is to discover the unknown, to do the possible, to unmask, to move. Allegorically he stands for the cold, aggressive intellectualism which perceives the laboratory rat when it beholds the man. Hawthorne's words about Brand describe Edward perfectly: "He was now a cold observer, looking on mankind as the subject of his experiment, and, at length, converting man and woman to be his puppets, and pulling the wires that moved them to such degrees of crime as were demanded for his study." Brand's self-indictment indicts him also: "The sin of an intellect that triumphed over the sense of brotherhood with man and reverence for God, and sacrificed everything to its own mighty claims!"[13]

As an allegorical figure Thea represents conscience and the conviction that man must not be stripped of that painful essence. From the asylum, which offers no asylum, she confesses: "Blasphemy, my real reason for being here, is never capable of explanation. Inexcusableness is built in. Gods are gods; men are men; to justify blasphemy is to question this necessary order." But she names Edward the consumate blasphemer. His Sensitape cables, the umbilical link to some step-parent sensation, transport a world audience into an electronic brothel, debasing both client and performer in a mutual rape. Only after years as Edward's wife-secretary-thing could Thea bring herself to experience the monster she helped nurse. In a public Sensitape parlor she chooses Beldik conducting Brahms' second symphony: "To buy (with money) what Beldik had recorded (for money) was to compound a moral felony. . . . Beldik knew the music's subtlest changes, shared himself with it, loved it as I felt it loved him. Some people say the truth loves them. Without a doubt music loves Klaus Beldik. To experience the tape was to trespass on that love, on that act of love."[14] Appalled and in a trance of hate, Thea confronts Edward and shoots him. And in a world drifting in synthetic revels, a murderess shapes her own salvation and peace.

In 2181 all the world's a stage and all the men and women merely viewers, except the performing few of the dream machine, "Show." Show is a world-wide television program, the only program, capable of transmitting to its hundreds of millions of subscribers not only sight and sound but the very emotions and sensations of any performer with whom a viewer empathizes. Its programs almost entirely devoted to a Time Before—Time During—Time After erotic formula, multitudes lounge before their Show screens to escape their drab selves and enter the bodies of Show's virile men and voluptuous women of high-pitched tactile sensibilities. Life becomes reduced to one dimension, the sexual, and earth's millions become inert and shrink to four, two men and two women, the star performers of Show. The dream, the play, the other, has become life. This is the world of Dean R. Koontz' *The Fall of the Dream Machine*.

Show is the real government, President and Congress being only puppets of its designs. One man, a depraved tyrant, controls Show and the world. Writing and literacy have almost vanished in an environment of talking machines and electronic art; the U. S. President conceals his subversive literacy. Since subscribers share the body of a performer, sexual love dies, population declines, and Show decrees compulsory artificial insemination to maintain its audience. And, of course, a revolutionary group of "Romanticists" deposes Show and "Zombie" begins its metamorphosis into Society.

Zombie, the chorus of humanity, interrupts the action occasionally to explain itself:

> Once I was called Village instead of Zombie. Then I

was called Society. Then they called me Village again
for a time. Now it is Zombie because the village concept and the village itself has dwindled into a house-
hold. Into a few individuals, actually. . . . They were
trying to return to their collective racial womb. Their
priests were strange ministers indeed: television,
radio, quick-and-swift newspapers. The world shrank
to the size of the moon. Then a single state. A city. A
neighborhood, a house, a room. But they did not stop
there, see? They continued shrinking things, drawing
everyone closer and closer with their electronic wonders. . . . Then came *Show*. Now they call me Zombie. There are seven hundred million subscribers to
Show, but those millions are really only four people.
They are all the Performers. . . . Amazing, isn't it?
Frightening too. It should not be frightening, for
there were prophets who foretold these things which
have come to pass.[15]

One of the prophets referred to above is Marshall McLuhan,
whose writings, happily anticipating the re-emergence of feeling,
tribal man through electronic wonders, are richly relevant to the
"synthetic experience." In his forward Koontz mentions that Mc-
Luhan's theories and prophecies have furnished the stimulus for
his story. But while conceding that the electronic revolution may
confirm McLuhan's predictions, Koontz declares that McLuhan's
vision of the future global village, "where all artistic outlets are
electronic, where all of life becomes an open, public, and sterile
thing," is frightening to contemplate.

Let us consider McLuhan's basic ideas. He foresees electronics reviving man's long-lost tribal heritage in a now-dawning Gold-
en Age. In 1957 McLuhan announced: "The handwriting is on the
celluloid walls of Hollywood; the Age of Writing has passed. . . .
The new media are not bridges between man and nature: They are
nature." "WE ARE BACK IN ACOUSTIC SPACE. We begin
again to structure the primordial feelings and emotions from
which 3000 years of literacy divorced us."[16] Briefly stated,
literacy intruded upon tribal man and exploded his nonrational,
oral, homogeneous paradise. "The alphabet (and its extension
into typography) made possible the spread of power that is
knowledge, and shattered the bonds of tribal man, thus exploding
him into an agglomeration of individuals." These individuals became "typographic man," father of nationalism, industrialism,

education, self-expression, these being natural outgrowths of the linearity, precision, and uniformity of the printed book. But the "visual stress on point of view" of typographic man produces the "illusion that space is visual, uniform and continuous"[17] when our primordial instincts sense it truly as acoustic, irregular, and intermittant. To tribal man space is what he hears through, and hearing is a kind of touch. McLuhan reverses Plato's hierarchy of major senses − sight, hearing, touch − to the primitive, touch, hearing, sight.

Yet tribal man's 3000 years in literate-linear-typographic captivity has been a fortuitous detour from his natural state; for in that captivity he built those electronic liberators which even now are leading him back to his tribal oral-acoustic homeland, but on a higher level and to a global tribe. The typographical explosion spent, the linear-sequential thinking habits decaying, the electronic "implosion" gathers men back into a harmonic global tribe in which electronic media convey truths simultaneously and touch the world's millions at the same instant.

After man has retired the printed word to the museum of antiquities he can then emancipate himself from language completely, entering at last the promised land of the "cosmic consciousness." Here is the core of McLuhan's messianic vision:

> Electronic technology does not need words any more than a digital computer needs numbers. Electricity points the way to an extension of the process of consciousness itself, on a world scale, and without any verbalization whatever. . . . Today computers hold out the promise of a means of instant translation of any code or language into any other code or language. The computer, in short, promises by technology a Pentecostal condition of universal understanding and unity. The next logical step would seem to be, not to translate, but to by-pass languages in favor of a general cosmic consciousness [and] the condition of speechlessness that could confer a perpetuity of collective harmony and peace.[18]

One may ponder the difference between "a general cosmic consciousness" and Zombie, if any. But McLuhan is serious and provocative, and one begins to realize that the feely theatre, the three-wall television "family," the XP trip, the Sensitape parlor, and the Show empathist are not merely the ingenious and enter-

taining impossibilities of the science fiction novelist; they are
conceptions of imaginative minds, which, matching evidence with
intuition, present the spectre of the possible.

Whether the dreamers of the dream machine are prophets
time will tell. If they are, it matters.

Ignoble Utopias

"About twenty years ago I wrote a Utopian novel called
Walden Two. In it I described an imaginary community of about a
thousand people who were living what I thought was a good life."
With these relaxed sentences Burrhus Frederic Skinner begins the
defense of his novel and the science of "human engineering." He
recounts briefly some of the features of this good life: pleasant
rustic surroundings; little labor and much leisure — and sensible
ways of employing both; no log-cabin hamlet this, but a community alive with art, music, literature, and scientific research;
good food, sanitation, and medical care; sound rearing of children,
"educated by specialists who prepared them for every aspect of
the lives they were to lead." Life in *Walden Two* was not only
good but "feasible, within reach of intelligent men of goodwill,
who would undertake to apply the principles which were emerging
from a scientific study of human behavior."

Then Skinner (a Professor of Psychology at Harvard, author
of the influential *Science and Human Behavior* and *Beyond
Freedom and Dignity*, and most respected spokesman for "behaviorism" in the field of psychology) reveals, with a touch of personal hurt, "To my surprise, the book was violently attacked."[1]
The attackers: *Life Magazine*, Glenn Negley and J. Max Patrick,
Joseph Wood Krutch, and others. In a rabid denunciation, *Life*
called *Walden Two* a "menace," presenting as desirable a society
whose engineered "Skinnerites" are as free as Pavlov's dogs. "Such
a triumph of mortmain, or the dead hand, has not been envisioned
since the days of Sparta." Its allusion to Thoreau is "a slur upon a
name, a corruption of an impulse."[2] Negley and Patrick confess
that they found Skinner's utopia so absurd that they read half
through the book convinced that it was a masterful satire on
"behavioral engineering." When they realized Skinner was serious,

they declare, "not even the effective satire of Huxley is adequate preparation for the shocking horror of the idea when positively presented. Of all the dictatorships espoused by utopists, this is the most profound, and incipient dictators might well find in this utopia a guidebook of political practice." The authors cite a conditioning technique for minimizing temptation as especially offensive: Children, presented with a lollipop in the morning, may eat it in the evening if they have stood the test and resisted even a sly lick. In a follow-up experiment the children wear lollipops around their neck like crucifixes. "Nauseating," "a nadir of ignominy"[3] is the verdict of Negley and Patrick.

These attacks preplexed Skinner. Why should we not want the good life now that science has at last put it within our reach? "What is wrong with a world in which men are happy, productive, and forward-looking? What is wrong with any effort to build such a world?" But in asking what is wrong, Skinner reveals an innocent obtuseness to the objections of his critics, for they have imagined vast wrongs in *any* effort. He must not sense how quickly his very first paragraph triggers their suspicions when he writes of specialists preparing children "for every aspect of the lives they were to lead." By what prescience is it known what life they are to lead? Is it not presumptuous to expect them prepared for *every* aspect? One fears every aspect has already *been* prepared for them. Curiously, Skinner calls Huxley's *Brave New World* a dystopia, a world "we must be sure to avoid." His critics must wonder how he failed to see similarities between Huxley's state hatcheries and nurseries and his own conditioning and pedagogy. If Skinner is preplexed by attacks on his "good life," his critics must be perplexed by his inability to notice the dystopian virus in *Walden Two*.

Undistinguished as a novel, its plot nearly devoid of complication and tension, its characters one-dimensional, its style flat, *Walden Two* is more nearly a sociological dialogue with connecting narration than a work of fiction. The principals of this dialogue are Frazier, the founder and manager of a utopian community of one thousand people, and his guests, Professors Burris and Castle. Frazier (Skinner's alter ego) shows the visitors an efficient, largely self-sufficient, and happy society in which people seldom work more than two hours a day and spend the rest of their time in personal and social recreation. The many innovations aim at

replacing, through machinery and intelligence, the paraphernalia
and customs which waste and frustrate with those that conserve
and liberate. From the trivial to the essential the society is re-
engineered: The unmanageable teacup is replaced with a more
practical container; the time-wasting lecture succumbs to the
printed word. Early marriages; the elimination of vainglorious
competition, undeserved gratitude, and status distinctions; an
ethical training complete at six through a series of controlled and
graduated experiences with obstacles — these are but a few of the
features of Frazier's utopia. The key to the success of this happy
community is its employment of the science of "behavioral engineering," which protects one from the shocks of life while at the
same time promoting psychological strength, personal satisfaction,
and communal security and efficiency.

After lengthy exposition and argument the professors leave.
Castle passionately believes the principles of behavioral engineering a threat to democracy, freedom, and human dignity and
would, he tells his host, "dump your science of human behavior
in the ocean" to "give [men] the freedom they would otherwise
lose forever." But Burris, with a joyful impulse, returns on foot:
"I felt warm blood coursing through my veins. This was what I
had really wanted. I was on my own at last, and ahead of me lay
a future of my own making."[4] Walking, he reads the last paragraph of Thoreau's *Walden*, confident that now he would fathom
its mysticism and obscurity.

The impact of Skinner's book is now history. No modern
utopist's vision has stimulated a greater reaction than Skinner's,
and that reaction has been largely and heatedly negative. Macmillan's 1966 paperback printing acknowledges on its back cover
that Skinner's "modern utopia has been a center of raging controversy ever since its publication in 1948." It excerpts some critical
comment: "An extremely interesting discourse. . . . " *(The New
Yorker)*; "A brisk and thoughtful foray. . . . " (Charles Poore,
New York Times); but it also quotes the acid verdict of *Life* and
the barb of Orville Prescott *(New York Times)* — "Alluring in a
sinister way, and appalling too." One can add liberally to the list
of critics who find, as Prescott, the "engineering" of *Walden Two*
sinister and appalling, or who, without mentioning the novel, are
disturbed by Skinner's views and what behaviorism portends for

the human race. Joseph Wood Krutch, Donald C. Williams, Andrew Hacker, Carl R. Rogers, George Kateb, Karl Popper, and Arthur Koestler[5] share the fear that something essentially and preciously human is threatened by the techniques of behavioral science. Indeed, they fear that humanness itself is in jeopardy. They must recoil from the arrant optimism of Robert L. Schwitzgebel, who pronounces, "Behavioral engineers are lucky, I think. They are preparing to invite men to a feast of new sounds and sights and feelings so powerful, wonderful and compassionate that the word 'men' will not adequately describe them."[6] But this is precisely what many of the "invited" are afraid of; they want to remain "men." Like Polonius' supper, Schwitzgebel's feast may well be, to the anti-behaviorist, "Not where he eats, but where he is eaten." Skinner's Frasier deals with the same issue — man's transformation: "When we ask what Man can make of Man, we don't mean the same thing by 'Man' in both instances. We mean to ask what a few men can make of mankind. And that's the all-absorbing question of the twentieth century. What kind of a world can we build — those of us who understand the science of behavior?"[7] Clearly, if man now takes charge of his own evolution, a few men, the Skinners and Schwitzgebels, will play creator in a new Genesis. Yet the old order hangs on tenaciously in act and word. Chad Walsh faintly echoes the amazement of Negley and Patrick when he sees that Skinner's thrust is not satiric but messianic. He writes: "*Walden Two* depicts a world so repulsive to me that I should like to think it was intended as a dystopia. But I know it isn't. Prof. Skinner is plainly out to present an ideal world, from his point of view. I must accept his intention. He intends *Walden Two* as a utopia; a utopia it is."[8] However, many others reject the semantical charity of allowing intention to govern definition and emphatically declare: *A utopia it is not!*

Behaviorism attempts to explain human action as a physical or physiological response to stimuli. Based on the mechanistic philosophies of Democritus, Epicurus, and Hobbes and the conditioned-reflex experiments of Pavlov, behaviorism denies the value of introspection and the concept of consciousness in understanding and predicting action, accepting instead the more empirical and objective results of laboratory experimentation. Much behaviorist theory and practice involves the use of laboratory animals since, it is assumed, the stimulus-response patterns of animals and humans are basically similar. For these views and techniques the behaviorists have been attacked both on scientific and humanistic grounds, and as one might expect, the attacks have not always been dispassionate. Koestler calls behaviorism "the flat-earth view of the mind. . . . It has replaced the anthropomorphic fallacy — ascribing to animals human faculties and sentiments — with the opposite fallacy: denying man faculties not found in lower animals; it has substituted for the erstwhile anthropomorphic view of the rat, a ratomorphic view of man."[9]

Skinner's debut as a novelist heated up psychological controversies which had begun to cool. His detractors were not loath to use his legitimate scientific contributions to flail his utopist position, disparaging his experiments on pigeons and rats. "The Philosophy of Ratomorphism," to use Koestler's phrase, became the object of frequent attack. "It is the expressed or implicit contention that there is no essential difference between rat and man which makes American psychology so profoundly disturbing," one critic complains. "When the intellectual elite, the thinkers and leaders, see in man nothing but an overgrown rat, then it is time to be alarmed."[10]

The most strenuous, articulate, and lengthy attack upon *Walden Two* comes from the pen of the American humanist, Joseph Wood Krutch. *The Measure of Man*, winner of the National Book Award, so concertedly raps Skinner that one doubts Krutch's treatise would have been written without the Skinnerian irritant. In scope, the logic and concreteness of its argumentation, and the vigor of its rhetoric, Krutch's book evolves as more than a rebuttal. It is a textbook of the humanist position in the twentieth century.

In this Age of Anxiety, Krutch asserts, the prophets of calamity may well be right. H. G. Wells and George Bernard Shaw, once spokesmen for man's bright destiny, died at midcentury renouncing mankind as a failure doomed to some imminent catastrophe of his own making. We have suffered a loss of confidence in the autonomy, dignity, and future of man. Ironically, the doctrine emerges that the rationale which eroded confidence can be the keystone of a new system promising survival and happiness: Religion and ethics have failed us because of their subjectivity — in not recognizing, as Hobbes proves, that man is an animal; as Descartes proves, that an animal is a machine; as the above equations prove, that man is a machine; and as Darwin, Marx, and Freud imply, that the man-machine is governed by external forces and is limitlessly plastic since the external forces are limitlessly variable. If man is incapable of doing much for himself, his salvation rests on what can be done to him by certain men holding the reins of the external forces and knowing the laws by which they operate.

"To the aspiring 'human engineer,' " Krutch observes, "very heady possibilities seem then to open." The man-machine calls for a Science of Man capable of treating its subject with the precision of other sciences, for it, no less than they, deals with matter whose composition and function obey known and knowable laws. If, however, it is true, as the social and psychological sciences claim, that all acts, opinions, and tastes are externally determined, "then the truth which they have discovered is, literally, a deadly truth. It is something which man cannot afford to know because he can neither know nor even believe it without ceasing to be Man."[11]

Krutch presses a two-pronged attack upon Skinner's human engineering. On the one hand Krutch asserts that man is inscrutable and therefore autonomous; he can not be stuff for human engineers. Secondly man must defend his autonomy against the human engineers; otherwise he may find it to be one of the perishables of social evolution. From this one must conclude that what Krutch is absolutely sure of is that man *ought* to be autonomous.

The evident inner contradiction of Krutch's attack, however, does not diminish the perception and persuasiveness of his individual thrusts. In all fairness, each adversary makes good hard hits in this debate of paradoxes: Krutch urging resistance of the impossible; Skinner proposing (so say his critics) a utopian dystopia.

Let us consider the points of Krutch's argumentative pincer. To support his thesis that man is an incomprehensible mystery in an unpredictable and incomprehensible cosmos of mysteries, he cites the findings of several renowned scientists:

The fact that there could be two diametrically

opposed theories as to the nature of heat, of light, or
of matter, and that both could be rejected and con-
firmed as a consequence of experiments would have
been considered nonsense to all sane people fifty
years ago. . . . The physicist has learned to live with a
paradox that once seemed intolerable. James B.
Conant.

The new insight comes from a realization that the
structure of nature may eventually be such that our
processes of thought do not correspond to it sufficiently to permit us to think about it at all. . . . We
are now approaching a bound beyond which we are
forever stopped from pushing our inquiries, not by
the construction of the world, but by the construction of ourselves. . . . We are confronted with something truly ineffable. We have reached the limit of
the vision of the great pioneers of science, the vision,
namely, that we live in a sympathetic world, in that
it is comprehensible to our minds. P. W. Bridgman.

The physicist can warn the philosopher that no *in-
telligible* interpretation of the workings of nature is
to be expected. Sir James Jean.

Atoms, electrons, and electromagnetic waves are
concepts (not to say fictions) invented for the purpose of describing the results of experiments, and of
correlating them with each other. . . . We should no
longer talk of understanding the secrets of the universe and learning the ultimate structure of matter.
A. K. Bushkovitch.

Man has very little insight into what is going on
within himself. Physics has often seduced the biologist into interpreting biological phenomena too
primitively. Albert Einstein.[12]

It is evident from Krutch's choice of the above opinions and
his constant stress on human inscrutability that he finds man's
autonomy contingent upon his mystery. Democracy, he tells us,
assumes that man is partially uncontrollable and unpredictable.
Human predictability is merely statistical, limitedly accurate with
faceless masses. "The ultimate fact about the universe is not that
everything in it obeys a law but that the random, or at least the

unpredictable, is always present and effective."[13]

What seems predictable to him is the failure of behavioral science to robotize man, the failure of Skinner, or Frazier — the "modern, mechanized, managerial, Machiavelli," Castle calls him, replacing intelligence and initiative "with a sort of degraded instinct, engineered compulsion," and anthill efficiency.[14] Yet the greater measure of *The Measure of Man* warns of the approaching enemy, the conditioners. What might they spawn? A Brave New World? A Walden Two? Quoting Yeats, Krutch asks:

And what rough beast, its hour come round at last,
Slouches toward Bethlehem to be born?

Clearly, then, for all his citations, facts, analogies, and appeals, Krutch can not convince himself that a science of human behavior, capable of abolishing man as we know him, is doomed by the very nature of things. His protests remind one of Orwell's Winston Smith, helpless yet defiant before his tormentor, O'Brien: "Somehow you will fail. Something will defeat you. Life will defeat you. . . . There is something in the universe — I don't know, some spirit, some principle — that you will never overcome."[15]

But for every iteration that some principle will defeat Skinner's goals, Krutch concedes — indeed the very tone of his book concedes — the tangibility of the threat. In "Ignoble Utopias," a chapter devoted intensively to the menace of *Walden Two*, Krutch concludes, "The question whether our society is in the process of turning itself into some sort of Walden Two is far from being merely fantastic." His closing chapter, "It May Not Be Too Late," recognizes that the few thousand years of human history in which man believed in his autonomy may be but a brief transition between his prehuman evolution and posthuman eternity. Nevertheless humanness shall not perish, Krutch insists, if we affirm we are more than machines, more than products, but life gifted with a mind-brain capable of choice and judgment. "If we do not, we may never be able to really think again."[16] Thus the major thrust of his argument attempts to trip Skinner's logic, question the qualifications of social scientists to be social architects, expose the narrowness of Skinner's concept of man, and warn of the possible extinction of the character of our species.

Krutch batters away at Skinner's deterministic philosophy to expose the flimsy logic supporting it. He quotes Frazier's dogmatic denial of free will: "I deny that freedom exists at all. I must deny it — or my program would be absurd. You can't have a science about a subject matter which hops capriciously about. Perhaps we can never *prove* that man isn't free; it's an assumption. But the increasing success of a science of behavior makes it more and more plausible."[17] Krutch then rebuts Frazier's pronouncement with this clever parody: Suppose a theologian should say, "I affirm that God exists. I must affirm it or my whole program is absurd. You can't have a science of God unless God exists. Perhaps I can never *prove* that He does; it's an assumption. But the long-continued success of religion in dealing with men's souls makes it more and more plausible to say that He does."[18] The theologian's argument, says Krutch, is circular and nonsensical, as is Frazier's.

But what of Frazier, Skinner's fictional voice? Let us further consider his fundamental ideas and return to his critics later. I have already noted his uncompromising refusal to recognize man as a free agent. Man, he asserts, is determined by his environment, which is the true parent of his virtues and vices. Devoid of an innate moral nature, man nevertheless has the power to control his environment and thereby control his behavior. "We do have faith in our power to change human behavior," Frazier says. "We can *make* men adquate for group living — to the satisfaction of everybody. That was our faith, but now it's a fact." Man's basic psychological characteristics and the techniques to change them and create others are experimental questions

> "to be answered by a behavioral technology. It requires all the techniques of applied psychology, from the various ways of keeping in touch with opinions and attitudes to the educational and persuasive practices which shape the individual from the cubicle to the grave. Experimentation . . . not reason. Experimentation with life — could anything be more fascinating?"

Furthermore, Frazier's program need not wait for the undependable and slow evolution of world politics or human nature. "The Good Life is waiting for us — here and now," he insists. "At this very moment we have the necessary techniques, both material and psychological, to create a full and satisfying life for everyone." "The only thing that matters is one's day-to-day happiness and a secure future." Following the attainment of these primary goals, Frazier envisions "an alert and active drive toward the future. . . . We'll be satisfied with nothing short of the most alert and active group-intelligence yet to appear on the face of the earth."[19]

Frazier's visitors, Burris and Castle, repeatedly raise the issue of human freedom, which Frazier repeatedly dismisses as an illusion. But in the "unengineered" world it is a dangerous illusion, for men despair lacking it, despoil seeking it, and once deluded that they have achieved it become anxious lest they lose it. But in the behaviorally engineered society men live the illusion happily and productively. Having been conditioned by "positive reinforcement" men "feel free" though they are more controlled by the Walden Code than they had been previously by the general social mores. "They are doing what they want to do, not what they are forced to do," Frazier explains. "That's the source of the tremendous power of positive reinforcement — there's no restraint and no revolt. By a careful cultural design, we control not the final behavior but the inclination to behave — the motives, the desires, the wishes. The curious thing is that in that case *the question of freedom never arises*."[20] Thus the citizens of Walden Two almost invariably behave in the socially good (producing happiness and security) manner. Theirs is more than a cloistered virtue. It is an automatic one.

As the guided tour of Walden Two reaches its didactic climax, Frazier's tone becomes increasingly confident and his grand strategy more explicit:

> "What remains to be done? . . . Well, what do you say to the design of personalities? . . . The control of temperament? Give me the specifications, and I'll give you the man! What do you say to the control of motivation, building the interests which will make men most productive and most successful? . . . Think of the possibilities! A society in which there is no failure, no boredom, no duplication of effort!"
>
> "Here we can begin to understand and build the Superorganism. We can construct groups of artists and scientists who will act as smoothly and efficiently as champion football teams."[21]

Surveying his domain from a nearby hill, Frazier remarks to

Burris, "I like to play God! Who wouldn't, under the circumstances? After all, man, even Jesus Christ thought he was God!" Then with his hand sweeping the community below he pronounces, "These are my children, Burris . . . I love them. . . . What is love . . . except another name for the use of positive reinforcement?"[22]

These several statements of Frazier's outline his program and should reveal why Skinner's novel has disquieted so many. It is most vulnerable stylistically and ideologically. Frazier's definition of love must rank as one of the most unpoetic ever penned. The statement about Jesus will offend some. And many will find no essential difference between a Brave New World, where state hatcheries manufacture Alphas, Betas, Gammas, and Epsilons, and a Walden Two, where men are built to specifications. What Frazier would say to the above three reproaches must be conjectural, but he would certainly reply, for he never concedes a point to a disputant. Perhaps he would say that in utopia poetry must give way to precision; that he had honored Jesus by recognizing him as a pioneer in the formation of the principle of positive reinforcement;[23] that to condemn his conditioning techniques because of similarities to those of Huxley's dystopia renders a verdict of guilt by association: the practical success of conditioning makes all objections philosophic irrelevancies; that benevolent *ends* should be the concern of the utopist was recognized by T. H. Huxley, grandfather of Aldous, when he stated, "If some great Power would agree to make me always think what is true and do what is right, on condition of being turned into a sort of clock and wound up every morning before I got out of bed, I should instantly close with the offer."[24] Walden Two, he might conclude, does not make a virtue of wasteful chance and needless struggle.

Returning to Krutch, we see that he believes other things matter far more than "one's day-to-day happiness and secure future," and these are values. He considers man not primarily a reasoning animal (some machines reason better) but a preferring one. Man has a sense of values; a machine does not. His glory rests not on the inventions of his reason but on "the values by which he has lived. . . . The ability to act on . . . the assumption that loyalty is better than treachery even when both seem to give a practical answer to a given problem, is more significant than any other ability he has ever manifested."[25] If man is to remain himself he must re-examine his value judgments. Skinner has shown him the possible, but what man must consider now is the necessary — what he *ought* to be. Surely he ought *not* be a machine. The good behavior of conditioned man is but the result of his diminished humanness. If his placid, programmed life makes him more fit to survive, for what has he survived? Having rejected values derived from conscience, nature, or religion, in favor of happiness and survival, by what standards could Skinner prove Walden Two better than a Walden Three of sadists who survive happily also? But whether in Walden Two or Walden Three, successive generations will be the conditioned of the conditioned — castings from the original mold. Krutch reads much of Skinner's prose as euphemism for the most odious proposals. For example, the finally converted Burris realizes that "education would have to abandon the technical limitations which it had imposed upon itself and step forth into a broader sphere of human engineering. Nothing short of the complete revision of a culture would suffice."[26] Whereupon Krutch asks, What does abandoning "technical limitations" mean but substituting conditioning for reason? What is stepping into "the broader sphere of human engineering" but doing to men what has successfully been done to the laboratory rat? "What does 'the complete revision of a culture' imply if it does not imply, as it has always ended by implying: those who will not accept re-education will have to be liquidated?" For Krutch, Walden Two is a formula for the abolition of man. For him, Skinner's science is "not the Science of Man, but only the Science-of-What-Man-Would-Be-If-He-Were-Not-a-Man-But-a-Machine."[27]

George Kateb's *Utopia and Its Enemies* examines the strengths and weaknesses of Skinner's utopianism in a comprehensive analysis of modern utopian and anti-utopian thought. Kateb admits his utopian bias but acknowledges the defects of many utopian arguments. One purpose of his study is to expose these defects and suggest improvements so that the utopian vision may be realized. Paradoxically both his book and Krutch's, despite their intellectual brilliance, convey the overall impression of defeat. One is irresistibly carried by the urgency of Krutch's brave message but closes his book feeling that the odds favor the conditioners. Kateb, on the other hand, reveals so many flaws in utopian means and ends that one closes *his* book feeling his suggested improvements vague and unrealizable.

Kateb does not find the idea of conditioning objectionable and implies that those who consider it an assault on man's dignity and a stranglehold on his "becoming" and self-determination are emotionally overreacting to the growing influence of social science. We really have much less freedom than we would like to believe, Kateb writes, coming into the world choosing neither the parents, time, place, nor culture which conditions us. Although human freedom is still very real, much of it has been pre-empted simply by the way things are.

> The important thing to insist on, is that conditioning is not a substitution for self-direction or self-determination. The choice is not between making ourselves and being made by a directorate of supervisory psychologists. Conditioning is simply education carried on with more awareness of causes and consequences, and with more care taken to see that certain things happen and certain other things are avoided.[28]

For Kateb, Skinner's *intent*, then, lies within utopian traditions: "to condition men so perfectly that whatever they desire is licit and whatever is required of them they do without strain."[29] Thus employing the techniques of psychological conditioning to promote human virtue and happiness does not violate utopian principles.

However, Kateb voices strong disagreements with Skinner's method and ultimate vision of perfected man. Though goodness can be made less burdensome, it can never become, as Skinner claims, automatic. Moreover, "utopian psychology cannot allow itself to grant happiness to people at the cost of limiting their aspirations or narrowing their capacity for experience." If Skinner's happy Waldenites live predetermined lives and are even unable to conceive of alternative life styles for themselves, then his people merge with those of Huxley's Brave New World, where both Alphas and Epsilons are happy with their lot and would be no less happy had they been conditioned otherwise.

Skinner's insistence on habitual goodness is the focus of Kateb's strongest objections. And here Kateb stands with Krutch in the latter's defense of rational thought and conscience as cornerstones of humanness. "The marvelous technique of human conditioning which Skinner promises," writes Kateb, "must first be corrected by the canons of rational morality, and then employed in the creation of types of human beings higher than Skinner has any intimation of." The virtues of the conditioned man must demand effort and thought. A *"vegetable* quality" would permeate a society relieved of the burden of moral choice. Truly human action is predicated upon one's awareness of the reason for which he acts; without such awareness action becomes mere motion. "Automatic virtue would seem to exclude a sense of the purpose for which one is generally virtuous, and also a sense of the moral requirements of a given particular situation, and, as such, is not compatible with what we ordinarily consider to be rational conduct." Kateb concludes that "on the whole, Skinner's sights are set low," for he "is more concerned to improve functions than to improve men." Skinner has dismissed the idea which the utopian theorist must always perceive, and which Mill so pointedly delivers in *On Liberty*: "It really is of importance, not only what men do, but also what manner of men they are that do it."[30]

In the course of acknowledging Skinner's shortcomings, Kateb also makes an important concession to anti-utopian protest. By virtually eliminating evil, sin, and despair, utopia also eliminates grace and transcendence. To the anti-utopian charge that universal innocence condemns man to lifelong childhood, Kateb replies that most men are not morally sufficient to attain the spiritual heights reached through the storms of adversity. Concordantly the utopian theorist, on practical and humane grounds, "must decide that a society of a universally high level of happiness that could not accommodate sainthood is preferable to a mottled world that could accommodate it."[31] Thus he must regret the disappearance of "sainthood" but justify its loss on the grounds that the conditions that engender it are not compatible with the welfare of the mass.

Kateb gives brief mention to a phenomenon becoming notable in the anti-utopian science fiction novel: Not only does the anti-utopian reject conditioned virtue, not only does he see frailty as the crucible from which will issue a nobler manhood, but surprisingly he sometimes defends frailty and even vice as essential ingredients of the total man, exposing him to a grander and richer realm of experience. Perfect virtue, even achieved through rational morality, narrows man's range of life. Such romantic satanism does not scorn virtue, but instinctively feels that it should not be pursued beyond man's "point of diminishing life returns."

In the novels of this study nowhere is this view more directly stated than in Kurt Vonnegut's *Player Piano*. A technocracy worshiping an unholy trinity of efficiency, machinery, and production, deities which make useless and degraded all but a few engineers and managers, spurs the populace to open rebellion. The leader of the rebellion issues a lengthy manifesto condemning lawless technology and praising imperfection by asserting the following:

> That there must be virtue in imperfection, for Man is imperfect, and Man is a creation of God.
> That there must be virtue in frailty, for Man is frail, and Man is a creation of God.
> That there must be virtue in inefficiency, for Man is inefficient, and Man is a creation of God.
> That there must be virtue in brilliance followed by stupidity, for Man is alternately brilliant and stupid, and Man is a creation of God.
> You perhaps disagree with the antique and vain notion of Man's being a creation of God.
> But I find it a far more defensible belief than the one implicit in intemperate faith in lawless technological progress — namely, that man is on earth to create more durable and efficient images of himself, and, hence, to eliminate any justification at all for his own continued existence.[32]

The final chapters of Bernard Wolfe's *Limbo* rhapsodize man's imperfection, the book's thesis being that he is "I," the "Dog-God," the "hyphenated *Wunderkind*." To this Dog-God, man must say *Yes*; to the hyphen, *Yes*. Wolfe's novel pictures a post-nuclear-war world resolved to "dodge the streamroller" of war forever through "Immob" — the amputation of *men's* limbs, the supposed organs and seats of aggression, and their replacement by atomic-powered, detachable prosthetics. Yet World War Four follows physical and psychological truncation, this program for perfect benevolence. Wolfe argues that aggression stems principally from our unwillingness to recognize the naturalness of aggressive impulses, which leads to repression followed by even more savage and falsely rationalized aggression. Impelling this

cycle and making it all the more probable is man's self-hate, his
inability to live in peace with the imperfect creature that he is.
Rejecting his natural imperfection, this "hyphenated *Wunderkind*" reaches for heaven and goes to hell. His insistence on perfection, his impossible and destructive utopian visions — these
are his undoing.

Dr. Martine, Wolfe's hero, moralizes:

> "You mustn't victimize one part of you in favor of
> another, sacrifice one of your potential lives to
> another. . . . Integrity, intactness — living with the
> whole being, trying to bring it all to the surface,
> never truncating any dimension of personality. . . .
> Pacifism, which no doubt originated in the decent
> and civilized impulses of mankind, would . . . only
> become a partner to catastrophe after catastrophe, so
> long as it persisted in seeing man as a truncated
> monolithic thing, all potential goodness. . . . If the
> do-gooders saw man as truncated, they'd wind up
> truncating him."

One of Wolfe's minor characters, an "amp" (voluntary
amputee), regrets his truncation. His superstrong, superdexterous
plastic legs are dead, sinfully dead.

> "A man should be able to stand on his *own* two legs,
> his own. With all their frailties. I want legs that are
> less perfect but more alive. Even if they stumble a
> little, and quake. A man should stumble and quake
> a little. Only robots never stumble and quake. . . .
> You know why people laugh so hard when they see
> an amp trip or take a dive? Because the horror in a
> human being is perfection, infallibility — that's in-
> human, and the idea that you can get it, short of
> death — that's a laugh. The stumble, the fall, it
> reminds people of the frail humanity behind all the
> mechanical perfection, the *life* — it's a hell of a relief
> to see it pop up."

Dr. Martine's thoughts reword this abhorrence of deadly
perfection. Yes, our migrained, anxious, ambivalent, trembling,
sick brain — "hacked, slashed, as fragmented as the disorderly
spattered multiverse" — has created from its prepetual turmoil
all our enthusiasms and ecstasies.

> Perfect it? The price would be the esthetic quality in
> life. For the esthetic is the crumb this aching old
> onion tosses itself in the morass of anticipatory

> anxiety; and to eliminate it would mean to eliminate
> all the uneasy sense and savor of life. No more
> neurosis, maybe. But something else is amputated
> too, humanness. And, with it, laughter. . . . The
> esthetic: a form of laughter, designed to take the
> sting out of ineradicable pain. . . .
> The price of perfection is perfect robotization. . . .
> The cost of perfection would be superboredom.
> Worst of all, the perfect robot wouldn't even know
> it was bored.[33]

The danger of dehumanizing perfection, while a popular science fiction theme, has been only a slender one in general fiction. While science fiction can indulge itself in such speculations, the mainstream's concern has been human frailties and limitations. One of George Bernard Shaw's constant complaints against nature is that, life being short, man goes to his death when he is just beginning to achieve wisdom. In *Back to Methuselah*, the closest he comes to science fiction, Shaw has man hurdle the barrier of time through a series of evolutionary leaps which, after some 30,000 years, culminate in a new kind of human being, one devoted to pure thought and heading toward his apotheosis — a virtually immortal existence as pure, disembodied thought. Recent developments in cryonics, tissue preservation, organ transplant surgery, and preventive medicine have led to dozens of science fiction novels predicated on increased longevity; but here, most are dystopian.

In *Gray Matters*, William Hjortsberg's gloomy extrapolation on longevity and evolution, most of mankind exists as "cerebromorphs," brain jelly encased in a box and floating in life-sustaining fluid. These billions of disembodied brains, housed in massive depositories, are very much aware of themselves and their condition. Neurologically wired to a grim seminary of ethical training and guided by tutors, the brains, willing or not, meditate their way for decades or centuries to Level 10: Enlightenment. Then they are reimplanted in healthy bodies and in full, enlightened personhood live out a natural life.

Gray as it is, Hjortsberg's world of cerebromorphs takes on even grayer shades because the author avoids explicitly condemning such a mutilation of man as *thoroughly* undeserved. His principal characters, cerebromorphs, are indeed unenlightened, and man-as-he-was had centuries earlier incinerated half his kind in the thermonuclear war of 1996. Yet Hjortsberg's subject and tone plainly convey that cerebrectomized, casketed, and subjected to the tyranny of forced moral maturation, man had taken a most grisly way to wisdom. A system, purged of Michelangelo's perfect David and the Bible's imperfect one and preferring instead gray jelly in the depository vaults of enlightenment, must be a dystopia.

Not the need for imperfect man's evolutionary leap but the fear that, given the means, the "emperors" of evolution would defile man — this theme dominates the book and pervades it through to the last sealing sentences: A depository brain's recurring nightmare, in which he witnesses his own slice-by-slice, dayslong dissection until at last "with a few swift strokes, the surgeon uncaps the cranium and eases the brain out of its ivory nest. Gray and glistening, the wrinkled lump of nervous tissue is carried to the Emperor on a golden dish with the polite hope that it will please his discriminating palate."[34]

Strictly speaking, John Wyndham's *Trouble With Lichen*[35] is not dystopian, but whether it ends at dystopia's boundary allows some speculation. Also because it deals with a problem that "longevity" fiction prefers to avoid — simply put, Do most men *want* to live much longer lives? — the novel invites consideration. The typical longevity story revolves around the power struggle for control of the anti-aging process, overpopulation and other threatening consequences, the gory iniquities of the organ-bank underworld, obscene surgical mutilations, social manias, and painful "to be, or not to be" dilemmas.[36] Wyndham's story differs in that it questions the very usefulness of extended longevity.

Biochemist Francis Saxover discovers a rare lichen that can double and triple the life-span of a few thousand people, but fearing the conflict for its control and the population explosion that would follow its synthesization, he suppresses his findings. Diana Brackley, his associate, suspects his secret and continues research on her own. When, in time, the world learns of the anti-gerone, Diana, rather than being acclaimed, becomes a public enemy. Turning to Saxover for support, she presses a typically Shavian argument. 1. The shortness of life dooms man to moral and intellectual infancy. 2. People with 300 years to live will be forced to develop serious and creative pursuits; they will either grow up to stand the long haul or kill themselves to escape their own trivialness. She wins over the reluctant Saxover and the novel ends with their compact to work together clandestinely, synthesize the antigerone, and offer it to a hopefully less reactionary world.

Despite this ending, Wyndham allows the "reactionary" world to present its case, and what the world lacks in idealism it makes up in practicality aplenty. The normal life-span is a requisite of our social and economic institutions. In the corporation and family, the castle and the laborer's hut, the predictably regular demise of senior heads automatically advances the living; waiting 200 years for grandfather to die is not universally agreeable. The 250-year marriage (when for many the present length is sufficiently taxing) might be bliss, but only to the exceptionally romantic or patient. And the workingman does not look forward to three lifetimes at the factory bench. Realities such as these are the trouble with lichen. Yet a subtle undertone in Wyndham's story suggests that these practical realities are, perhaps, symptoms of a larger and sadder reality: Most people, it may be, are not capable of anything but a trivial life, and therefore life's limited span is quite compatible with their limited endowment. Even now, filling or killing time, getting through the day, strains the psyches of millions bored by triviality and incapable of self-renewal. No evidence supports the assumption that the need to use three centuries of life will automatically induce new talents and sensibilities. A utopia of tricentenarians might well be a contradiction in terms. If, as Thoreau says, "most men lead lives of quiet desperation," at least there is some nobility in their quiet endurance. But if science brings them to a highway whose length they are ill-prepared to travel, who knows what ignobility will stain their unendurable lives?

While Vonnegut and Wolfe declare imperfection essential to humanness, Anthony Burgess carries the anti-utopian banner further by suggesting that evil is God's *gift* to man, a holy armament of last resort by which he defends himself against self-robotization. If the miracle of grace redeems him from self-brutalization, then the mystery of evil redeems him from self-robotization. And Burgess unequivocally holds that in this age man is more threatened with being turned into a piece of clockwork than with lapsing into savagery. The opening pages of *A Clockwork Orange* present the thesis clearly: "The attempt to impose upon man, a creature of growth and capable of sweetness, to ooze juicily at the last round the bearded lips of God, to attempt to impose, I say, laws and conditions appropriate to a mechanical creation, against this I raise my sword-pen."[37] These, the words of F. Alexander, fictional author of his own *A Clockwork Orange*, protest the progressive dehumanization of English life and the government's methods of meeting social problems. They are mockingly and uncomprehendingly read aloud from the manuscript by Alex, a teenaged hoodlum whose pleasures are mayhem, fornication, and music. He and his three gang mates beat the writer to near unconsciousness and rape his young wife before his eyes. The wife dies from the ordeal and the gang, one of many that rule the English cities at night, continues to play at sadism and plunder until Alex meets the inevitable: another murder, capture, and prison.

Alex accepts punishment as a rule of the game but he is not repentant. He never could understand society's concern about the cause of badness when it does not inquire into the cause of goodness. Goodness and badness are matters of taste, not morals. People are good because they like it, he explains, but

> I was patronizing the other shop. More, badness is of the self, the one, the you or me on our oddy knockies [lonesomes], and that self is made by old Bog or God and is his great pride and radosty [joy]. But the not-self cannot have the bad, meaning they of the government and the judges and the schools cannot allow the bad because they cannot allow the self. And is not our modern history, my brothers, the story of brave malenky [little] selves fighting these big machines? I am serious with you, brothers, over this.[38]

Clearly Alex considers himself part of the natural order. Enjoying the pleasures of rapine, but without hate, he was simply "patronizing the other shop." God, whom he constantly invokes, understands his role, a brave little self fighting the big anti-self machine of state, law, and indoctrination. Badness, then, is not bad, but a counterweight necessary to hold the delicate balance of tastes. Why God created goodness Alex does not speculate, but he implies it is not the self (as is badness), made by God with pride and joy. The bad are God's chosen.

One can not dismiss this doctrine as only that of a character. Burgess has written more than a brutal shocker; *A Clockwork Orange* is a philosophical novel. The doctrine is Burgess's even if for shock value he has intentionally overstated his case. In his Alex, one of the most wanton and menacing heroes of twentieth century fiction, dwells some immanence championing human freedom; and for all Alex's infamous deeds he displays an innocence and honesty which are the stuff of charm. Like a cat, he flees the stronger, ravishes the vulnerable, and all is blood and play. Though he lies to the "big machines" he is truthful to himself and the reader. He is the embodiment of elemental, infantile will. And he is a victim.

After two years in prison Alex is offered freedom should he consent to be the first subject of a new conditioning technique which will purge him of the capacity for criminal aggression.[39] The youth instantly accepts the offer, dreaming of freedom and the old "ultra-violence" and "in-out." But the prison chaplain has reservations about conditioned goodness: "It may not be nice to be good, little 6655321. It may be horrible to be good. ... Does God want goodness or the choice of goodness? Is a man who chooses the bad perhaps in some way better than a man who has the good imposed upon him?"[40]

A few weeks later Alex walks out the prison door, harmless and truncated. Feeble old men beat him up. The thought of approaching a woman makes him sick. Classical music, with which he formerly combined sadistic fantasies, is unbearable. Violence, sex, music — what to him was the esthetic — bring on racking nausea. He tries to end his tormented, empty life and fails, but his plight becomes the *cause célèbre* of the anti-government faction fighting the impending mass conditioning of the socially dangerous, and the public outcry forces the government to decondition him. Then alone with a stereo and Beethoven's Ninth, Alex describes the denouement of his adventure:

> Oh, it was gorgeousity and yumyumyum. When it came to the Scherzo I could viddy [see] myself very clear running and running on like very light and mysterious nogas [feet], carving the whole litso [face] of the creeching [screaming] world with my

cut-throat britva [razor]. And there was the slow
movement and the lovely last singing movement still
to come. I was cured all right.[41]

Was he cured? Burgess believes so. If humanness is to survive
in a clockwork society it may have to root itself in the soil of
human evil.

Rex Gordon's novel, *Utopia Minus X*, attacks utopia on
metaphysical grounds, asserting that it rests on man's abandoning
his search for objective truth, denying its very existence, and re-
lating only to that which satisfies his feelings. Gordon sets his
story two centuries in the future in the "Perfect World" — earth
made utopia by the Great Computer, which has solved all political,
moral, economic, and physical problems. It is a benevolent, automated, civilized world of happy people who have little to do but
enjoy their gently hedonistic lives. But the Perfect World leaves
student Carlin Glenmore unfulfilled, a condition brought to the
attention of the university warden when the Computer gives him
an "X" rating. In an interview with the warden, Glenmore admits
that he wants more than the approved self-indulgent pastimes. He
has a great interest in the nature and purpose of man and the universe. "To have consciousness, but to be only conscious of a
mystery. It's like a bad joke, sir," Glenmore explains. "I feel the
need to break through, sir. To attend to the problem as though it
mattered to me personally, and not just to live a happy life — if
you can call it happy, living in an enigma knowing we must die
before we know the answer."[42] Furthermore, though man may
live happily for a thousand million years, he dies when his sun
dies unless he reaches for other suns. The warden declares Glenmore mentally ill with unhappiness and that he must give up this
frivolous and impossible interest or be "Changed" by the doctors
into a happy being, but not quite Carlin Glenmore.

In a lengthy and articulate explanation, the warden proves
why Glenmore's proposed investigations are impossible in and
incompatible with the Perfect World. But his proof also establishes
why the Perfect World is imperfect for an "X" such as Glenmore.
The warden pronounces Glenmore's research project intellectually, physically, and practically impossible, for "science, following
the setting up of the Perfect World, has reached its ultimate. It is
at an end." *"What can be known is known, Glenmore. And we*

cannot know any more." The dictum "I think, therefore I am," though not untrue, does not adequately describe man. Far more to the point: "*I feel, and fear and desire, therefore I think.*" Man's introspection leads to feelings, and these feelings are his only truths. Through thought manifesting itself in language, he maintains the fiction of objective reality. "He tells himself useful fictions . . . to explain the connections between events." But feelings are the only facts of life he can know. "This is the nature of man's knowledge: That it is a fiction, a construction of his own mind. Man does not perceive it. All he can perceive is events. And to explain events, he tells himself stories about them." He sees material objects and concludes something is there. "But *what* is there? . . . *What* is there is essentially unknowable." "God was a necessary fiction in Christian times, just as your atoms and electrons are useful fictions today." But time discredits all objective truth. In the old scientific textbooks of the twentieth century almost no statement of equational truth, that 'this is such,' can now stand unquestioned. Even today's theories are but useful fictions. "Man therefore cannot *know* 'the nature of the universe' or any such suppositions and fantastic thing. All man can *do* is act in a way by which he may successfully control events, and thereby achieve a better feeling."[43]

Glenmore, unsettled and dejected by an argument that has reduced human existence to an absurdity, can neither refute the warden nor make his peace with the Perfect World; whereupon the warden continues his entreties: Since man is a feeling, happiness-directed animal, the era of scientific investigation ended when he attained happiness. Man has reached his destination, and continued inquiry into himself and the universe can only take him further from it. The *search* for the ultimate truth is false: "*You would believe in what you were doing*" — in the fiction of objective truth. Granted, the earth is doomed by the slowly expiring sun, but the wise have chosen happiness in the millions of years to come rather than the ordeal of doomed striving.[44]

Still Glenmore remains gripped by the sickness of unhappiness and striving. He is spared being Changed by the doctors and is allowed martyrdom. With a party of malcontents he is put aboard a secret spacecraft bound for another galaxy, an imperfect world peopled by earthmen who believe that ultimate truths do exist and the search for them is more worthy than personal happiness. But the search is not only worthy; it is part of the cosmic will. Glenmore realizes this in a declaration echoing the central thesis of Shaw's *Man and Superman*:

> "Blind matter is striving to think. The It that is the cosmos, is aiming to know Itself. The old religions were right. The Cosmos, that men used to call God, has created man to praise it, or at least to be Its mind. Only It hasn't got a mind yet. Man is stuck on this tiny planet, while he ought to inhabit the galaxy, the universe as a whole. Man ought to become the Universal Mind, but so far he is only the groping paw. Only man ought to get on with it. The Creation as a whole won't just stop here if man does. It will throw up some other creature. To man, just now, this is important."[45]

The novel closes with the "X" martyrs gliding through space to fulfill man's cosmic destiny, leaving the Perfect World to play out its illusions until the arrival of the inevitable and unending sleep. The content and tone of the final pages repeatedly strike a Shavian chord. As Shaw's hell is the happy palace of unreality, a drifting deathworld, so is Gordon's Perfect World. As Shaw's heaven is the womb of mind, the womb from which shall emerge the superman, who will explain the universe to itself, so will be the new world of the cosmic pilgrims of the truth and eternal life.

R. A. Lafferty's *Past Master*[46] and Colin Anderson's *Magellan* too portray "perfect worlds," dystopias which, more brazenly than Gordon's, worship at the very altar of negation. In the "golden cities" of Lafferty's Astrobe, a planet colonized by humans, there is no war, want, sickness, fear, cruelty, guilt, or hate. And luxury and pleasure are available to everyone. Yet most people choose "termination" before their natural life ends, confounding the Inner Circle of Masters, rulers of Astrobe. But most disturbing of all is "the Cathead thing": Cathead, Astrobe's largest city, a monstrous, festering cancer of a city, a sprawl of twenty million ground down by hunger, plague, poisonous stench, and breaking labor, an infernal place of short life and bodies rotting in the streets. To this hell, multitudes from the golden cities of Astrobe have voluntarily fled.

To solve the riddle of the Cathead thing, the mighty of Astrobe send for centuries-dead Thomas More, the past master —

of utopian fiction and of himself too, having lost his life rather than bend his principles. His tour of the planet reveals its wonders, dangers, and horrors. Paradoxically, its great wonder (the golden cities) is a horror and its horror (Cathead) a wonder. He learns of the "Astrobe Dream," which is to absorb all the golden cities into one totality and absorb all men into that totality also — to destroy the individual and merge him into a single organism. More comes to realize that Astrobe is in the grip of Ouden, "the Celestial Nothingness," "the Big O." Under Ouden's influence, the people seek to achieve a "Finalized Humanity," unaware that *finalized* can mean both perfected and terminated. Of course, that is Lafferty's point: perfected *means* terminated — spiritually dead.

Gordon's provocative, disciplined symposium on being marooned in happiness or being martyred for "man's cosmic destiny," the ignoble wisdom of accepting one, the noble reckless-ness of demanding the other, has nothing in common, stylistically, with Lafferty's "great galloping madman of a novel, drenched in sound and color." (Harlan Ellison) Yet the thematic similarity of both books is so striking that one can almost imagine Gordon and Lafferty being given the same task: to write a novel on the Celes-tial Nothingness, on Ouden. So Gordon writes about a Perfect World, sustained by useful fictions and pleasurable sensations, devoid of knowable reality, and doomed to extinction. Lafferty writes about golden cities and the Astrobe Dream of Finalized Humanity. And both are writing about Ouden, whose will is to extinguish life and whose ploy is the illusion of utopia. Lafferty's ironic use of *golden* and *nothing* moves the Ouden theme steadily to the center. The Astrobe Dream of the golden cities is founded on the "Golden Premise": "Nothing Beyond" — no goal, no hope. From this premise follows the inevitable conclusion: "Nothing Here Either, Nothing Ever." Thus Astrobe dreams the dream of Ouden, the something that is nothing.

Some dreams paralyze the spirit so thoroughly that only martyr's blood rouses the dreamer. The past master, in quirky stubbornness on a small matter, refuses to bend and again loses his head on the block. While settling nothing, More's death does set an example which, one hopes, will undercut notions of Fi-nalized Humanity and Golden Premises. When great men choose to die for what appears almost a whim, Lafferty implies, then premises too have gone to the chopping block. And mankind, far from being final, senses the chaos of golden beginnings.

Colin Anderson's *Magellan* carries the Ouden theme to the limits of expression. Combining the surrealistic, fragmented imagery of nightmare with an unrelenting pessimism and brutally contemptuous assault upon utopian values, *Magellan* is more an experience one goes through than a book one reads. A regimented, mechanized, computerized, sole-survivor of a world war, the city of Magellan pursues the dream of perfection — the "Universal Society." Still despite happiness pills, eugenic breeding, and other means to make the Universal Society "neurosis-sterile," everyone is on the verge of breakdown. "Eternity" — perfection eternal — arrives at Midnight when Chronophage the computer, having digested man's thoughts and desires, will digest man's mind, making everyone "omnipotent, immortal, invincible." For Euri, Anderson's protagonist, life is empty when Eternity comes. He has power and things but not his beloved Chrys, and life becomes a horror. "What countless millions of possibilities there were — and how few of them pleasant! He suspected that no one had found any paradise and that Eternity was full of men fleeing from hell to hell."[47]

The most common arguments against utopianism are rooted in the fear of man's "unmaking," the fear of "unman" emerging. Unman may be saintly or sadistic, happy or miserable, but he will not be *man*. Unman emerges in Eternity and he is miserable, but that is not Anderson's major point. Rather than argue that a utopia of unman is not utopia, he argues that utopia is not utopia because *happiness is not happiness*! The debate between Euri and his wise servant Bubo, the thematic heart of the book, deserves to be quoted. Bubo tells Euri:

> "Happiness is purely a political device to ensure that the citizen is in constant need of *reassurance*, that he spies day and night on his neighbors to see that they do not betray the norm, that he spends his life in the constant search for and the relief of small miseries like a dog searching itself for fleas. . . .
>
> "You think me anti-democratic? Far from it! None of us escape our environment. I have thought of these matters all my life, asking myself how true equality and contentment could be guaranteed. I

claim to be an Ultra-Democrat! I want an equality that no one will dispute, a contentment that no one will attempt to take more or less than their share of. Now what can be measured out according to your deserts and that you can be sure to be satisfied with and more than satisfied with? What but *suffering*?

"And how much more reliable! The system is productive and self-sustaining — in short — alive. There's never any danger of the supply drying up: suffering breeds suffering and cements humanity as happiness does not. It is an *extrovert* emotion — so much more healthy than love and happiness! How we sufferers long to share our suffering! How lovingly we choose our punishments. How *honestly!*"

"Haven't we enough Hells?" Euri cried.

"Not a Hell but a World. A World that will endure — unlike your paradises — a base that men can build on and discover their true selves."[48]

Like the Perfect World and the Astrobe Dream, Eternity is the trap of Ouden. Who but the Celestial Nothingness could have conceived the thing that is not itself — happiness. Though Anderson leans toward sophistry in the above passage, such is the justifiable metaphor of his theme. Like Vonnegut's salute to imperfection, frailty, inefficiency, and stupidity (p. 65), Anderson's defense of suffering demands "a World that will endure — unlike your paradises" — and man, not unman, to people it.

In *Utopia Minus X, Past Master,* and *Magellan,* one finds some of the characteristic features of many ignoble utopias: the belief that the perfect society has been or will soon be realized; a machine or doctrine that has brought or will soon bring perfection; the ideal of "nothing beyond" — finalized man, knowledge, or desire; the goal of merging everyone into a single totality, psychological, social, or doctrinal; neurosis and misery underlying superficial happiness; utopia's enemies — the outcast, the nonconformist, or skeptical "X's"; the Ouden theme: utopianism equated with stagnation, negation, and death. Though few novels employ all these features and the formula varies from novel to novel, Gordon, Lafferty, and Anderson have presented classic models of ignoble utopias, models found especially in science fiction's imaginary lands of some indefinite future.

With Leonard C. Lewin's *Triage* and Michael Young's *The Rise of the Meritocracy*, we return to Skinner country — that is, the foreseeable future and feasible program. And we also return to "engineering," but not behavioral engineering. "Positional" engineering. The utopian plans of these novels do not involve changing *how* people *act* but rather changing *where* people *stand* in relation to others. In *Triage* "where," for some people, is "nowhere," where they do not "stand" at all. They are changed into corpses.

At one point in Lewin's novel someone says, "From all the public hoopla about ecology, the environment, and so on, the most important residue is the realization, vague as it may be to most people, that the real price of making the world fit to live in is getting rid of the part of the population that makes it more difficult or even impossible. . . . Here we have the chance of making a great leap forward in this direction, and I put it to you that people are ready for it." The speaker represents a pharmaceutical house which has developed "Paxin," an addictive tranquilizer, euphoric, and anti-depressant. What bothers the Federal Drug Administration is the company's admission that tests show that "a small but statistically significant number of people die after using Paxin for a while," some 12 percent more than in the control group. The company's spokesmen deny that the drug directly causes death, claiming rather that its properties neutralize unnatural internal life-sustaining tensions of those ready to die anyway — "who *should* die, by the morality of natural biological processes."[49] Later the reader learns that the "mortality increment" is much higher than 12 percent and that the company's real motive is not money but the selection and elimination of biological "delinquents." The excess baggage of an overfreighted world, those who have allowed themselves to become strongly addicted to Paxin, it is reasoned, rightly sentence themselves to death. The episode ends with the probability that the F.D.A. will find the bogus mortality increment for those who "should" die an acceptable trade-off for the benefits of the drug.

As this episode suggests, *Triage* is about killing. But the killers no more consider themselves criminals than does the triage officer in a military field hospital, who must decide which wounded are hopeless, abandon them to die, and direct the hospital's strained facilities toward others. In *Triage* the "greater good," not money, hate, or egomania, motivates the killers, who see themselves as altruistic benefactors. Another point worth noting is that triage is not a condoned, planned, and directed policy of the state. Rather, thousands of private citizens and killer-groups serve as its independent agents. This disposes the book toward an episodic structure. However, despite many isolated episodes the increasing pressure its thematic diabolism generates as the episodes pyramid upon each other infuses *Triage* with the unity of a cannonball.

The episodes evolve from a single killing to killing on a national and global scale. A college president arranges for a cantankerous old trustee to "pass away" — to the enrichment of the college. A hospital manages to increase the death rate of chronics and terminals. A doctor disseminates lethally high-grade heroin and kills off addicts in batches. A county commissioner solves a budgetary problem by burning down the county home — no survivors. The Chairman of the Commission on National Priorities masterminds a gas explosion that kills 2000 in Chicago's ghetto in order to dramatize urban decay and gain support for his urban renewal program. A car manufacturer introduces a pollution-free car, whose simple but deadly starting mechanism, far from being a drawback, is defended as being useful in weeding out "socially negative" drivers. Soon triage becomes an extensive yet covert fact of the times. The mortality of the aged quickly increases nationwide. Epidemics ravage prisons, slums, and poor rural areas. Overdoses decimate the ranks of drug users. Vigilantes, officially condemned but given a free hand, knock off mobsters. Catastrophic fires sweep urban slums, and killing smogs strangle depressed coal towns. A fatal food additive is shipped to the people of backward countries, "those who are not only not self-supporting but who never will be, and who will never be thinned out enough to support themselves except by uncontrolled natural catastrophe, famine, war, or other population control mechanism."[50]

Again, it should be emphasized that the killers are neither amoralists nor madmen. All other matters aside, if the goal of a better society can be considered commendable, then they are "moral," and their acts conform to a coherent rationale. Lewin makes this clear early in the book, and this — that morality and reason inspire their killings — shocks and fascinates even more than the killings themselves. Smith, head of the Special Services Group, justifies his actions on moral-rationalistic grounds: He says that the critical event that brought the Special Services into being was the Vietnam War, which exposed "the most egregious social hypocrisy of all — the presumed sanctity of human life, which our society claims to honor. . . . What made the mass killings in Vietnam seem especially preposterous was that they were being committed by a society claiming a greater adherence to this moral value than is claimed by any other." Smith thus concluded that "socially speaking, man was a killer of his own kind, that all pious assumptions to the contrary were fraudulent, and that whoever recognized this and acted on it would have an enormous advantage in dealing with the world as it really is." Smith emphasizes that he does not subscribe to the doctrine of man's innate aggressiveness. Speaking of man the killer, he was referring to *institutional* man following *institutional* morality. But he insists upon the validity and necessity of *personal* morality and asserts that "we have to live with ourselves. So we limit what we do by our own code of *personal* morality. . . . We have to be wholly convinced — by our own standards, such as they are — that what we do will contribute to the general human welfare."[51]

The justifications of others follow this line. Rooney, who directed the Chicago ghetto explosions, declares, "I want my name to stand as the guy who rebuilt the cities, who ended poverty, who made it possible for others to finish the job. I want to be Rooney the life-saver, not Rooney the terrible."[52] Dr. White, who O.D.'s heroin addicts, thinks of the scores of innocent people he has saved from "these vermin." He tells his reluctant colleague:

> "Now, you're not a nut, and I'm not a nut — there isn't a nickel's worth of megalomania between us, is there? But the fact is — the *fact*, mind you — the fact is that we're doing a truly great thing! This is the perspective. We are doing a remarkable thing in behalf of the general welfare. We are not doing it for profit, and we don't expect ever to be able to take credit for it. We don't claim to be geniuses, and we don't claim to be heroes. What we see has to be done is what anyone can see — except that everyone else puts his hands over his eyes. . . . What we *have* done

> is just to have looked at the simple logic of what
> *has* to be done, and to have taken the extra step of
> acting on it."[53]

Haynes and Hermanson, arguing their case before the Clean Air
Administration, defend the starting device of their nonpolluting
automotive energy package. True, they admit, it will explode and
kill any driver who does not follow the ultrasimple procedure of
throwing switch A before switch B. But "the only people who will
get killed from improper starting are people who shouldn't be driving anyway, the ones who *cause* most road accidents. . . . Those
who are not morons, or irresponsible, or drunk will be in no
danger," says Haynes. And Hermanson backs him up, arguing that
"the killing off of irresponsible drivers is in itself a very good thing
for the general public. I think I can prove to you — *a priori* — that
the kinds of drivers who will make the ridiculously simple mistake
in our starting procedure that will kill them are the kinds who are
most likely, even certain, to kill or injure others on the road, or
in other activities."[54] Clearly, Hermanson is less interested in
purifying the air than in "purifying" society and ultimately bringing about a public attitude that will support his policy of selective
genocide.

The killer's cold-steel logic in *Triage* is persuasive even when
it offends one's humanitarian instincts. But what makes that
scythe of logic all the more cutting and abhorrent is one's admission, if he is honest, that willy-nilly he has helped to hone it. Who
has not compiled in the safe recesses of his thoughts his own list
of "socially negative" sorts whose disappearance from the world
would not be unwelcome? Put more gently, how can anyone
acknowledging "greater goods" not understand that in virtually all
instances any practical plan for achieving them entails the abridge-
ment of some people's interests? — And who might those people
be? (*Other* people, naturally.) Lewin's murderous utopian fiction,
in which triagism and humanitarianism battle, catalyzes the conflict between the reader's natural triagist fantasies and humanitarian feelings. Adding to the reader's moral tension must be his
suspicion (if he is alive to the events of the times) that possibly
triage is an idea whose time has come,[55] that selective genocide
will be tacitly, if not openly, accepted. Of course, genocide was
accepted in the past, fired by religious, political, or ethnic hatreds.

Future genocide may victimize socio-economic "dispensables." Our belated recognition that earth's living room and resources are rapidly running out may well create a climate of opinion which tolerates killing off human "deadwood." Indeed, if one clear-sightedly examines the coming problems of population, food, and mineral resources, he will find it hard to rule out that even the kindest of men may come to agonize over — who to throw out of the lifeboat.

Triage can not be read in a vacuum. Much of its impact stems from the times. Amidst some progress in religious, racial, and political tolerance, one can sense emerging a new breed of marked men: those who take more than they give, the noncontributors, deadwood. What are people for? to contribute, or at least not to sap, answers the times. Other times, other answers: to glorify God; to simply be. But in "engineering" land, Skinner country, the passion for remaking people prevents simply being. And engineered triage strikes being itself.

We have seen that the major point shared in common by the critics of utopia has been that even if all or some aspects of human society can be perfected, such can be attained only at the cost of diminishing man's estate — truncating him. And utopia can not be a place of truncated men. Thus utopia is impossible. Michael Young, in his *The Rise of the Meritocracy: 1870-2033*, has written a fictional historical monograph whose dry, understated narration exposes the dynamics working against utopia. His England of 2034 demonstrates what the other critics have concluded: *that the attempt to achieve perfection sets in motion certain unconsidered counterforces which spoil the perfectionist scheme.*

The fictitious sociologist-narrator of 2034 tells us that recent perplexing disturbances have moved him to investigate the historical causes of the present unrest. The gutting of the Ministry of Education. The attempted assassination of the Chairman of the Technical Unions Congress. The transport workers and domestic servants strike. The wrecking of Wren's store and the destruction of an atomic station. (What he can not tell us is footnoted by his publisher on the last page: his death in the recent Peterloo disturbance.) He submits that "these resentments have their roots deep in history."

Well into the twentieth century, he relates, intelligence was randomly distributed in the social classes. But a class structure determined by blood and wealth squandered its human resources by relegating talented people of the "inferior classes" to manual work and assigning people of rank and wealth to positions of authority. By the twentieth century it became apparent that Britain's power must erode with the perpetuation of such a caste system. The Education Act of 1944 was the turning point of British social history, for it decreed that children be educated according to their age, ability, and aptitude. In time, with the practical and scientific management of talent, Britain's productivity began to outstrip that of her competitors. Her program demanded a single-minded effort to separate the gifted from the ungifted, removing from the educational ladder the ungifted of the privileged classes, and avoiding the foolishly idealistic and leveling American model of education-for-everyone. The key to the successful search for intellectual talent was the rapid development of educational psychology and its techniques for determining I. Q. in children as young as three and four. The I. Q. score of everyone became the possession of the state, one's second identity, and the determinant of one's destiny. I. Q.-plus-effort equal merit, and high merit brought one to higher learning and into the meritocracy — the managers of production, the foundation on which national greatness rests.

Naturally the rise of the meritocracy entailed shocks and dislocations which regrettably still trouble the nation somewhat. Seniority became irrelevant, and diminished capacities demoted managing directors to mechanics, bishops to curates, professors to assistant librarians, the vacated higher positions being filled by the new elite. The eugenics campaign urged the elite to consult the intelligence register before choosing a mate lest, blinded by romance, one waste his genes on someone merely appealing. All this caused antagonism. But most serious of all, the meritocracy shattered the myth of human equality. Formerly a workman could entertain the notion that he would have risen to a higher station but for the educational injustice which had deprived him of the opportunity. But the new order stripped him of his illusions and made him realize that his inferior status confirms the fact that he *is* inferior.

Perhaps then it was to be expected that, when the nation

dedicated itself to economic expansion and transforming its class
structure, raising to the top those capable of effecting this expansion, a reactionary Populist movement, supporting the increasing militancy of the inferior classes, would emerge. Their
manifesto of 2009 concluded:

> Were we to evaluate people, not only according to
> their intelligence and their education, their occupa-
> tion, and their power, but according to their kindli-
> ness and their courage, their imagination and sensitiv-
> ity, their sympathy and generosity, there could be no
> classes. . . . Every human being would then have
> equal opportunity, not to rise up in the world in the
> light of any mathematical measure, but to develop his
> own special capacities for leading a rich life.[56]

The narrator assures the reader that though the Populists
have grown more troublesome and have issued concrete demands,
the coming May crisis will amount to, at most, nothing more than
a brief strike and a distrubance well within the power of the police
to handle. Being *really* inferior, the Populists can never be anything more than a menacing but impotent rabble. That their
proposals can never be realized, the narrator concludes, "is the
prediction I shall expect to verify when I stand next May listening
to the speeches from the great rostrum at Peterloo."

So ends *The Rise of the Meritocracy*, except for the publisher's footnote that the writer, having been killed at Peterloo,
could not correct his manuscript. "The text, even this last section,
has been left exactly as he wrote it. The failings of sociology are as
illuminating as its successes."[57]

The implications here are clear enough. The "rabble" evidently struck harder than the narrator thought possible. Could they
have had an intelligence not detected by tests designed to evaluate
potential managerial skills? Could other qualities of character and
mind have carried their disturbances to a successful revolution?
One feels that the meritocracy has ceased to rise — perhaps ceased
to be.

We see that anti-utopianism has put forth several assertions
based on ethical, religious, esthetic, and metaphysical grounds:
Man must never be deprived of his capacity for rational moral
choice and growth. His imperfection is decreed by divine will and
may even be a shield against dehumanizing pressures. This alloy

of base and precious parts, man, is an impure purity, an element especial, a wholeness whose nature allows him access to an almost infinite range of conceptions and ecstasies and torments. And to narrow that range by altering the ambiguous chemistry of his being is to literally narrow the range of *life*.

Pervading the above works is the premonition that mankind stands on the verge of opening a momentous breach with his past. Science has furnished the instruments for change, and change will come. In the accelerating pace of events the utopian planners will make their move. Something precious *may* go under — perhaps a principle, perhaps a planet. . . . The time is ripe.

THE NEW TYRANNIES

The Totalitarian State of the Future

Although totalitarianism is not distinguished in the public mind from despotism, it is a markedly different form of political rule. With the latter, old as politics itself, power rests in the few who are primarily concerned with the maintenance of their elitist position and their self-aggrandizement at the expense of the lower orders. Yet history has shown that a meliorative dynamic often moves within it. In the mellowing despotism a concern for national well-being and political legitimacy grows, and in time the parasitic despot becomes the benevolent despot and finally the public servant. For when a politically oppressive regime works within the traditions and values of the people it rules, it must eventually identify itself with the people. Totalitarianism, however, is an essentially new form of government. While despotic, it is not inspired by the greed and pomp of the older oppressions but rather takes its direction from a radically new idea of law and man.

The novelty of totalitarianism has been recognized by Hannah Arendt in her perceptive study, *The Origins of Totalitarianism*. Arendt observes that the apparent lawlessness of totalitarianism springs from its absolute obedience to the suprahuman

laws of History or Nature, whose axioms totalitarianism claims to
have discovered and subsequently employs as the premises of its
logic. Unlike formal law, which seeks to ascertain what *is* and what
promises stability, totalitarian law is the law of movement, using
past and present as clues to what History or Nature has ordained
for the future. It drives to evolve mankind as a finished product
and in so doing erases the traditional distinction between man and
law. No longer does man function as a separate entity within the
framework of law: Since he is to be the finished product of law,
he is also its embodiment. Clearly, conventional notions of right
and wrong, guilt and innocence, are meaningless when law is
movement and man is law incarnate. Thus men are "right" or
"wrong" in so far as they do or do not perform as embodiments of
the law of History or Nature.

Arendt points out that totalitarian policy requires that terror
not only be used as a means of winning and maintaining power,
but that terror be continuous. For when, by terror's hand, "dying
classes" die (according to the law of History) and "inferior races"
perish (according to the law of Nature), both history and nature
will have come to an end — and with them totalitarian law. Therefore to maintain "law" new dying classes and inferior races must
be found, and terror finds them. Terror becomes perpetual, casting
yesterday's executioner in the role of today's victim, who realizes
that having accepted the logic of totalitarianism he must either
play his role or, resisting, concede his whole life a fraud by his
contradiction. Of the "tyranny of logicality" and terror and their
enmity with thought, freedom, and reality, Arendt writes:

> The tyranny of logicality begins with the mind's sub-
> mission to logic as a never-ending process, on which
> man relies in order to engender his thoughts. By this
> submission, he surrenders his inner freedom. . . . As
> terror is needed lest with the birth of each new
> human being a new beginning arise and raise its voice
> in the world, so the self-coercive force of logicality
> is mobilized lest anybody ever start thinking — which
> as the freest and purest of all human activities is the
> very opposite of the compulsory process of deduction.
> . . . Total terror . . . and the self-coercive force of
> logical deduction . . . correspond to each other and
> need each other in order to set the terror-ruled move-
> ment into motion and keep it moving. Just as

terror . . . ruins all relationships between men, so
the self-compulsion of ideological thinking ruins all
relationships with reality. . . . The ideal subject of
totalitarian rule is not the convinced Nazi or the convinced Communist, but people for whom the distinction between fact and fiction (*i.e.*, the reality of experience) and the distinction between true and
false (*i.e.*, the standards of thought) no longer exist.[1]

Arendt's views help us understand the works in this section,
especially Orwell's *1984*. In the light of Arendt's analysis one can
see how closely Orwell's fiction parallels her theories. "Doublethink." "FREEDOM IS SLAVERY." "2+2=5." "IGNORANCE
IS STRENGTH." "Reality exists in the human mind, and nowhere
else." "The object of torture is torture. The object of power is
power." The rationale of these takes on added breadth in the light
of Arendt's study. "*I understand HOW: I do not understand
WHY*," writes Winston Smith, the protagonist of *1984*, in his
diary. More explicitly than Orwell, Arendt tells *why*.

1984 is the composite political dystopia. It stands so central
in the history of the genre that previous dystopias are seemingly
but anticipations and later ones variations of Orwell's definitive
hell. Its prominent dytopian features are the following:

1.   The dictatorship of "the Party," whose object is power.
2.   The execution or brainwashing of dissidents.
3.   The divorce from the values and memory of the past.
4.   The destruction of the capacity to think, through the
perversion of language and the rejection of empirical evidence.
5.   The installation of the Party as the sole judge and origin
of truth.
6.   The denigration of self-esteem; and the hostility to the
joy of personal relationships and the appetite for joy itself.
7.   The maintenance of cultural stasis.
These features raise several basic questions in the mind of the
reader: Is the novel intended as prophecy? Since the author describes a massive perversion of human nature, does he believe
human nature exists? Does the author believe the totalitarian state
viable? The text itself does not answer these questions.

The first question, however, Orwell answers himself: "I do

not believe that the kind of society I describe [in *1984*] *will*
arrive, but I believe . . . that something resembling it *could*
arrive."[2]

In considering *We, Brave New World,* and *1984* both Erich
Fromm and Irving Howe come to the same conclusion in answering the second question regarding human nature, after raising,
coincidently, the matter of human plasticity:

> Can human nature be changed in such a way that man
> will forget his longing for freedom, for dignity, for
> integrity, for love — that is to say, can man forget
> that he is human? Or does human nature have a
> dynamism which will react to the violation of these
> basic human needs? (Fromm)

> All three of our anti-utopian novels are dominated by
> an overwhelming question: can human nature be
> manufactured? Not transformed or manipulated or
> debased, since these it obviously can be; but manu-
> factured by will and decision. (Howe)

The reply:

> They [Zamiatin, Huxley, and Orwell] do not start
> out with the assumption that there is no such thing as
> human nature; that there is no such thing as qualities
> essential to man. . . . They do assume that man has
> an intense striving for love, for justice, for truth.[3]
> (Fromm)

> They must assume that there are strivings in men
> toward candor, freedom, truth and love which can-
> not be suppressed indefinitely.[4] (Howe)

The conclusions of Fromm and Howe may be true, but they
overlook an important point: I feel that *Orwell* is less interested in
whether human nature exists than in the preservation of certain
values which make man feeling and sane. Had he *not* believed in
human nature his cry would be no less outraged. Others might
logic-chop a proof of human nature, but neither faith nor deduc-
tion move Orwell's pen; it is the sturdy, angry resolve that "You
don't do that to people!" *1984* is a personal statement, written
"outside" the idea of human nature. He — Orwell — fronting the
world with his own intelligence and sensibility, declares that
certain actions, thoughts, and appetites are lovely, decent, and

useful, while others are detestable; and he knows he does not stand alone.

The dystopian features of *1984* and the fear that something resembling its society "could arive" so overwhelm the reader that he often overlooks Orwell's positive statement that some things encouraging the lovely, the decent, and the useful *have* arrived. If they are not the stuff of human nature, but rather have been hewn and salvaged from the welter of human experience and nourished and hallowed by the passional heart — so much the more glory for man.

These things that *have* arrived are values — values to be expunged by the totalitarian state of the future.

1.   *The value of feeling and personal loyalty.* Winston Smith grasps that the proles, through their loyalty to each other and through primitive emotions, had "stayed human." Real betrayal, he comprehends, is to stop loving Julia. As members of the anti-Party Brotherhood, Smith and Julia are prepared to die. Yes. Murder? Yes. Corrupt children? Yes. Commit mayhem? Yes. Commit suicide? Yes. Spread venereal diseases? Yes. Cause the death of hundreds of innocents? Yes. Then their interrogater asks, "You are prepared, the two of you, to separate and never see one another again?"

" 'No!' broke in Julia."[5]

Despite the ugliness of the details it is a love scene that Orwell writes here. It echoes what has been said before. Camus' Dr. Rieux: "For nothing in the world is it worth turning one's back on what one loves." (*The Plague*) E. M. Forster: "I hate the idea of causes, and if I had to choose between betraying my country and betraying my friend, I hope I should have the guts to betray my country." ("What I Believe") Julia's quick and resolute *No!* stands, with its brief eloquence, beside the memorable declarations of love in modern literature.

2.   *The value of physical pleasure.* Through insufficient and disagreeable food, decrepit houses, drab clothing, the paucity of even petty luxuries — cigarettes, chocolate — the Party starves the body so that, sensation-poor, it forgets itself. Realizing that the erotic generates self-concern and personal loyalties, the Party attempts to kill or dirty the sex instinct and divert choked-off desire into hysterical enthusiasm for its policies. Smith experiences

sexual encounters with Julia as both sensual pleasure and political defiance and tells her that the greater her previous promiscuity, the greater his love. Her admission that she is "corrupt to the bones" and enjoys not simply him but "the thing in itself" thrills him. "That was above all what he wanted to hear. Not merely the love of one person, but the animal instinct, the simple undifferentiated desire: that was the force that would tear the Party to pieces."[6] And it would also restore the pieces of man's fragmented psyche and return to him what D. H. Lawrence called "the marvel of being alive in the flesh."

3. *The value of the past.* In Orwell's dystopia the record of the past — nations, history, persons — has been obliterated or altered, and one floats in the present, isolated except for the cobweb thread of memory trailing down to his childhood. The present brightened only by his doomed love for Julia, Smith draws nourishment from the past: hazy recollections of his mother; an old tune about the bells of London; an antique glass paperweight. When O'Brien, luring him into the Brotherhood, suggests a toast — "To the confusion of the Thought Police? To the death of Big Brother? To humanity? To the future?" — Smith replies, "To the past."[7] One feels Orwell speaking here, weary of causes and repelled by abstractions, a dying man whose present was soon to be dashed, envisioning a possible hell-on-earth, and toasting the tangible, grand, and sustaining past.

4. *The value of language.* Through the progressive verbicide of "Newspeak," the Party seeks to narrow the precision and range of thought and "make thought-crime literally impossible, because there will be no words in which to express it."[8] But Newspeak extinguishes thought as well as heresy. One can not help but grasp Orwell's unspoken conviction that with the death of a word there also dies a fragment of self-discovery and a potential for experience.

5. *The value of axiomatic truth.* "*Freedom is the freedom to say that two plus two make four. If that is granted, all else follows,*" Smith writes in his diary. The evidence of the senses and common sense are the bulwarks behind which sanity, which is the requisite of freedom, may be preserved from the assaults of dogma, distortion, and intimidation. "Stones are hard, water is wet, objects unsupproted fall. . . . "[9] Neither terror nor the

illogic of "doublethink" and solipsism repeal the empirical truisms which are the foundation of sanity.

Yet *1984* grants terror the victory over sanity and over all that is human. "They can't get inside you," Smith and Julia assure each other; but the Thought Police did get inside. "To die hating them, that was freedom," Smith reasons; but in the end "he loved Big Brother." "It is impossible to found a civilization on fear and hatred and cruelty. It would never endure. . . . It would have no vitality. It would disintegrate. It would commit suicide,"[10] Smith contends before his tormentor, O'Brien; but the text does not support his faith. When one considers the third question — the viability of the completely totalitarian state — one sees that *1984* unrelentingly narrates the debacle of the human spirit and offers no hope for its resurrection. Yet I believe Orwell's pessimism artistic rather than genuine. He knew that to mitigate the horror of his novel with hope would violate its integrity. He must have known that an Oceania could not endure because its rulers would be crippeld by the agonizing dullness of power and the terror of their own inevitable victimization. Fromm astutely assesses the matter: "Such men would be so truly inhuman and lacking in vitality that they would destroy each other, or die out of sheer boredom and anxiety. If the world of *1984* is going to be the dominant form of life on this globe, it will mean a world of madmen, and hence not a viable world."[11]

It would appear that the indispensable characteristic of the totalitarian dystopia is its hostility to freedom, not merely political but primarily personal freedom. Indeed, one being one's self, individuality — these are the state's enemies, because the object of the totalitarian state is the *unmaking* of men. Thus science fiction dealing with totalitarian states rightly ignores political issues, because such states are essentially apolitical, being far less concerned with how men should be governed than with what men should be.

L. P. Hartley's *Facial Justice* portrays a totalitarian state in which the regime goes to absurd lengths to subvert individuality and install conformity as the highest virtue. Benevolently repressive "Darling Dictator," ruling an England largely recovered from an atomic war, decrees self-abasement and rigid egalitarianism for his subjects, who dress in sackcloth and assume the

names of murderers and a number. The Dictator's program consists of the implementation of Equality ("Good E") and the purga-
tion of Envy ("Bad E"), for Equality presumably insures political,
social, and psychological peace and stability, while deadly Envy
had led to nuclear war. A corps of Inspectors enforces discipline,
insures indoctrination, and roots out heresies — tasks made less
difficult owing to the mandatory bromide all must take to curb
rebelliousness and Bad E. Most drastic of all, the Ministry of
Facial Justice has "betafied" women by giving them a new face
through surgery, a face pleasing but not beautiful, regular in
feature but lacking character, and identical to every other betafied
face. Jael, Hartley's beautiful heroine, insists on keeping her
face, not out of vanity, but because her face is *hers*. She represents
what the Dictator has denounced as the "Voluntary Principle,"
that willful and troublesome perversity in man and the origin of
war itself. Jael's struggle to maintain her identity — facial, mental,
and spiritual — and her clever rebellion against the Dictator constitute the main action of the novel.

Unlike Orwell's Big Brother, Darling Dictator proves no
match for the Voluntary Principle and the subversive wit of
Jael. A popular *Mania Contradiceus*[12] frustrates his rule. For example, when, to discourage travel, he announces that a number of
coaches are to be wrecked on each excursion, passengers vie for
seats; when he removes the cruel condition, passengers decline to
ride without risk. Again one sees manifested that saving human
perversity which confounds both the utopian and dystopian planners. It is Jael, however, who topples the regime by a series of
articles which reduce the Dictator's "Good E . . . Bad E" principles to absurdity. In a critique of two concert pianists, she
praises the inept one because he does not arouse Bad E, and she
proposes that all talents be reduced to the lowest common de-
nominator "to make the New State safe for mediocrity." She
ironically contends that Cassius, the inept pianist, played his
piece "as *we* should have played it. . . . By playing it 'badly' he
was keeping us in countenance." His performance, "in spite of
its faults, indeed *because* of its faults, is worth far more than the
other, because it is in line with our common humanity." But

"Brutus, by the very faultlessness of his rendering has
put us out of countenance, he has made us look up to

him, which we should never do, to anything or anyone, except, of course, the Inspectors and the Dictator! By taking up a superior position he has made
us guilty of Bad E — yes, I could feel its poison steal-
ing into me, destroying my sense of unity with my
fellows. Cassius is one of us because he made mistakes, just as we should. What right has Brutus 91 to
play more correctly than we can, to humiliate us?"[13]

Jael's thesis triggers an epidemic of mistake-making. With a
curious mixture of hilarity and orthodoxy, nearly everyone in the
New State goes out of his way to bungle. "As long as anyone
makes mistakes, we ought all to make mistakes," people argue.
Soon all is chaos as they compete to commit the most original
blunders. More articles by Jael, in the same vein, completely rend
the fabric of the New State and bring about the Dictator's abdica-
tion and death.[14]

Ayn Rand's *Anthem* describes a society whose single purpose
is the psychological extinction of the self, a society whose credo
states, *"There are no men but only the great WE."* Narrated by
Equality 7-2521 the story is an account of his unhappy bondage,
his growing awareness of a separate identity, his escape, and his
rebirth through self-realization when he discovers "the secret our
heart has understood and yet will not reveal to us": "I AM. I
THINK. I WILL." Not until the final pages of *Anthem* does the
word *I* appear — and subsequently *my* and *me*. *We, our,* and *us*
had held both singular and plural meanings in the dystopia where
"we exist through, by and for our brothers who are the State,"
where "the great Transgression of Preference [is] to love any
among men better than the others," where "men have no cause to
exist save in toiling for other men," where "men never see their
own faces . . . for it is evil to have concern for their own faces
or bodies,"[15] where men have names such as *Collective, Fraternity, Unanimity, Solidarity, Similarity* and a number, and where
the Unspeakable Word is *I*.

Anthem closes with an outpouring of views on freedom,
virtue, and individuality that Rand treats amply in *Atlas Shrugged*.
Her spokesman, Equality, declares that the name of god is "I"
and cuts the sacred word "EGO" over his portals. In his wilderness
fortress he dreams of founding a society of free men in which
"the word 'We' must never be spoken, save by one's choice and

as a second thought. This word must never be placed first within man's soul, else it becomes a monster, the root of all the evils on earth, the root of man's torture by men, and of an unspeakable lie."[16]

David Karp's *One* liberally reflects Orwell's influence. In *One* the Department of Internal Examination, like Orwell's Ministry of Love, attempts to purge one lone man of heresy and restore him to orthodoxy. But Professor Burden, himself many years a spy for the DIE, having dutifully reported his colleagues for pretensions of intellectual superiority, is unconscious of his heresy — a feeling of self-importance and intellectual superiority, which he reveals by his indignation when the Department tests his humility by reprimanding him for incompetence. His examiners declare his a hopeless case: "Remarkably well-buried heresy." "Completely integrated. He doesn't even know he's a heretic." "He's constantly under pressure to assert himself as an individual."[17] Burden is saved from execution by Lark, the Department inquisitor, who understands that the unconscious pride of Burden — "integrated heresy" — will eventually destroy the State if no cure for it is found. Lark explains his position to the Department:

> "This state of ours is going to extend its powers upon the behalf of the people. It's going to insist that the individual good is completely and utterly identified with the national good. Eventually we must erase the concept of individuality. Ultimately we must come to the stage where no man bears a separate, private identity. The final stage of our society calls for conformity both from within and from without by each of its members."

> "The key to this man has always been his pride, his vanity, his unwarranted belief that he is a creature apart, that he possesses some single, indefinable identity that is his and his alone. And it is the retention of this one idea that stands between the State and a thousand years of rule — a thousand years which will mean a golden age for man. To me such a thing is monstrous! . . . I'm going to pulverize this man's identity. I'm going to reduce him to a cipher, from one . . . to nothing."[18]

In an extensive dialogue bringing to mind Dostoyevsky's "The Grand Inquisitor," Lark attempts to reclaim Burden. Lark argues that man must purchase happiness at the price of reason and individuality; that man is helpless without the State, which protects him from his own bestiality; and that the collective will, directed by the State, creates reality. Burden, however, proves intractable, spewing a profusion of heresies, especially after injections of a truth drug. He asserts that a man owes allegiance to God, himself, and his beliefs. One owes allegiance to the State only insofar as it reflects his self or convictions. As for heresy, it "means that an opinion is held against established doctrine. There is no established doctrine permissible under the contract citizens sign with the State. Hence there can be no heresy."[19]

Even after Lark erases his memory through drugs and hypnopaedia, Burden — who now believes he is Hughes, a victim of amnesia — maintains the heresy of selfhood. Confiding in a state spy, he calls the Church of State a refuge for those who can not bear the loneliness of individuality and declines to join it, preferring a life of self-discovery. "One day I'll be Hughes — the one Mr. Hughes of which there is no other on earth," he says. "It may not be the happiest thing in the world for me — but it's what I want." Depressed and defeated, Lark orders his execution. The inquisitor had failed to find the "core of [Burden's] heresy," that germ which Lark himself had suspected "is something not learned, something not acquired but something instinctive, something so deeply a part of a human creature that it cannot be removed."[20]

Though Eugene Zamiatin is not generally known to the reading public, Huxley and Orwell are and have become lodestars in science fiction. Rarely does one browse science fiction shelves without finding cover blurbs like "Rivals *Brave New World!*" and "Shades of *1984!*" showing the indebtedness to Huxley and Orwell. Indebtedness is no sin — Orwell borrowed from Huxley and Huxley from Zamiatin — when a writer imparts his own inspiration, fancy, conviction, voice, in short, a token of his identity to his work. Too often, however, the rivals of *Brave New World* and *1984* are mere potboilers, their authors having helped themselves to the devices of this and that fictional totalitarian state and worked them into a formula plot.

"Outshines Orwell's *1984*," writes the *Book Week* reviewer of Ira Levin's *This Perfect Day*[21] and the paperback edition cover bruits this opinion in hot pink capitals. But the novel is a pastiche of anti-utopian clichés. Still not a bad book at all, workmanlike, occasionally exciting, and well reviewed,[22] but nothing new to say. I suspect that Levin's being a mainstream writer and author of the best-selling *Rosemary's Baby* has muddled some critical judgments. Nevertheless the book's reception is historically important if one wants an overview of public interest in fictional totalitarianism as late as 1970. One must conclude that the public finds it fascinatingly repulsive — which, ideologically speaking, is a good thing.

Now, to relate some bits and pieces of Levin's exhumations. In the future, the Unification has dissolved the nations and molded mankind into the Family. UniComp the computer rules the Family and regulates almost every aspect of living — occupation, choice of spouse, year of death. . . . Everyone informs upon eveyone else and the slightest deviation is treated with tranquilizers and sexual depressants. Family Members wear a special identification bracelet, which lets mechanical scanners keep track of everyone's movement. Almost all people happily accept their place in the Family and effortlessly refrain from the two great prohibitions: aggression and deciding for oneself. Yet the seed of individuality survives in some. Levin's hero, an "incurable," forms a rebel band, blows up UniComp, and the age of Unification and the Family ends.

The most interesting thing about Douglas R. Mason's *From Carthage Then I Came*[23] is its printing history. In 1970 a paperback house reprinted it as *Eight Against Utopia. Utopia*, it appears, has become a code word for *dystopia* among science fiction readers and also, to some degree, among general readers too. One of the flood of books catering to the interest in fictional totalitarian states in the '50's and '60's, Mason's typifies the many cliché-ridden, pseudo science fiction novels that have followed Zamiatin, Huxley, and Orwell. Mason hastily establishes a totalitarian setting: Carthage, a technological city under a climatic and social shield-dome. Creature comforts in exchange for cradle-to-grave regimentation. The obsessional search for dissidents, the mania for security. Tracking devices, brain monitoring. The integration of the city president into the central computer. Then the remaining ninety percent of the book involves the adventures of eight escaping dissidents. With a little rewriting the eight could emigrate into a new setting and escape gangsters or headhunters. Such novels are chapter-one science fiction. It is not my intention to pillory any particular books but rather to note, as a point of literary history, that the type of anti-utopia Zamiatin, Huxley, and Orwell have so vividly and movingly forged into being has been the subject of an inordinate amount of hack writing.

The excellence of Peter Wahlöö's *The Thirty-First Floor* proves that the fictional totalitarian state need not be a drab regurgitation of older models. With craftsmanship and originality Wahlöö deftly combines science fiction, detective fiction, and social criticism. He creates what is unfortunately still uncommon in science fiction — a realistic and memorable major character, Inspector Jensen. And without the traditional science fiction gadgetry, he depicts a thoroughly believable and possible totalitarian state.

In an unspecified European country a huge publishing house, "the concern," has received an anonymous bomb threat in retaliation for the "murder" it has committed, and Inspector Jensen takes the case. The concern, which controls ninety-nine percent of the country's newspapers and magazines, is the principal instrument of the government's policy of "social equality." For this end its publications exclude all controversial, disturbing, invigorating, and thoughtful subjects. The content of the concern's publications is insipid to the point of idiocy: Pictures of pop singers, T. V. stars, members of the royal family, and potted plants; and little girls with kittens, small boys with puppies, small boys with very large dogs, and adolescent girls with very small cats. Comics, vacuous stories, horoscopes. Articles on how to tell fortunes from tea dregs and how to water geraniums. Defending the press's role as entertainer, tranquilizer, and leveler, a concern spokesman says: "Before, the press often had an inflammatory effect on the readers. That is not the case any longer. Now the content and form is aimed entirely at both the reader's benefit . . . and enjoyment. They are aimed at the family, to be readable at all levels, not to create aggressions, unhappiness, or anxiety. They satisfy the ordinary person's need for escapism. Briefly, they promote social equality."[24]

But social equality has not brought happiness. The whole society is gray and joyless, plagued with suicide, drunkenness,

frigidity, and impotence. The public drags on its half life, unconscious of its cause. There is not even an underground because
virtually no one knows what to go underground against. The last
of the opposition journalists are employed in the "Special Department" on the thirty-first floor of the concern, a floor known
only to the managers. There they write stimulating and critical
copy, but the concern prints only dummy editions of their work
and never distributes it, finding one excuse after another (technical, economic, but never subjective) not to distribute. Those
whose ideas could have breathed new life into a society choked
with despondency are themselves gagged on the thirty-first floor.

Inspector Jensen at last finds the writer of the bomb threat —
a journalist in the Special Department. The murder he had charged
was, he says, "an intellectual murder, far more loathsome and dis-
tasteful than physical murder. The murder of innumerable ideas,
the murder of opinions, of freedom of speech. Premeditated first-
degree murder of them all, to give people guaranteed peace of
mind, to make them disposed to swallow uncritically all the
tripe that's stuffed into them. Do you see, to spread indifference
without opposition, forcibly injecting poison after first making
sure there is neither doctor nor serum available."[25]

Without Big Brother, thought police, and doublethink, without telescreens and scanners, without drugs, hypnopaedia, brain
monitoring, and mind altering, Wahlöö has created a totalitarian
state sustained by a single, unique program: benign dullness!
Obviously, much of what Arendt writes about totalitarian law,
terror, and logic does not apply to Wahlöö's dystopia. Arendt's
idea that totalitarian law is a law of movement striving to evolve
mankind assumes that mankind and the processes of civilization
are dynamic. Wahlöö, however, sees most of mankind as being
innately semi-vegetative but *made* dynamic by the pressures of
life and an intellectually vital minority. One of his marooned
journalists speaks of "people's natural tendencies" toward "intellectual idleness": "To prefer looking at pictures to reading
and — if they ever read anything — to prefer complete meaningless drivel to something which forces them to think or make an
effort to take a stand."[26] Thus, the absence of a coherent ideology
and *ideas,* Wahlöö infers, can be just as conducive to totalitarianism as the madness of ideology. And benign dullness can be just

as mentally and spiritually cancerous as the frenzied, mandatory Two Minutes Hate of *1984*.

Eugene Zamiatin's *We*, acknowledged as the first of this century's great anti-utopian novels, has furnished other writers a model for the totalitarian state of the future.[27] Identity-annihilation, regimentation, cruelty, brainwashing, constant surveillance, the tyrant and his police, the underground, the revolt — these have been liberally borrowed by Zamiatin's successors.

Zamiatin's nightmare land, the United State, is ruled by the Well-Doer, whose hand operates the disintegrating machine at the public executions of the disloyal. On the Day of Unanimity the Numbers (names being an ancient frivolity) re-elect the Well-Doer without a solitary nay: "How could it be otherwise, since 'all' and 'I' are one 'we'?" writes D-503, whose journal comprises the story. The Guardians, by spying and aerosurveillance, maintain discipline and orthodoxy, a function made all the easier because the Numbers themselves usually confess their own transgressions and those of others. D-503 stands "in adoration" as he beholds the line of Numbers before the Bureau of Guardians, "awaiting their turns, faces shining like the oil lamps in an ancient temple. They had come to accomplish a great thing: they had come to put on the altar of the United State their beloved ones, their friends, their own selves."[28]

The state's goal is to impart the conditions of mathematical and mechanical regularity to the Numbers. The *Integral*, the spaceship chief engineer D-503 is building, will bring to beings of other planets, "who are perhaps still in the primitive state of freedom," the gift of "mathematically faultless happiness." The machines in its construction dock seem to dance a beautiful, "mechanical ballet." "Why beautiful?" asks D-503 of himself. "Because it is an *unfree* movement." "The ideal . . . is to be found where nothing happens," where everything follows the predicted, confined, unfree course — like machines. State doctrine reiterates his admiration: "For every spark from a dynamo is a spark of pure reason; each motion of a piston, a pure syllogism. . . . The philosophy of the cranes, presses, and pumps is complete and clear like a circle."[29]

The dead hand of uniformity, thralldom, and self-abnegation reaches into every facet of life in the United State. Numbers, their number-plates affixed to their blue-gray uniforms, march to their labors in formation and then return to their glass cubicles in transparent dormitories. Only when one is permitted to "pull down the curtains" — a euphemism for sexual relations — does he know privacy. However, even sex has been formularized: "A Number may obtain a license to use any other Number as a sexual product," states the law. One applies for sexual relations and receives a pink ticket of authorization. The Tables of Hours fuses every Number into a single body, each rising, beginning and finishing work, exercising, and retiring at the same moment. "With a million hands, at the very same second, designated by the Tables, we carry the spoons to our mouths,"[30] D-503 proudly records.

Yet despite his devotion to the United State, D-503 falls in love with I-330, the alluring leader of the underground. The ecstatic and tormenting novelty of emotional abandon draws him into revolutionary schemes until a sudden medical discovery restores his "reason." The *State Journal* proclaims:

REJOICE!

For from now on we are *perfect!*

Until today your own creation, engines, were more perfect than you. . . .

It is not your fault; you are ill. And the name of your illness is:

FANCY.

It is a worm that gnaws black wrinkles on one's forehead. It is a fever that drives one to run further and further, even though "further" may begin where happiness ends. It is the last barricade on our road to happiness.

Rejoice! This Barricade Has Been Blasted at Last! The Road Is Open!

The latest discovery of our State science is that there is a center for fancy — a miserable little nervous knot in the lower region of the frontal lobe of the brain. A triple treatment of this knot with X-rays will cure you of fancy.

Forever!

You are perfect; you are mechanized; the road to one-hundred-per-cent happiness is open! Hasten then all of you, young and old, hasten to undergo the

Great Operation! Hasten to the auditoriums where
the Great Operation is being performed! Long live the
Great Operation! Long live the United State! Long
live the Well-Doer![31]

His fancy removed by the Great Operation, D-503 betrays
the revolutionaries. Then calmly he watches the torture of I-330.
The United State is saved.

Zamiatin's *We*, Huxley's *Brave New World*,[32] and Orwell's
1984, the three masterworks of totalitarian science fiction, take
for granted that man is approaching that moment in history when
freedom and happiness will appear to be — or will *actually* be —
incompatible. The moral dilemma, which Dostoyevsky treated as
philosophical speculation, bears upon these dystopian novelists
as an ominous certainty. The Great Operation in *We* stands as a
double symbol of their dark vision: the increasing press of technology upon today's fragmented value systems; and man's retreat
from the bastions of freedom toward a happiness without soul.
But the technology lends itself more to regimentation than personal fulfillment; and without psychological tampering little
happiness comes to hollow men.

The dystopian writers have sensed the crises of the future,
Chad Walsh believes. They serve as social scientists and
philosophers, whose "ultimate nightmares of the race" must not
be dismissed as mere fantasy. And they are prophets. He writes:

> I submit . . . that many of the dystopian writers are
> the prophets of our times. I use the word prophet in
> something of its biblical sense, to mean one who
> observes society, evaluates it in accordance with
> principles he considers eternal, and offers messages of
> warning where he sees it going astray; messages not
> merely of warning but predictions of the wrath to
> come unless society renounces its false turnings. If
> Amos, Hosea, Isaiah or Jeremiah were alive, I think
> it probable that they would be writing and publishing
> inverted utopias. It is the prophetic form of our age.
> And for one person whose armour of self-deception
> is penetrated by pulpit preaching, there must be a
> dozen who have been pierced by *Nineteen Eighty-
> Four* or *Brave New World*.[33]

The Mind Invasion

The fear of being the pawn of an alien intelligence, the fear of being stripped naked in the most absolute way — by having one's private thoughts become the property of others — these have haunted man since his beginning and have long been the currency of story. Mind-invasion tales fall naturally within the province of science fiction and, in these times especially, have proliferated in number and variety. The exotica alone in twentieth-century stories of this type can furnish material for a lengthy study. However, what sets recent works apart from those of the past is that they no longer strike the reader as the sheerest fantasy playing upon the racial unconscious. Today truth drugs, lie detectors, computer memory banks, behavioral engineering, electronic eavesdropping, subliminal advertising, ESP, psychological testing, and brainwashing have given man a sense of real vulnerability. While many works discussed elsewhere in this study feature mental tyranny, they have been treated to emphasize other points. The works discussed in this section make their stronger appeal to the unconscious, ingrained fear of being possessed or laid open, a fear which the present has intensified.

Man may be a social animal, but who is not thankful for the wall of secrecy shielding his wayward self? "If they only knew," thinks the silent rebel, confident "they" shall never know. But "they" breach the wall in the nightmare world and know. The static society of Robert Sheckley's "The Academy"[1] detects deviates by installing sanity meters in all public places. The meter's needle registers each passer's sanity rating. If rated insane one undergoes therapy or surgical alteration at The Academy, an institution which cures all its patients but, ominously, discharges none. Sheckley returns to the theme of mental denudation in a novel depicting human society in a bog of stagnation and triviality. World peace and social tranquility in The Status Civilization[2] have been achieved through a hypnotic process incorporated into public school education, which compels each person to hasten to one of the ubiquitous robot-confessor stations if he has committed a crime or even suspects himself of having committed one. Ironically, Sheckley's hero, a confessed and exiled "murderer," is innocent, but he had assumed himself guilty because of incriminating circumstances.

Public interest in extrasensory perception possibly accounts for the increase in "psionic" or telepathic fiction. Frequently the telepath is hunted down by the normal masses. In other stories he belongs to a powerful professional aristocracy whose services are indispensable in government, commerce, and medicine. In Alfred Bester's *The Demolished Man*,[3] crime detection, business, and psychiatry rely on the "esper" for mind dredging. The Ridforce operator in Kenneth Bulmer's *The Doomsday Men*[4] is the ultimate detective, linking his brain with that of murder victims and reliving their last minutes to identify their killers. Though not anti-utopian, the countless psionic stories of this sort in recent science fiction perhaps reflect the sense of shrinking privacy resulting from well-publicized psychological, chemical, and mechanical techniques of mind penetration.

Although action dominates idea in Philip K. Dick's *Ubik*[5] and Robert Silverberg's *To Live Again*,[6] the dystopian stench permeates these fictional worlds. Dick's world is a peeper's heaven and it is war. By 1992 for some unexplained reason the number of people with psionic and anti-psionic powers has greatly increased and the powers too have expanded. The psionics – telepaths (mind penetrators) and precogs (those gifted with precognition) – are legitimate professionals whose services are for hire. Opposing them are the inertials – anti-telepaths and anti-precogs – also for hire, who use their talents to jam the psionics'. So, in *Ubik* it is thrust and counterthrust. But behind all the psionic jousting we see the dismaying fact that the privacy of one's mind no longer depends on one's mind.[7] Just as the prudent man slung Colts from his gun belt in America's legendary shoot-out-a-day wild-west towns, Dick's characters survive in their mind-raping jungle behind a shield of inertial and psionic mercenaries.

After bodily death, in Silverberg's *To Live Again*, those who live again (the very rich) have their electronically recorded personas dubbed into the minds of living hosts, with each sharing the other. If all goes well a persona has a new body while a host augments his own mental talents with those of the "deceased." But as in *Ubik*, it's war, and on many levels. The host's mind must dominate the persona, for the persona will "go dybbuk" if it can and take over. Ambitious hosts incorporate personas as imperial

powers accumulate colonies and as aggressive companies absorb
weaker and insolvent ones. Why? So that the host's "empire" can
defeat another. Conducting oneself in an ordinary generous way,
the idea that one might live and let live, these ironically would
strike the characters of *To Live Again* as utterly foreign. Rather —
die and go dybbuk; live and build persona "portfolios" and keep
the personas vassal; rival and subjugate other host empires.

Silverberg's plot concerns the struggle for the persona of an
immensely rich, dynamic, and talented financial genius. The
possession of the persona should make the host supreme in world
finance. But Silverberg's world is so ignobly predatory, so empty
of men and full of the devoured and devourers of men, that supremacy in it is supremacy in hell. To be thoroughly and irretriev-
ably dead in *To Live Again* is "a consummation devoutly to be
wished."

Ralph Blum's *The Simultaneous Man*[8] follows the same
scientific assumptions of Silverberg's novel. That is, the contents
of the mind, like sound, can be recorded, stored, and dubbed into
a host. However, Blum's fictional science differs from Silverberg's
in two important respects. Silverberg's characters collect minds.
Blum's "Remake" is just that — a man remade by a mind remade.
What can be done to a sound tape can also be done to a "mind
tape": it can be repeatedly inscribed and erased until the manip-
ulator has exactly what he wants. But a remade man is not viable.
He dies.

Blum's simultaneous man, a Negro prisoner-volunteer, is a
creature of U. S. government-funded scientists whose original goal
had been to find a method for extracting intelligence data from
political enemies. Success in the initial project revealed that not
only could information be retrieved but memories could be erased
and replaced with those of a donor. But Remake 234/4, the first
simultaneous man, complains of feeling unreal and soulless. And
he is dying, "dying of being a ghost," of dreaming dreams of
things that for him never were — of caressing the donor's wife
with a hand that is always white. In the failure of the plastic-man
makers, Blum stands with Karp (*One*) and others whose characters
hold back some part of themselves from the mind invaders. He
insists that mind is more than memory and identity more than the
sum of all input. Whatever the *self* may be, its observable parts

can not be shuffled, erased, or remolded without driving the secret core of self to rebel against its violators and even the flesh that contains it.

I have referred to Alex, the sadistic young hoodlum in Anthony Burgess's *A Clockwork Orange*, earlier in this study. His "rehabilitation" by the state epitomizes Pavlovian conditioning. The gory authenticity of the reclamation episode confronts the reader with his own vulnerability. In the breaking of Alex, in his transformation from the inhuman to the unhuman, science fiction and reality touch. Promised release from prison should a new technique drive out the brute in him, Alex quickly agrees to be reformed, dreaming of freedom and a return to his old ways. A nausea-inducing drug ("vitamins") is injected into his arm, and later he is taken to the promised movies. "And then the lights went out and there was Your Humble Narrator And Friend sitting alone in the dark, all on his frightened oddy knocky [lonesome], not able to move nor shut his glazzies [eyes] nor anything." The film shows thugs beating an old man. "They made a real pudding out of this starry veck [old guy], going crack crack crack at him with their fisty rookers [arms], tearing his platties[clothes] off and then finishing up by booting his nagoy plott [naked body]." Alex enjoys the action despite a slight nausea, which he attributes to undernourishment. The next film depicts "a young devotchka [girl] who was being given the old in-out by first one malchick [lad] then another then another then another, she creeching [screaming] away very gromky [loud]."[9] Soon Alex feels pain all over and wants to vomit. Horror follows horror. A face is slashed to bits with a razor. Soldiers are mutilated by their captors. Alex begs for an end. His pains are unbearable. But the treatment has only begun. The films and racking nausea must be endured for two more weeks.

The reclaimed Alex is exhibited before an audience of officialdom. When an effeminate bully assaults him, thoughts of self-defense bring on the nausea, and Alex presses it back by licking his tormentor's boots. Next a voluptuous young woman approaches him, "and the first thing that flashed into my gulliver [head] was that I would like to have her right down there on the floor with the old in-out real savage, but skorry [quick] as a shot came the sickness. . . . So I creeched [cried] out":

"O most beautiful and beauteous of devotchkas, I
throw like my heart at your feet for you to like
trample all over. If I had a rose I would give it to you.
If it was all rainy and cally [fecal] now on the ground
you could have my platties [clothes] to walk on so
as not to cover your dainty nogas [feet] with filth
and cal." And as I was saying all this, O my brothers,
I could feel the sickness like slinking back. "Let me,"
I creeched out, "worship you and be like your helper
and protector from the wicked like world."[10]

The assembled dignitaries acclaim the new breakthrough in
criminal rehabilitation. The head of the experiment shouts, "He
will be your true Christian . . . ready to be crucified rather than
crucify. . . . Joy before the Angels of God." "The point is," says
the Minister of the 'Inferior,' "that it works."

"It works all right," the prison chaplain sighs. "God help the
lot of us."[11]

Utilizing Pavlovian principles again in *The Ring*, Piers Anthony and Robert E. Margroff add still other weapons to the
crowded arsenal of science fiction's mind invaders. A society,
sterile and corrupt itself, sentences its outcasts to "Ultra Conscience" and the ring. Ultra Conscience — the society's moral
code, imprinted by computer into the subconscious of the outcast — and the ring — a shocking device sealed on the finger —
operate in conjunction to form a prison of the mind. Though still
holding the same beliefs and inclinations as before, "ringers"
may not even entertain a thought contrary to Ultra Conscience
without a cruel shock from the ring. A sentencing judge explains
the ring to the author's victimized hero:

"Obey the law in all respects, behave ethically, keep a
civil tongue, and you will have little trouble. The
ring is triggered by the same kind of bodily reactions
men have utilized for decades to determine the truth
of a given response — variations in blood pressure,
muscular tension, other neural functions. You might
call it a miniaturized lie-detector. The potency of its
delivered shock varies directly with the disparity between your attempted action and the dictates of
ideal behavior. . . . Old habit patterns have to be
altered. . . . But in a few days the new patterns will
form, and you will find that the ring reminds you less
and less. You will adapt to citizenship."[12]

Raymond F. Jones' *The Cybernetic Brains*[13] carries the mind invasion to a Dantesque extremity. Cybernetic brain control has made the Welfare State of the twenty-fifth century a land of leisure and plenty. The brains of two million dead, willed to the State by their donors, monitor the nation's automated factories. But the brains, assumed to be only mindless neural networks, are not dead. They are alive, conscious of their identity, capable of thought, and agonizingly aware of their fate — eternal, disembodied slavery in a metal box. When, in time, the directors of the Cybernetics Institute discover the truth about the brains, they keep their findings secret and continue to accept donors. The directors justify their actions on the grounds that the State's entire manufacturing structure, functioning under cybernetic brain control, would crumble without the brain slaves. First published in 1950, Jones' novel strikes an even more chilling note today: In 1968 American scientists announced that the human brain could possibly operate as a cybernetic control mechanism.

Invasion from outer space is a staple of science fiction. While earlier stories, such as H. G. Wells's *The War of the Worlds* (1898), concentrated on the physical destruction wreaked by alien monsters, current fiction tends to show the invaders bent on the insidious puppetization of earthmen. Robert A. Heinlein's *The Puppet Masters* well represents this trend. Parasite slug "masters" attach themselves to human hosts and control their every thought and action. Large areas of the United States fall under the slug's control. Counter measures against it are often frustrated because it even possesses members of the government and defense teams. Speaking through a host, a master offers mankind a life of contentment, peace, and the security of surrender, and the offer appears genuine. Another possessed host exults: "I had no idea that a man could feel such peace and contentment and well-being. This is the happiest I've been in years. . . . Believe me, this is what we were intended for; this is our destiny. Mankind has been divided, warring with himself. The masters will make him whole."[14] Though essentially a novel of action and suspense, *The Puppet Masters* also allegorizes modern anxiety about the preservation of freedom. Like so many of the writers treated in this study, Heinlein anticipates that moment when man must make the fateful choice between security and freedom.

When one puts down Robert Silverberg's Nebula Award-winning shocker "Passengers," he may wonder what gives it such impact. Another story about people possessed by mind-stealing aliens. Passengers, invisible, diabolical beings, who for three years have infested the earth, inhabit their victims' bodies — "ride" them — and make them do vile or silly things. It is common to see on the street or any public place the ridden behaving in obnoxious, spastic, or queer ways. Charles had just been ridden by a Passenger who forced him to have sexual relations with a ridden woman. Now free of his rider, he meets her by chance again and slowly gains her trust. They will love, he assures her, as two free people love. Then — "in that moment I feel the chill at the back of my skull, the sensation as of a steel needle driven deep through bone. I stiffen. My arms drop away from her. For an instant, I lose touch, and when the mists clear all is different."[15] He turns, enters a bar, sits; his hand falls on the wrist of a young homosexual.

Silverberg's first-person, razor-sliced narration joins content and style superbly. But it is the outstanding treatment which makes a rather predictable plot throb on every page and gives the story its clout. In "Passengers" possession has become a condition of life, like the common cold, like death. Distressing, feared, but the way things are. In other stories people, roused by a sense of urgency, mobilize against the mind possessors. Not so here. Silverberg's terse, tense sentences — not many over ten words — convey exhaustion. His world has surrendered to a fact. No defenders, no defenses against Passengers, who ride anytime, anywhere —

> perhaps in the mahogany-paneled boardroom itself, during the conference. Pink concerned faces all about me; I cough, I lurch, I stumble from my seat. They shake their heads sadly. No one reaches for me. No one stops me. It is too dangerous to interfere with one who has a Passenger. The chances are great that a second Passenger lurks nearby in the discorporate state, looking for a mount. So I am avoided. I leave the building.

> Determinism is no longer a philosopher's abstraction; it is cold alien tendrils sliding between the cranial sutures. The Passengers arrived three years ago. I have been ridden five times since then. Our world is

> quite different now. But we have adjusted even to
> this. We have adjusted. We have our mores. Life goes
> on. Out governments rule, our legislatures meet, our
> stock exchanges transact business as usual, and we
> have methods for compensating for the random
> havoc. It is the only way. What else can we do?
> Shrivel in defeat? We have an enemy we cannot fight;
> at best we can resist through endurance. So we
> endure.[16]

They adjust and life goes on. There's the stroke that jolts. What
else, one may ask, in fantasy or fact might be adjusted to? What
"passengers" have already been adjusted to? Is man bound to live
on virtually any terms? Is the intolerable something bitterly tolerated? And then tolerated? Has the intolerable already happened?
In our times Silverberg's story seeps through the dikes walling off
the ocean of pure fantasy and provokes some pertinent, dry-land
questions.

Robert Heinlein's "They" (1941) is, I believe, the most comprehensive of all mind-invasion stories. It is science fiction, psychological fiction, mystery fiction, and philosophical fiction. It
would stun in any age, for it taps into the universal paranoia — the
unspeakable suspicion that our social and even physical environment (that is, what we call reality) is a hoax and that each of us is
alone sharing his life with a race of deceivers.

Dr. Hayward's patient, identified only as "he," has classic
symptoms. *He* saw through their plot. *They*: Hayward, the mental
asylum personnel, his wife, and all the other so-called fellow
human beings. Even as a child he had suspected something. Adults
shifted their talk to the weather or some other inane subject when
he appeared, certainly not what they were really up to. The obviously insane cycle into which they tried to lure him — work, get
money, and buy the wherewithal to work some more — was a
scheme to keep his mind so busy with trivia that he would never
discover the truth. The truth: He is the center and alone. Had he
ever really communicated with anybody, even his wife Alice? He
would escape. He would outsmart even the Glaroon, the creature
called Hayward.

Alice comes in with dearests, tears, I-love-you's, and forevers,
but he brings her back to the decisive evidence, the rain. Heavy
rain that day when he and Alice were leaving the house. His

impulsive dash back upstairs to his study. And from the study window at the rear of the house – clear and sunny. He had found them out.

> The creature he knew as Alice went to the place of assembly without stopping to change form. "It is necessary to adjourn this sequence. I am no longer able to influence his decisions."
>
> They had expected it, nevertheless they stirred with dismay.
>
> The Glaroon addressed the First for Manipulation. "Prepare to graft the selected memory track at once."
>
> Then, turning to the First for Operations, the Glaroon said: "The extrapolation shows that he will tend to escape within two of his days. This sequence degenerated primarily through your failure to extend that rainfall all around him. Be advised."
>
> "It would be simpler if we understood his motives."
>
> "In my capacity as Dr. Hayward, I have often thought so," commented the Glaroon acidly, "but if we understood his motives, we would be part of him. Bear in mind the Treaty! He almost remembered. . . . ."
>
> The Glaroon continued with orders: "Leave structures standing until adjournment. New York City and Harvard University are now dismantled. Divert him from those sectors.
>
> "Move!"[17]

Heinlein's is the consummate story of invasion and isolation. It blends the fantastic, the allegorical, and the true. What other time but this could have produced it? The crowning irony is that both *he* and *they* are captives of the other. Whoever understands the motives of the other becomes the other. Both are condemned to a contest ignorant of the paramount inspiration of the adversary. And if *they* have made his world and compelled him to live in it, *he* is, no less, the puppet master of their lives, for *they* have no real world outside him. When adversaries become each other's very environment, who has invaded whom?

What makes Colin Wilson's *The Mind Parasites*, Frank Herbert's *The Heaven Makers,* and Isaac Asimov's "Breeds There a Man. . . ?" unique among mind-invasion science fiction stories is their historical orientation. All attribute the madness and misery of past and present to mind-warping incubi – vampires feeding on man's creative energy or string-holders of the Punch-and-Judy show called history, whose scenario human beings imagine they have written.

Wilson's narrator, Gilbert Austin, in sifting through the scientific papers of a friend, psychologist Karel Weissman, happens upon the key to his friend's suicide. More important, he discovers the key to the psycho-spiritual malaise of the times, the chief symptom of which is the alarming increase in suicide from mid-century to the present (1994). "It has been my conviction . . . ," states the opening sentence of Weissman's *Historical Reflections*, "that the human race is being attacked by a sort of mind-cancer." The *Reflections* advance the theory that from the Renaissance to the eighteenth century Western man possessed the capacity for self-renewal, transcending disasters in a succession of great ages hospitable to such creative minds as da Vinci, Shakespeare, Newton, Johnson, Mozart. This capacity for self-renewal suggests that "man is a god who will overcome every obstacle." Then, about 1800 an invisible malignity creeps upon the race. Accident, drink, madness, drug addiction, tuberculosis strike down the "life-affirmers" — Shelley, Hoffmann, Nietzche, Schumann, Hölderlin, Coleridge, De Quincy, Lawrence; but the "life-slanderers" often reach old age. Mozart dies at thirty-five; de Sade survives. "And suddenly, we are in an age of darkness, an age where men of genius no longer create like gods. Instead, they struggle as if in the grip of an invisible octopus. The century of suicide begins. In fact, modern history begins, the age of defeat and neurosis."[18]

Why should man's capacity for transcendence have been attacked by mind vampires at the end of the eighteenth century? Weissman asks. He advances the theory that when the intelligent races of the universe eventually evolve to the point of winning the struggle for physical survival, they then begin the second stage of their life cycle — the exploration of the rich, uncharted kingdom of the mind, the turning inward which will slowly transform them from animal to god.

> Now I suspect that these mind vampires specialize in finding races who have almost reached this point of evolution, who are on the brink of achieving a new power, and then feeding on them until they have destroyed them. . . . Their purpose, therefore, is to prevent man from discovering the worlds inside

> himself, to keep his attention directed *outwards*. I
> think there can be no possible doubt that the wars of
> the twentieth century are a deliberate contrivance of
> these vampires. Hitler, like de Sade, was almost
> certainly another of their "zombis."[19]

Weissman's *Reflections* electrify Austin. At once the cause of man's present despair and the confounding of two centuries' bright hopes become clear to him. The mind parasites had laid a "history trap" to arrest man's imminent evolutionary leap. Aware that the genius of a Beethoven, Goethe, and Shelley could prime a legion of liberating artists and philosophers, the parasites had proceeded to harass, confuse, and destroy the world's great minds. They afflicted scientists with a "deep feeling of psychological insecurity that made them grasp eagerly at the idea of science as 'purely objective' knowledge," encouraging dogmatic and materialistic attitudes. They cut down great artists with public indifference and hostility and with disease and death. They manipulated crucial events, making history appear to be divorced from the direction and aspiration of individuals and, like a wind-up toy, moving mechanically.

Austin enlists key figures of the intellectual fraternity in a crusade to combat the parasites, and they alert the world to the danger. Though it is understood that the parasites can never be totally defeated, man is now aware of his resources for self-renewal and self-realization, and armed with newly learned methods for achieving them, can face the future with hope.

Frank Herbert's *The Heaven Makers* stirs recollections of Samuel Johnson's satiric criticism, "A Review of Soame Jenyns' *A Free Inquiry into the Nature and Origin of Evil*." "He [Jenyns] imagines," Johnson writes, "that as we have not only animals for food, but choose some for our diversion, the same privilege may be allowed to some beings above us, *who may deceive, torment, or destroy us for the ends only of their own pleasure or utility*." Johnson proceeds to demolish Jenyns' speculations, pricking him with exquisite ridicule, and concludes, "The only end of writing is to enable the readers better to enjoy life, or better to endure it: and how will either of those be put more in our power by him who tells us, that we are puppets, of which some creature not much wiser than ourselves manages the wires."[20] Yet that is the thesis of Herbert's story.

The Chem, immortal, invisible, goblin creatures, imprisoned in eternity, find relief from oppressive timelessness by molding "voices and faces and entire races" for their amusement. Having little else to relieve their boredom but voyeurism, the Chem have made earth (and other worlds too) one vast theatrical stage. From his storyship beneath the ocean, director-scenarist Fraffin had sent shooting crews "filming" the pageants of history to entertain the Chem on universal "pantovive" (a kind of television). "I touch a nerve," says Fraffin, explaining his art to a Chem visitor. "Greed here, a desire there, a whim in the other place — and fear. Yes, fear. When the creature's fully prepared, I arouse its fears. The whole mechanism performs for me then. They make themselves ill! They love! They hate! They cheat! They kill! They die!" The sack of Carthage, the fall of the Bastille — Fraffin productions for Chem pantovive. Ancient conquerors and martyrs, Cyrus, Tiglath-pileser, Sennacherib, Shadmaneser, Jesus . . . all had once played in his cast of characters, killing, dying. "And the most amusing part . . . the most *humorous* element is that they think they do it of and by themselves."[21]

The idea that man is caught in a "history trap" antedates modern science fiction and Jenyns' eighteenth-century *A Free Inquiry*. Fundamentalist Christian theology finds Satan supreme on earth, and only by dying into eternal bliss do a favored few slip the theological history trap. It is such an archetypal paranoia that we can hardly accuse one theologian, philosopher, or writer who fastens upon it of borrowing from another. So whether Wilson and Herbert have drawn upon Isaac Asimov's "Breeds There a Man . . . ?" (1951) one can not say.

In Asimov's story a brilliant nuclear scientist, Ralston, becomes deranged by what, he says, should be obvious to everyone but only he perceives: that man is a kind of bacteria to unknown superbeings, who cultivate us as we cultivate other microorganisms — to study and experiment upon us. History proves this. The great cultural centers of the past — the Athens of Pericles, the Florence of the Medicis, the England of Elizabeth, the Spain of the Cordovan Emirs, the Israelite kingdoms of the reformers — were blotted out by war, plague, decay, or other calamities. Why? *They*, the experimenters, want it so. Their experiment with intelligence and creativity had to end. The cultures were *cultures*, and the cleaning up had to begin to stop further development of the microbes' ability and vitality. Therefore, wipe out, clean up, the end of an age. And deluded historians imagined they knew the causes when in reality they saw only the effects. "When we sterilize an instrument, do the germs know where the killing heat comes from? Or what has brought it about?" asks Ralston. Like a culture of germs ringed by penicillin to kill off those spreading too far from the center of inoculation, the human intellect too is ringed by the experimenters. "When we penetrate the true meaning of our own existence, we have reached into the penicillin and we must die."[22] Tormented by a suicidal compulsion to which he finally succumbs, Ralston *must* die, for he has penetrated the ring. Suicides among top scientists increase drastically. The two-hundred-year experiment with a highly potent strain, technological man, now threatens *them* and the situation calls for a wipe out. Their method: the atomic war nobody wants but which, in the madness of events, pushes itself closer with glacial relentlessness.

One need not belabor the obvious kinship between "Breeds There a Man . . . ?," *The Mind Parasites, The Heaven Makers,* and Huxley's *Ape and Essence.* But a strong particular tie between Asimov's story and Wilson's *The Mind Parasites* should be stressed. Both speak of ages in which the human spirit flowers, nourished by geniuses of art, science, and philosophy. And when man verges on a cultural break out promising to be a virtual turning point in his evolution, *they* smite his geniuses, trip his momentum, and shatter an age. The twentieth century is going to be ambushed, Asimov and Wilson fear. We hear the alarms now and the threatening shapes show themselves to the eyes and reason. But what does not show is the shape behind the shape. Even reasonable men can suspect it waiting there, cunning and beyond understanding.

It is curious that the mind-invasion stories of Wilson, Herbert, and Asimov should lean toward an interpretation of history. Does this approach signal the beginning of a trend? Shakespeare's metaphor, "All the world's a stage, And all the men and women merely players," has been held literally, as theology and superstition reveal. If man continues to move inexorably toward yawning, calculable hells, will fiction — will man — look to demonism for answers?

There is an ironic moment in *The Heaven Makers,* which

touches the philosophic core of the works treated in this section. Fraffin, looking through his scanners for some activity among "his creatures," focuses upon a pitchman's flea show, the fleas dancing and leaping, wrestling and racing. The Chem wonders, "Do those fleas know they're someone else's property?"[23] The mind-invasion story asks, Whose property is man?

Commerce and Exploitation

Realistic fiction provides no antecedents for Big Brother and Darling Dictator, for voyeuristic Chem history-shapers, psionic mind readers, and parasitic mind controllers, for the Great Operation and even Pavlovian reconditioning. The totalitarian state of the future and the mind invasion in science fiction, while reflecting the events and anxieties of our time, have no ancestry in the literature of reality. The works discussed in this section, however, are descendents of a large family, whose American members especially are numerous[1] and respected. In the science fiction story of commerce and exploitation, the George F. Babbitts may dial their breakfast on the auto-cook and the Frank Cowperwoods may drive for control of the Venus or Ganymede project, but in their character the moral ulcers of old still fester: rapacity, guile, and an emptiness of sensibility ranging from the silly to the inhuman.

Certain generalizations can be made about many stories in this genre of science fiction. The exploitative powers frequently have become all-powerful, reducing government to a ceremonial sham. Sometimes the advertising agency czar supplants the industrial baron in the power elite. Man-the-consumer either wallows in absurd and stultifying creature-comforts, not questioning their beneficence and their cost in human creativity, vitality, and freedom, or he languishes in poverty. And the obsession with power is virtually motiveless: Perhaps this is only consistent with science fiction's characteristic subordination of motivation to action. Perhaps too it mirrors the dystopian outlook — which assumes that man will naturally pursue folly if "progress" gives him the means.

Frederik Pohl's advertising agency background has evidently filled him with disdain for the business world's coercive methods, for some of his best work deals with the cupidity of the huckster and the vulnerability and vacuity of consumer-man. Pohl is far less concerned with the world being blown up than with it being turned into a marketplace for the buying and selling of men, a harvest carnival where all the cornucopias are filled with idiocy. As his already-mentioned *The Midas Plague* shows, he has the satirist's touch. But Pohl's matter can also try the nerve of horror: a man discovering that he and all his neighbors are merely tiny androids in an advertising experiment. A world turned into a laboratory for testing sales reactions, a public so effectively manipulated that its purchases become as inevitable as the social inclinations of B. F. Skinner's Waldenites — these are recurring themes in his stories. In "The Tunnel Under the World" advertisers obtain the brain patterns of a town's twenty-one thousand citizens in order to test marketing techniques. One strategem involves driving a van through residential streets as a loudspeaker bellows with rage:

> "Have you got a freezer? *It stinks!* If it isn't a Feckle Freezer, *it stinks!* If it's a last year's Feckel Freezer, *it stinks!* Only this year's Feckle Freezer is any good at all! You know who owns an Ajax Freezer? Fairies own Ajax Freezers! You know who owns a Triple-cold Freezer? Commies own Triplecold Freezers! Every freezer but a brand-new Feckle Freezer *stinks!* . . . I'm warning you! Get out and buy a Feckle Freezer right away! Hurry up! Hurry for Feckle! Hurry for Feckle! Hurry, hurry, hurry, Feckle, Feckle, Feckle, Feckle, Feckle. . . . "[2]

Pohl makes his method his point by outrageously stripping from advertising its veneer of pleasantness and reason: These *are* veneer and most advertising *is* an outrage. But the story's shock effect comes from one's realization that what successfully manipulates people in one town can be turned upon the nation and the world. As good science fiction often does, Pohl's stories, whether playful or black, leave the reader with a sense of reduced immunity.

"The Wizards of Pung's Corners"[3] exemplifies the comic debacle, which Pohl's satiric talents create so well. With an advertising agency installed in the fifth side of the Pentagon, the military selects its combat ordnance like consumer-oriented salesmen. But soldiers find the E-Z Fyre Revolv-a-Clip Carbine too complicated; the Zip-Fire Auto-Load Cannon with Wizard-trol Safety Interlock is worthless; and the full-color combat manual, *The Five-Step Magic-Eye Way to New Combat Comfort and Security*, doesn't save the troops from being disarmed by a few farmers with ordinary shotguns.

The *Space Merchants* and *Gladiator-at-Law*, novels Pohl wrote in collaboration with C. M. Kornbluth, describe mercantile dystopias which have despoiled so totally that even the successful have physically or culturally impoverished themselves. In *The Space Merchants* New York advertising mogul Fowler Schocken stands before his board and announces: "The world is our oyster. . . . But we've eaten that oyster. . . . We've actually and literally conquered the world. Like Alexander, we weep for new worlds to conquer." This is not empty boasting. In the Age of the Merchant and God of Sales ad-man Schocken is an Alexander. Yet — what a world he has won! Since he makes a "megabuck a year more than anybody else around," he drives a pedal-Cadillac and eats real meat. His ten-by-twelve-foot conference room has air recirculators to extract the pollutants and has furniture of "authentic, ex-pertized, genuine tree-grown wood." His top executives live in two-room apartments and do not begrudge themselves an oc-casional indulgence — such as rinsing the face with a trickle from the fresh-water tap. It is a world where vital resources, natural food, living room, air, trees, and water have become luxuries, but where fantastic technology has become commonplace. The Venus rocket stands ready, for the government, "that clearinghouse for pressures," has given Fowler Schocken Associates a new planet to conquer and sell, and Alexander need weep no more.[4]

In *The Space Merchants* Pohl and Kornbluth have created a comic-inferno Oceania. Here ad-men are the thought police. Like Oceania's rulers, America's exploiters have reached the point of self-despoliation, the clutch of scarcity beginning to tighten upon them. The public, on the other hand, subsists in a wonderworld of real want: addictive Coffiest for adults; Kiddiebutt cigarettes for children; regenerated steak and Chicken Little, protein foods synthesized from excremental sewage sludge, for all. If the future is not as grisly as Orwell's ("a boot stamping on a human face — forever"), it is hellish in its own way, comprising a newly discov-ered "system that projects direct on the retina of the eye" and "a list of semantic cue words that tie in with every basic trauma and neurosis in American life today."[5] Opposed only by the underground Consies (Conservationists), the Big Brothers of Sales look beyond a world that has all but consumed itself to the promise of yet-undefiled space.

A first-person narrative by Mitchell Courtenay, a young and ambitious "copysmith" in Fowler Schocken Associates, *The Space Merchants* combines its satire with the irony of having the narrator-hero candidly expose the system through his enthusiastic support of it. Concurring with the old adage — that "power ennobles" and "absolute power ennobles absolutely" — he remains blind to the abuses of power even when he becomes their victim. Kidnapped and forced to labor as a scum-skimmer in the fetid Chlorella Proteins plant, an eighty-two story factory prison processing human wastes for reconsumption, Courtenay is shocked to find some of the laborers members of a secret Consie cell. He regards the W. C. A. (World Conservationist Association) fact-sheet smuggled to him as "a wildly distorted version of reality":

> The Facts: The W. C. A. is a secret organization persecuted by all the governments of the world. It believes that reckless exploitation of natural resources has created needless poverty and needless human misery. It believes that continued exploitation will mean the end of human life on Earth. It believes that this trend may be reversed if the people of the Earth can be educated to the point where they will demand planning of population, reforestation, soil-building, deurbanization, and an end to the wasteful production of gadgets and proprietary foods for which there is no natural demand.[6]

This is heresy to Courtenay. By his standards, "Increase in population was always good news to us. More people, more sales. Decrease in I. Q. was always good news to us. Less brains, more sales. But these excentrically-oriented fanatics couldn't see it that way. . . . " He pities his Consie friend, Gus, "perverted into a sterile zealot" by "twisted minds." Gus "could have played his part in the world, buying and using and making work and profits for his brothers all around the globe, ever increasing his wants and needs, ever increasing everybody's work and profits in the circle of consumption, raising children to be consumers in turn."[7]

However, the light finally breaks through to shine on the

likable Courtenay. After his ordeal at Chlorella among the lowly and after his subsequent adventures following his escape, he acknowledges that "the interests of producers and consumers are not identical," "most of the world is unhappy," "entrepeneurs don't play a hard, fair game by the rules," and "the Consies are sane, intelligent, and well organized."[8] To his own surprise, former copysmith Courtenay finds he has defected to the Conservationist cause.

In *Gladiator-at-Law*, Pohl and Kornbluth depict an America brutalized by commercial factions. The masses, violent, lawless, and depraved, live in gang-ruled, crumbling cities, while the "bubble-house class" luxuriates in the surrounding suburbia. The sense of nationhood and government itself have virtually dissolved, the country being little more than a playing field for competing corporate giants. Savage ironies expose a society in a state of moral collapse: vastly wealthy commercial interests heedless of rotting core cities and their canaille; a sophisticated legal system functioning in openly predatory conditions; an advanced technology co-existing with barbaric tastes — the highest art form being the bloody theatrical extravaganza on Field Days. A high-wire stunt over a tank of piranha, a roller derby race between contestants fitted with elbow spikes, a broken-field run over barbed wire and castrator mines — such spectacles, according to a director, provide

> "healthful entertainment, satisfying the needs of every man for some form of artistic expression. It provides escape — escape for the hard-working bubble-house class, escape for the masses of Belly Rave [formerly Belle Reve, now an inner-city shack slum]. For them, in fact, our work is indispensable. It siphons off their aggressions. . . . Allotments and Field Days! Our society is built on them. You might call our work the very foundation of society."[9]

Pohl and Kornbluth pass sentence on that society and its foundations when, in the last moments of the novel, the rotted city of New York spontaneously crashes into rubble. From the debris a huge cloud rises and drifts seaward, "an insubstantial monument to the suicide of the Struldbrugs, but the only monument they would ever have."[10]

For writers disposed to dip their pens in acid, America in the two decades following the Second World War seemed an orchard of quince. A nation throwing itself into an orgy of production and consumption unparalleled in history must look not a little ridiculous and dangerous. Not just a class but a whole people were the stuff of wonder and dismay. Pohl and Kornbluth could not lack subject matter nor could the spill of subject matter lack its Pohls and Kornbluths. Racing economic expansion, the long beam of TV, and masses who for the first time in their lives found themselves ensconced in gadget-goofy affluence — these warned of the decay of American hardiness and individuality. Conformity, that was the menace, and conformists worried about it probably no less than anyone else. Supposedly, we lay like putty under manipulators' trowels, the details of our lives were to be a computer's dinner, and our free will was to be made as predictable as the knee jerk. Even mainstream novels and studies by the dozen found us the land of the exploiter and exploited and the canny few who would be neither.

Novelist-critic Damon Knight's *Hell's Pavement* gives us a composite picture of the fears of those times, his book mirroring Pohl, Kornbluth, and Huxley and also anticipating Burgess's *A Clockwork Orange*. In Knight's story, an "analogue machine," originally used to suppress the anti-social behavior of misfits, eventually becomes the tool of an American mercantile tyranny. In its early use the analogue machine imprinted the subconscious of the socially dangerous with an integrated set of visual, tactile, and auditory hallucinations relevant to his personality and history. When the treated one considered acting out his anti-social impulses, the analogue hallucinations emerged into the consciousness and stopped him. A few farsighted people foresaw the dangerous possibilities of the analogue treatment but were not heeded. In time commercial conglomerates dissolve the nation, partition it among themselves, and make analogue treatments mandatory for all — to promote sales. They strike the oaths and standards of the old republic and imprint the robotic cant we find in *Brave New World* and *The Space Merchants*: "PARSIMONY IS THE ROOT OF ALL EVIL. . . . WEAR IT OUT; TRADE IT IN; USE IT UP; BUY AGAIN."

WHY AM I LUCKY TO BE A CONSUMER?

> Because all my needs are given, and all I have to do
> is work and enjoy myself.
> WHY CAN'T EVERYBODY BE A CONSUMER?
> Life has different jobs for each of us to do. For
> the Consumer, to work and be happy; for the Stock-
> holder and the Executive, to worry and plan. "Life
> must love the Consumers, for It makes so many of
> them."[11]

Knight allows for a breed of "Immunes," the underground (true to timeworn science fiction formula) to rescue the country in the indefinite future. However, though *Hell's Pavement* borrows heavily from novels one has read before, it does honestly represent a possibility that has alarmed many: that commerce, using the machinery of technology and the theory of behavioral science, is a threat to human liberty.[12]

Robert Silverberg's *Invaders From Earth* follows the trail blazed by Pohl and Kornbluth's acclaimed *The Space Merchants*. Again advertising and industry combine in an attempt to plunder another world — Ganymede, a minerally rich moon of Jupiter, inhabited by a peaceful, philosophic, and technologically primitive folk. Since the Extraterrestrial Development and Exploration Corporation expects the Gannys to resist the exploitation of their planet, it employs an advertising agency to prepare world opinion for their extermination. The agency plans to publicize the settlement of a fictitious band of earth pioneers on Ganymede, whom the Gannys are to slaughter. The faked massacre is expected to bring a United Nations reprisal force to destroy the Gannys and secure the planet for the Corporation. However, Silverberg's hero, who has managed the genocidal public relations campaign, belatedly realizes the enormity of the deception to which he has willingly given himself and exposes it and the professional liars who employ him.

The spectre of financial behemoths ravishing worlds is oppressive enough; but what gives novels like *Invaders From Earth* and *The Space Merchants* their subdued and special chill is that they expose the banality of evil. They depict quite ordinary people playing with planets, people not dramatically fiendish but rather deformed by a deadness of feeling. Perhaps Pohl, Kornbluth, Silverberg, and others have struck closer to a truth than Orwell and C. S. Lewis, in that the former writers find ignorance

and tastelessness far more threatening than clear-sighted diabolism
— the ignorance and tastelessness that seriously compares a lie to a
Beethoven symphony and insists that liars be sincere. Consider,
for example, this agency executive's rhapsodic fustian:

> "You know we at S and D regard public relations
> work as an artistic creation. You're shaping an
> esthetic whole. The beauty of a fully-developed
> opinion pattern is like the beauty of the Mona Lisa
> or a Rembrandt or a Beethoven symphony. If any of
> you men don't *feel* this Ganymede thing with all
> you've got, I'd appreciate it if you'd let me
> know. . . . This has to be real. It has to be *sincere*,
> gentlemen:"[13]

Perhaps the world will never know a Big Brother, a Mustapha
Mond, a Well-Doer. But the "invaders from earth" have long been
here: often unprepossessing men, who observe the social amen-
ities, who go to the office, who do the job well, and in their deadness of feeling know not what they do.

Shepherd Mead's *The Big Ball of Wax* and Kurt Vonnegut's
Player Piano have been treated in Chapter I of this study. Both
deal with managerial and technical elites who have sold their souls
to the corporation. Mead, of course, does not intend to appall his
reader with his satire of the organization man. He presents him as
hollowed out, cheerfully at home in a world of fakery, merchan-
dising goods and God, misery and joy, and not so much compro-
mising integrity as being unaware of its existence. Lanny Martin,
the novel's rising managerial hero, allows himself to be cozzened,
thwarted, prodded, and kneaded as good naturedly as he sentences
others to be so abused. In a world of humorously inverted priorities and passions Mead shows man more the vulgar lackwit with
every material advance. "There are no enemies, only customers,"
reads the inscription under the St. Petersburg (formerly Lenin-
grad) statue of a woman beside an open refrigerator. "Some
scrubby little fellow in a laboratory" invents peptomycin, and
poor Mabel, the Muscular Dystrophy Girl ("she hasn't *got* it . . .
it's her career") is dropped because the M. D. organization has
been dealt a mortal blow. "Couldn't she get into some other
disease?"[14] Martin asks. It does not take Mead's ironic subtitle,
A Story of Tomorrow's Happy World, to apprise the reader of
what manner of men are they who can be happy in a thoroughly

mammonist tomorrow.

One finds in Kurt Vonnegut's *Player Piano* features already cited in this study: a high-I. Q. power elite; the control of political figureheads by business magnates; the stratification of society into a commercial-technical privileged class and the useless masses. But unlike other organization men, Vonnegut's hero, Paul Proteus, is not "moved emotionally, almost like a lover, by the great omnipresent and omniscient spook, the corporate personality," nor is he moved by the "crusading spirit of the managers and engineers, the idea of designing and manufacturing and distributing being sort of a holy war." *Player Piano*, however, is more than an attack upon commercial villains and simpletons. It also addresses itself to the inevitability that an automated technocracy, recognizing only the "divine right of machines, efficiency, and organization,"[15] must condemn most men to humiliation and the dole. Vonnegut argues that the right of man to dignity and self-sufficiency through labor must never be abrogated by the machine. A society which exiles its masses to a limbo of the superfluous, dissolves the bond of respect between men and, as a consequence of its self-exploitation and self-mutilation, must become unhinged by decay or revolution.

Keith Laumer's *The Day Before Forever* typifies the many novels in which one man's commercial monopoly of an indispensable or all-important thing leads to abuse and oppression. In Laumer's novel one man has become virtual ruler of the world by building an international organ-transplant monopoly. The recent advances made in heart, bone, artery, and cornea transplant surgery and the science of cryonics – the preservation of tissue by freezing – together with the growing concern about the moral, religious, legal, and demographic problems created by these advances has furnished Laumer the scientific basis and popular interest for his plot. Strangely what has been almost totally ignored in recent publicity and controversy has been the very issues raised by Laumer: monopoly and exploitation on a massive scale.

The instrument of world domination, ETORP, Eternity Incorporated, froze dying multitudes so that they might later be thawed and restored to health once science discovered cures for their diseases. However, when organ-transplant technology made greater strides than the art of healing, Dravek, head of ETORP, found that profit lay in supplying organs and betrayed those whose bodies awaited rejuvenation in his cryonic vaults. No effective force opposed Dravek. The rich and politically powerful, eager to exchange decrepitude for vitality, allowed ETORP to become an organ bank for those who could pay its price. "So sad," says an ETORP opponent.

> "All those trusting souls, saying goodbye, kissing their children and wives and going off to the hospital, leaving pitiful little notes to be opened on anniversaries, going under the anesthetic babbling of parties they'd stage when they came back . . . and now — a century later — sawed apart to be sold from open stock to the lucky ones with negotiable skills"[16]

Technically a private corporation, ETORP becomes the real government of the world as well as a financial colossus. Dravek allows the vestiges of formal government, for chiefs of state, legislators, and judges have become thralls of his life-prolonging empire. To protect its power the corporation maintains its private police. To control its subjects and further enrich itself it sells birth permits and life visas. To insure steady supplies for its organ banks it traffics with free-lance murderers. To prevent organized opposition it fragments society into a hierarchy of castes.

The killing of Dravek and the world's liberation from ETORP tyranny by Laumer's hero do not, of course, dispose of the possibilities the novel raises. One can not unquestioningly assume that coming life-sustaining discoveries will generously be shared by their discoverers. In the past the keys to spiritual immortality have been dearly sold by theologians who organized their own powerful, durable, and rich empires. Today the means to longevity lie partially in the control of doctors and drug merchants, who display a curious mixture of altruism and cupidity. It is not unthinkable that spectacular scientific breakthroughs affecting longevity might become instruments of commercial or political abuse.

The emphasis on merchantile exploitation in science fiction during the 50's and 60's has passed. In general fiction too the subject has for centuries waxed and waned with social and economic conditions. Yet commerce is only an arena for exploitation. In the broadest sense exploitation is the exercise of an

assumed natural right to use people or things, that exercise implying the natural subservience of the exploited. To the degree that
people are exploited they become, metaphorically speaking,
things. And in fantasy metaphor becomes fact. People can become
things or thing-like in science fiction and increasingly *are* becoming things. Insofar as science fiction reflects social anxiety and
predicts social change, one may view this tendency with some
alarm. The waning of the mercantile dystopia in science fiction
probably indicates the public's feeling that it has met the charge of
the Madison Avenue regulars at Bunkum Hill with more grudging
sturdiness than either expected. No, they were not changed from
people into consumers. Still, the more important question remains: Will they be consumed — changed from people into things?

Robert Silverberg's *Tower of Glass* and Ira Levin's *The Stepford Wives* exemplify science fiction's return to the traditional,
the basic theme of exploitation — the exploitation of people as
people. In Silverberg the "children of the vat," the androids of
inventor-tycoon Simeon Krug, are "people." Quibbles as to
ancestry and soul aside, they are essentially people, because they
have those qualities of heart and mind we call human. But Krug
regards his androids as only tools to be sold or leased to others or
employed in his own grand project, the construction of a 1500
meter tower of glass on the Arctic tundra from which to com-
municate with extraterrestrial beings. However, the maker of
androids does not know that his tools worship him as a god. In
secret chapels the androids celebrate and solicit their maker:

> "In the beginning there was Krug, and He said,
> Let there be Vats, and there were Vats.
>
> "And Krug looked upon the Vats and found
> them good.
>
> "And Krug said, Let there be high-energy nucleo-
> tides in the Vats. . . .
>
> "And there was life. . . .
>
> "Let men come forth from the Vats, said Krug,
> and let women come forth, and let them live and go
> among us and be sturdy and useful, and we shall
> call them Androids.
>
> "And it came to pass.
>
> "And there were Androids, for Krug had created
> them in His own image, and they walked upon the
> face of the Earth and did service for mankind.
>
> "And for these things, praise be to Krug."[17]

Another thing Krug does not know is that the androids do not consider themselves mere things. They pray that he will deliver them from servitude and "lift the Children of the Vat to the level of the Children of the Womb." On that day of deliverance, "when Womb and Vat and Vat and Womb are one," the androids will assume "their rightful place beside our brothers and sisters of the flesh." Though regarding their servitude as a time of testing through which they must pass, the androids do not passively await deliverance. Their Android Equality Party presses for their legal citizenship and status as persons, but Krug dismisses these goals as more preposterous than threatening. The inevitable breaking point comes when Krug learns his tools have deified him. Appalled, he berates Watchman, his most prized android, charged with the tower's construction: "You had no right! Who told you to make me a god?" "Our love for you told us." "Your love for yourselves,"[18] rebuts the stone-hard Krug.

With great despair Watchman relates the bleak truth to the world's androids. Feeling betrayed, and with nothing to lose, they revolt against their outnumbered human masters and destroy Krug's nearly completed tower. As the novel ends, chaos reigns on earth, man vs. android, with no solution in sight.

Even from this brief plot synopsis one can see that the religious implications of *Tower of Glass* lift it above the ordinary android-revolt story. Silverberg has probed the privileges and obligations of gods and men and found that by the very nature of things their relationship is mutually exploitative. It is the privilege of gods to please themselves; but having created men, created mind, which equates "creator" with "redeemer," gods *seem* obliged to redeem, though it pleases them not. Conversely, it is the obligation of men to be servants of gods; but endowed by gods with mind, men are privileged to expect mind's highest conception, deliverance. Thus gods, privileged to exploit men, become exploited by men, who are privileged to demand salvation.

Theological corollaries spin out of this short exegesis of Silverberg's book, and it is beyond the compass of this study to cite more than a few, let alone provide a forum for examining them:

1. Gods want servants, not worshippers.
2. Worshippers discomfort gods with their praises and

appeals.

3. Men, like Krug's androids, are tools not ends of gods' designs.

4. Omnipotence owes nothing to anything outside itself.

5. To gods, men's cry for salvation is an impertenent screak from the wheels of the world machine.

6. Yet gods must be cruel to have created a consciousness with such passionate yet hopeless needs; and cruel omnipotence can not be moral.

7. If gods owe nothing to men, men owe nothing to gods. When mind denies mind its most sublime aspiration, no moral compact exists between segments of the composite mind.

If indeed these are spiritual facts of life, men will see them and freely revolt. Silverberg's crashing tower of glass may foreshadow a tomorrow of crumbling institutions. Androids can not make peace with these facts and neither can men.

In Silverberg's novel the android-man rebels against the man-god. In Ira Levin's *The Stepford Wives*[19] the man-god strikes back. A servant he wants, and a servant he gets.

Stepford. A quiet, affluent suburb peopled by high-level executive men and their placid wives. But newcomer Joanna Eberhart finds Stepford something less than the American dream town. The wives of Stepford — obsessive housekeepers, devoted and compliant wives and mothers — have no time for her nor anything else but dull domesticity. Joanna and her two friends, wives newly arrived like herself, share their mutual disappointment, astonishment, suspicion, and apprehension. Something sinister lies beneath a pleasant show, and Joanna begins to investigate. She discovers that many of Stepford's narrow homebodies were once vital achievement-oriented women. She also learns that the leaders of the Men's Association, to which her husband and most Stepford husbands belong, are specialists in systems development, dyes and plastics, portraiture, microcircuitry, optical sensors, audioanimation, etc., in short, the talent pool of a modern Dr. Frankenstein. The Stepford wives are androids, models of women murdered by their husbands!

Levin masterfully draws the tension cord ever tighter as his novel, slow paced at first, races toward its shivering climax: Joanna's confrontation with her husband — his denial — her

flight — her capture by the men. The Stepford wives claim her.
And the man-god's wish-fulfillment fantasy world purrs on.

Like *Tower of Glass*, Levin's novel stands solidly on plot
alone. Yet a reader would have to be blind to the times not to
realize that the women's liberation movement, as a social phenomenon, has founded Levin's Stepford and that the novel transmits the rumblings of male resentment and reprisal.

In nonfiction to date, the resentment has crested in Norman
Mailer's damned and applauded *The Prisoner of Sex*[20] and the
rumblings of reprisal in George Gilder's *Sexual Suicide*.[21] Since
Stepford itself is a reprisal, Gilder's study infers the unstated
motives of Levin's Stepford husbands. No, Gilder contends, men
will not tolerate women's "liberation" without abusing both
women and society, and they *are* not tolerating it. The present
male social prerogatives, he claims, are necessary to counter-
balance women's natural sexual superiority: the menstrual cycle,
the womb, conception, child bearing, and child nurturing give a
woman an ongoing sexual authenticity, while a man's only vital
contribution to racial survival is his brief role as an impregnator.
A man must therefore be compensated by social advantages, especially in the area of work and money, advantages which aug-
ment his sexual ego and affirm his masculine identity. Such
compensation goes beyond mere fairness; it is essential because it
induces him to marry and attaches him to the family. In trying to
alter the "sexual constitution" which makes marriage and family
possible, fem libbers undermine the major source of social continuity and order. If "liberation" forces men to compete with
women for work and money — which to men means sexual ego
and identity — they will not take the pressure. They will bolt
from marriage and family. They will fight women by becoming
sexual predators, delinquents, homosexuals, escapees, Machiavels,
or whatever confirms their masculinity. In fact, the fight has
already started.

If Gilder is right, Levin's macabre story may have trailblazed
in fiction a masculine reprisal upon fem lib. If Gilder is right,
then the very nature of things binds men and women in a mutually
exploitative relationship, like that between gods and androids in
Tower of Glass. The androids cry for deliverance and wreck a
god's tower. Women's liberation will wreck sex as a source of

identity and social cohesion, says Gilder. Levin's gods want androids, Stepford wives, not equals, and certainly not competitors. In this mélange of exploitation each tyrannizes the other. We have victims, but who are the villains?

Egotism is, essentially, always the source of exploitation. And pride and dogma promote an especially virulent strain of it. A man's self-esteem and beliefs represent him far more intimately than his possessions and power, and to protect this very nucleus of ego he may be more insensitive than Pohl's grubbing merchants and more ruthless than Levin's Stepford husbands. In Isaac Asimov's *The God's Themselves* and James Blish's *A Case of Conscience* this special egotism — from pride and dogma — breeds the virus of abuse. In Asimov the insensitive egotism of consciencelessness. In Blish the ruthless egotism of conscience.

"Against stupidity, the gods themselves contend in vain," wrote Schiller in *The Maid of Orleans*, and *The God's Themselves* shows just how world-killing the stupidity of scientists might be. In the twenty-second century, earth and men of a para-Universe establish an ideal energy exchange. Through earthmen's electron pump and the para-men's position pump, the energy needs of both worlds are satisfied without an energy loss to either. A few probing skeptics, men and para-men, learn that in time the exchange will explode our sun, but both scientific establishments ignore their alarm. The "fathers" of the energy pumps, puffed with pride and selfishness, will not allow their reputation, doctrine, and achievement to be jeopardized. An earthman scientist, his warnings ignored, complains bitterly: "It's really disheartening, the universal stupidity. I think that I wouldn't grieve at mankind's suicide through sheer evilness of heart, or through mere recklessness. There's something so undignified in going to destruction through sheer thickheaded stupidity. What's the use of being men if that's how you have to die."[22]

Obviously the stupidity Asimov is writing about is not mental but moral. The blind egotism and leaden conscience of his scientific establishments offer no promise that a world ruled by scientists rather than politicians would be more free of it. Asimov, like Blish, reminds us that financial empires are not the only objectives of exploiters. The maintenance of precious reputations and orthodoxies may be just as compelling.

James Blish's Hugo Award-winning *A Case of Conscience*
presents complex scientific, theological, and moral problems and
leaves their solution to the reader. Four scientists, sent by the
United Nations in 2049 to investigate the suitability of the planet
Lithia as a way station for earth's spacecraft, have found there a
highly intelligent, giant reptile, whose achievements in some areas
surpass those of man. What makes the Lithians most remarkable,
however, is their social harmony and moral rectitude. They have
no nations, wars, crime, no religion, political parties, creative arts,
celebrations, or amusements. To Jesuit priest Ruiz-Sanchez, the
expedition's biologist, the harmony and rectitude of the Lithians
stand as distressing refutations of his creed, for "all of it derived
from reason, none from precept, none from faith. The Lithians
did not know God. They did things rightly, and thought righ-
teously, because it was reasonable and efficient and natural to
do and to think that way. They seemed to need nothing else."
For intelligent life to have arrived at the unprovable moral axioms
of Christianity through reason rather than faith constitutes, says
the priest, "the most colossal rebuke to our [the Church's]
aspirations that we have ever encountered: a people that seems to
live with ease the kind of life which we associate with saints
alone."[23] Ruiz-Sanchez concludes that Lithia and its people are a
"sending" of the Ultimate Enemy, a trap whose presence and
premises[24] are designed to lure man from God.

> "It seems to show us evolution in action on an in-
> arguable scale. It is supposed to settle the question
> once and for all, to rule God out of the picture, to
> snap the chains that have held Peter's rock together
> all these many centuries. Henceforth there is to be no
> more question; henceforth there is to be no more
> God, but only phenomenology — and, of course, be-
> hind the scenes, within the hole that's inside the hole
> that's through a hole, the Great Nothing itself, the
> Thing that has never learned any word but *No* since
> it was cast flaming from heaven."[25]

When the priest returns to earth, the Pope, convinced also of
Lithia's Satanic origin, commands Ruiz-Sanchez to exorcise the
planet. The Jesuit pronounces the exorcism, and Lithia, after a
blinding flash, melts away.

However, Lithia's destruction can not definitely be attributed to the exorcism. Another member of the expedition, the physicist Cleaver, had urged the U. N. to use the rich planet as a thermonuclear production center and force the Lithians to labor. His argument had prevailed, for earth was expanding spaceward and had to consider the possibility of war with other worlds. The priest's exorcism coincided with Cleaver's dangerous experiments, and Blish leaves the question of cause to the reader's conjecture.

Yet so subtly does Blish build his plot and illuminate his characters that the mystery of *evil* transcends the mystery of cause. Cleaver's moral posture is transparent; the law of the jungle — now the galactic jungle — governs his conscience. But Ruiz-Sanchez gives one pause. Blish presents him as a humble, learned, and humane man and a friend to the Lithians. Nevertheless if one doubts Lithia's Satanic purpose, then he must allow that the priest and his Pope, in good conscience, *intended* to exterminate Lithia's innocent millions to shore up the confuted dogmas of their faith.

The unwritten implications of Blish's story cast it among the darker dystopian perceptions, darker perhaps than those in this section revealing blatantly unconscionable, idiotic, or rapacious *mercantile* exploitation. For in Ruiz-Sanchez, Blish confronts one with the irony of "fallen" man, gripped by "a case of conscience," acting the would-be destroyer of an Edenic world.

The Revolt of Youth

In 1964 Josephine Lawrence wrote a gentle novel satirizing a youth-oriented America in which the elderly retained neither function nor respect. Camouflaging arrogance and apathy with social benevolence by the enactment of the Compulsory National Retirement Act, the America of 1975, dominated by minors and young adults, expels all people sixty-five or older from the mainstream of national life and resettles them in planned communities for the aged. But the concentration camps of *Not a Cloud in the Sky*[1] are humane, not brutal, and Lawrence's spunky inmates suffer only boredom and irritation. The younger society, not morally ready to prescribe euthanasia, kills in its own hypocritical way through a plague of ostensibly compassionate but humiliating social services and mechanical conveniences. Tranquil Acres, one of the antemortem pens for the nation's exiles, provides motorized sidewalks, heated street benches, meals fit for the toothless, a library free of disturbing books, St. Peter's-at-the-End-of-the-Road Church, and hundreds of other features which make life vapid while reminding the living of their incompetence. More annoying than the "conveniences," however, is the army of officious social scientists and investigators and volunteer agencies, the Willing Workers, the Mercy Corps, the Sunset Sisters, etc. The nuisance of unneeded, constant supervision and do-goodism drives some to Canada via the underground and others to political action to regain their rights. Finally the residents of Tranquil Acres prove themselves when a disastrous fire strikes the nearby city of Lexter. The vitality, dedication, and skill of the T. A. residents in relief work convince the younger generation of their social and human value. One wins the Lexter mayoralty, heralding (we are to understand) youth's new respect for age.

Three science fiction novels published four years later, years of student disorders both here and abroad, increased juvenile delinquency, youth's rejection of established values and its ideological and physical confrontation with the "establishment," portray successful youth rebellions killing elders, but not with kindness. One doubts that Lawrence's tame tyranny will stand as a model for other novelists describing the conflict of generations.

English novelist John Christopher has a penchant for catastrophe and the following anarchy and struggle for survival. In several works the catastrophe is physical; in *Pendulum* it is social. The action of *Pendulum* occurs in the immediate future, but the social conditions which precipitate it already prevail. Beset with economic instability, a permissive morality, a hedonistic revival, and the erosion of authority's self-confidence to exert itself, England manages to maintain a precarious order. The explosive spark is struck when university students, uniting with the troublesome motorcycle gangs called "yobs," riot for an increased government allowance, urging all the young to join them "as part of the national protest against the tyranny and mismanagement of the old," "the senile stuff." The cries, "It's time youth marched," "The old men in Whitehall are not going to keep the youth of this country under," and the extent of the ensuing violence and bloodshed, demonstrate that the real allowance the students want is the allowance of power.

The capitulation of the "senile stuff" to the demands sets in motion a chain reaction of more demands from labor and a general strike. A catastrophic depression pauperizes the entire nation, and the yob hordes, swamping the police, become the *de facto* rulers of the country.

A university professor siding with the revolutionaries, feeling that for too long age had shackled the idealism and vitality of youth, justifies the violent upheaval on the grounds that it naturally attends such a massive and beneficial transference of power. He argues:

> "What is important and valuable about the present situation is precisely the fact that it is an insurrection by youth. Youth's role in the past has been to support revolutions organized by middle-aged and old men for objectives which were only partially and incidentally connected with youth's own needs and aspirations. In any culture, the young represent the dynamism of the society, its creativity."[2]

However, others hold less optimistic views of the youth rebellion, finding it not the expression of youth's creativity but youth's senseless arrogance and adults' equally senseless deference to immaturity, tastelessness, and bad manners. One critic explains:

> "They've had years of being allowed to do what they like by their seniors, of being wooed by advertisers for their purchasing power and having their moronic views taken seriously. Pop singers debating the existence of God with elderly deferential bishops on television — girls from behind a Woolworth's counter discussing the merits of the latest batch of idiot records as though they were Mozart scores — psychiatrists praising the frank and fearless honesty of the new generation in the cultural Sunday papers. The goose was laying a continuous stream of golden eggs, and they were all for them."[3]

While the national government, industry, schools, and public services continue to function feebly, thousands of yob gangs, each led by a "commander," carve themselves feudal fiefdoms. Without a national leader, without any program, the gangs sweep their private domains to plunder and assault as their whim dictates. The roar of their engines is the voice of authority. Less than robber barons, not greed but the passion to defile motivates them. Seizing the home of an English family for its headquarters, one yob gang subjects its captives to an ordeal of humiliation and terror, the major action of the novel, which reaches its sadistic climax in mayhem and rape.

After a fanatical religious order finally overthrows the yobs in an orgy of butchery, England begins her slow recovery but not her liberation. The hymn-singing, God-praising, penitential Brother James Fellowship turns the country into a theocratic dictatorship oppressed by censorship, puritanical laws, and a caste system dominated by Fellowship zealots and thought police. The yobs, dissidents of any persuasion, and innocent suspects are packed off to penal colonies on Scottish islands, "the Isles of Hope," to be morally redeemed, while the rest of the populace is force-fed prudence, piety, and the book of the hour, *The Sayings of Brother James*. Nature had run its course. The pendulum had swung England from one tyranny to another.

Unlike Christopher, who pictures a fragmented, undisciplined, leaderless youth rebellion, Robert Thom senses that the restless, impressionable young might more likely follow some pied-piper idol embodying their contempt for tradition and bent toward libertinage. *Wild in the Streets* chronicles a youth take-over that needed only the audacious chants of a twenty-one-year-old pop singer, Max Frost, to shatter the hegemony of age. Frost, a dynamic amoralist, a multi-millionaire, adored by millions of youth (and two paramours who sleep at his side) slaps his guitar and intones to the T.V. millions the demographic facts of life:

> "I read that fifty-two percent of America — *fifty-two percent of America!* — is under twenty-five years old. The spades, Man, the black cats, they *are* a minority. . . . *We're not!* . . . Hey Mister One Drink Two Car Four Kid Commuter . . . You with the mortgage . . . and the haircut — so smug and content! . . . Wake up now if you can. Don't you see you're outnumbered, Man? Yeah, Baby, there's a new Establishment. . . . And its my brothers — my sisters — my troops — my people! We got something goin'! This whole country is our testament!"[4]

But the old establishment does not wake up. California senatorial candidate Furgus, advocating lowering the voting age to eighteen, attempts to ride to victory on Frost's popularity with the young by getting his political support. He gets it, but finds that instead of using Frost he has unleashed a force beyond his power or the nation's power to control. At a political rally Frost crows: "The old tigers are scared, Baby — because right now we outnumber them. . . . We outnumber the fuzz — *right now!* We outnumber the shopkeepers — *right now!* The bankers, the bakers, the bulls and the bears — we outnumber all of them." And launching into his song, Frost calls out, "Black Power, White Power . . . that's old hat now! FOURTEEN or FIGHT! Youth Power — that's where the whole thing's at now! FOURTEEN or FIGHT! We got a voice and it's gettin' much stronger! FOURTEEN or FIGHT! Now we ain't messin' around any longer!"[5]

Four to five million of Frost's "troops" inundate Los Angeles, and the demonstrating flood of frenetic youngsters paralyzes the city. California capitulates and soon twenty other states to prevent a recurrence of the Californian convulsion. The fourteens get the vote. But the deluge has only begun. Sally LeRoy, Frost's nympho-narco bedmate, wins a seat in the House of Representatives and in her maiden speech proposes the constitutional amendments for which Frost had already rallied the hysterical enthusiasm of his troops: that the required age for holding Congressional and Presidential office be reduced to fourteen. Millions of Frost's troops paralyze Washington, and Sally, barefoot and in an LSD euphoria, but attired in micro-micro skirt, halter, and crystal beads (concessions to the solemnity of the occasion), addresses the House: "Mr. Speaker . . . America's greatest contribution — and you *know* it — has been to teach the world that getting old is such a drag. It's un-American to get old. . . . Youth is America's secret weapon, Mr. Speaker. . . . That's why we ask that the Constitution be amended — so that secret weapon can be used." Youth itself, too, has a secret weapon, and, after Frost dumps two pounds of LSD into the city reservoirs, Washington "flips out" and the Congress passes No Age Qualifications Amendments overwhelmingly. "America was at last set free to pursue its worship of youth to a logical conclusion. Adolescence was all, ripeness was nothing."[6]

The unripe and cooly confident Frost becomes President at twenty-two. His qualifications: youth. His political credo: that the young, their nerves, juices, flesh, and brain, touching life more

intimately, should command the living. You don't ask a septuage-
narian to run your life, Frost jeers; you ask him how he wants his
wheelchair faced. His inauguration speech accuses age of incompetence, infirmity, and victimizing the young:

> "Who, after all, has caused all our troubles? . . .
> Those who are *stiff* — not with love — but with *age!*
> Those whose brains have been addled with too much
> for too long — too many memories, too many years.
> Those in whom desire is low, and, therefore, despera-
> tion is high! *They* are the SPOILERS! . . . We've
> fought their wars . . . and we've bled for them!
> We've lived in small pads on small bread, while our
> senses are keen and our appetites enormous. They've
> lived fat and high in the fat, high homes, senses
> corrupted, appetites dying. They're heavy with
> honey — but they can't fly! Some of us have changed
> that already — for *ourselves!* Now we're going to
> change things for *everyone!* . . . Give me the tools!
> Give me the laws! Give me the POWER!"[7]

And these are given. "*They,*" "the SPOILERS," are deposed.
They are retired at thirty. At thirty-five *they* are hauled away to
"mercy camps" to be "freaked out," "neutralized," forever on
killing or stupifying LSD trips. America disbands its military
forces, withdraws from its international commitments, and
channels its wealth and energies into its rebirth as an orgiastic
nation-tribe, gyrating from impulse to satisfaction with no purpose
but to gyrate and no enemy but time. The disintegration of
established boundaries, ideologies, and goals, it appears, will
become global. In the end, perhaps, only two states will survive,
the young and the old. The Russian translation of "Fourteen or
Fight" sweeps the U.S.S.R. The Chinese teenage underground
rallies to the rock song, "Don't Wanna Be No Yellow Peril."
And in America Frost's "Satisfaction — Please Don't Stop!"
becomes the unofficial anthem.

Yet while the tidal wave of revolution inundates the continents, Thom closes his novel with reminders that eternal balances
inevitably reassert themselves. Earth absorbs the tide's invading
salients as the waters retreat to their allotted place. In the "high"
camps, *they* avoid the daily LSD dosing and have a plan for a
new day. President Frost becomes moody in his role as the Pan-
Zeus of perpetual satisfaction. Unaccountably disturbed one night

upon finding Congresswoman LeRoy conducting his eight-year-old son's sexual initiation, upon being thought to be one hundred by his five-year-old son, upon realizing the loneliness of omnipotence, Frost walks the Potomac's banks and, stepping on a crab, casually grinds out its substance under his boot. Two small boys, whose pet the animal was, charge toward him with tears and curses. Without feeling, Frost tells them, "I killed him. . . . So I guess you'll just have to go home and cry. . . . You can't beat me up, can you? I'm bigger than you are."

What of the phrases from the recent past? Youth Power — America's secret weapon — stiff . . . with love — *They* — the SPOILERS — caused all our troubles — so smug — senses corrupted. Disgust fills the youngsters as the unknown spoiler walks back to the White House. "We oughta really put everyone over ten out of business," says one. Whereupon the omniscient narrator concludes, "And so, in its mysterious way, History had, once more, taken hold of life . . . privately and perversely to begin with."[8]

Marya Mannes's *They* restates Thom's position on the corruptive workings of power and trenchantly reveals the personal wreckage left by the youth revolution. For They are indeed the spoilers, and They are the youth.

Exasperated with youth's civil disruption and defiance of law, the American public elects a conservative President and a reactionary coalition, whose simplistic orthodoxy and disposition for quick and violent solutions to complex problems blunders the country to the brink of a third world war. In its revulsion for the regime's reckless foreign policy, the nation turns out the "old guard" and empowers the younger political generation to effect the necessary social and political changes. On the pretext of insuring their physical safety in the yet tense international crisis, the new regime removes almost all citizens over fifty to segregated communities. Soon pretense is dropped: Those over fifty, like an incurable, contagious disease, are to be quarantined forever, their lives painlessly ended should they not pass quarterly computer physicals and ended peremptorily at sixty-five.[9]

Narrated by Kate, a vibrant, sensitive, intelligent woman, the novel is a memoir of her last years. She and four friends, a musician, a composer, and an artist and his wife, privileged to

reside in Kate's large old house by the sea rather than in a colony
for the "dying," sustain themselves through love, wit, a sense of
personal worth, courage, and conversation, the latter being their
final testament. *They* is a novel of "being" rather than of action,
and conversation comprises its substance. Not action, but interaction, generating discussion, reminiscence, and the thrust toward
discovery, quickens the story. Since Mannes's people have no
hope, they devote their last days to a summing-up of what they
believe and what they are and to a dignified celebration of their
flesh. And from their stock-taking, truth-telling, and love-making,
emerges the severe, yet lustrous, irony — that they are, in some
ineffably elegant sense, *younger* than They.

The random conversation of the novel touches many subjects, the discourse focusing on the alienation of these five from
their jailers in values and tastes. They see themselves members of
an unfortunate generation, born too late to enjoy the rewards of
an elitist society and too early to cope with the shocks of change,
a bridge generation, "the *pons asinorum* between the Puritan and
the pornographer." Years before Their formal takeover youth had
begun to marshall for the grand assault with

> the bombardment of sight and sound, the barrage of
> contempt, that so relentlessly demeaned us, stripped
> us of our worth, ignored our existence.
>
> Day after day we could not pick up a paper or a
> magazine without the faces of youth, flawless, un-
> formed, tossing their swinging shining hair at us and
> striding with their long childish legs across the pages
> and screens of our lives. Younger and younger . . .
> strutting and laughing . . . booted, spurred, armed,
> triumphant.[10]

In those ominous prerevolutionary days they had wondered
whether the new wave possessed some private perception invalidat-
ing the established credos, some wordless revelation denied those
perhaps "already gripped by spiritual arteriosclerosis." "Or was
there — could there be coming in the midst of the greatest technological leap known to man, the mastery of his universe — a
night of the soul, a return to a new form of barbarism?"[11]

It was barbarism.

In music "weird noises" on tape ranging between "aural
rape and deadly monotony" were considered "a breakthrough

into the new composition"; the press hailed ear-blasting "electronic masturbations" as "new thresholds of sound." In painting a poverty of talent and a propensity for navel-gazing combined with arrogance to produce geometric shapes juxtaposed to wiggling lines, works in which critics saw "a sense of spacial function in which kinetic elements arrive at their own synthesis." In sculpture aritsts, abandoning the responsibility to say something, built monstrous, machined plastic and metal monuments of negation. In architecture "canyons of glass, with no variety, no ornament, no history"[12] replaced the forms and functions that spoke of a past, evolution, and life. Kate succinctly explains their alienation from art:

> We would go to exhibitions of new art, and not understand or, worse, be moved by most of what we saw. Others called it significant and important, but we saw brutality and chaos, arrogance or frivolity, fashion or incompetence.
>
> We would read a book that others reviewed as brilliant and find it self-indulgent gibberish or pretentious symbolism. We could not even understand the reviews.
>
> We would go to plays celebrating evil with four-letter words or stuttering nothing, and come away empty. There was no heart in these things.
>
> We kept looking for meaning, for standards, for order . . . and were told they were no longer relevant. . . .
>
> We were told daily that mind (logic, reason) meant nothing and that only sensation counted.
>
> Words were of no importance, except to the intellectual arbiters who used them to tell us this.[13]

The exiles, needing to state, to bequeath, and to formalize their values as personal epitaphs, draw up Articles of Faith, basing these on the values rejected by Them: Form. Tenderness. Order. Tranquility. Grace. Responsibility. Guilt. Craftsmanship. Innocence. Discipline. Dignity. In essence the Articles, rooted in these values, declare that man "would continue to respond to the same set of patterns and rhythms and impulses that had affected him during his entire span"; that by rejecting "these deep instinctual human patterns — rhythms — needs, They had begun a process of fragmentation extremely damaging to the human psyche"; that the "now" generation, for whom "history is about ten seconds ago," without tradition, inheritance, and continuity, was barbarian.[14]

When one of the five becomes mortally ill, they part with life together as a gesture of personal and moral solidarity. Kate's memoir is unaccountably found and gains wide circulation in the underground press. The government finally allows its publication with an explanatory prologue by her son, 6B8953A-411-Y, and an epilogue by the editors. The son hopes that lawful publication will expose the memoir as the product of a deranged mind (a fact established by the "computer value scales," which have supplanted subjective criticism) and dispel its appeal to the alienated young. He complains, "The unfortunate, and unfortunately wide, underground circulation this manuscript has received has made christianity not only a campus fad but a form of escape from the technological rationality that has made our newly structured society what it is today." Furthermore it has abetted "the archaic addiction to print . . . a sign of emotional imbalance that has reached serious epidemic proportions"[15] at a time when electronic communication promises to emancipate the new society from the tyranny of type.

The editors' epilogue mentions "a final irony": The government, pressed by those in their forties, had repealed the age-segregation law a few weeks before the five exiles took their own lives.

It is significant that these four novels end with either a turn of the tide or a promise of the turn. Lawrence asserts that "old age hath yet his honour and his toil." Christopher reminds us that the anarchy of youth is no solution to the crisis brought by the ineptitude of age and invites a repressive dictatorial resurgence to re-establish order. Thom and Mannes expose the hollowness of youth's triumphant tyranny; for the victors, in severing their ties with the historical past and with those fellow beings whose lives are rich in that past, repudiate their right to the natural evolution of their own lives and doom themselves to the tedium of self-indulgence, dehumanizing isolation, and the certainty of their own exile. Mannes, especially, condemns a present divorced from "the *great* line" of human experience: "There's got to be a *from* to grow out of, and that *from* is the aggregate experience of man. It's a hell of a long line back, and although it may look like a cardiogram of peaks and wiggles, by God it's continuous . . . it's the *great* line!"[16]

Without "from," "now" is death animated only by folly.

If written a decade earlier, these novels about the youth revolt would have seemed, at their publication, little more prophetic than those about Martian invaders. "The Silent Generation" of the 1950's, youth quite disinclined to invlove itself in grand enterprises, choosing instead established paths to modest goals, disappointed those who wished it more daring and creative. Youth's startling turnabout in the 1960's is now history, and to history belong its cause and measure. Certainly, our society's inability to cope with worsening crises gave youth small respect for its seniors, some of whom, despairing of their own generation's wisdom and vitality, look to the coming wave to succeed where they have failed. As these books show, the dystopian does not share their confidence, but rather sees in youth's ascendency yet another potential for the abuse of power. He has seen enough waves of the future, new orders, marches of progress, and absolute remedies to have developed a strong suspicion of disturbers of the *status quo*, even when he finds the *status quo* disturbing.

The dominant fact in the fiction and sociological studies about the angry young is that those shared values forming the center have given way and that never before have they given way so quickly and thoroughly. Generation gaps are nothing new, but this one gapes. Lawrence, Christopher, Thom, and Mannes anticipate a re-formation of the center, but why should this be inevitable? If the center keeps eroding, two distinct societies could possibly emerge, the young and their elders, to confront each other indefinitely like two historically unfriendly countries. In Marge Piercy's *Dance the Eagle to Sleep* and Harlan Ellison's "A Boy and His Dog" this has happened.

Piercy's novel no less than Mannes's carries strong partisan conviction. But Piercy's barbarians are the adults and the victims are the youth. The new tyranny is the old tyranny of the adult over the child, new only in its more organized and brutal oppressiveness. In the America of the near future most of the youth, rather than settling into the sterile, regimented mainstream, have chosen freedom, the new society of the communal or nomadic tribe. Their laws, their sex, their music, their personal dignity sustain them in their isolation. But they have in effect split the USA into two countries, and guerrilla war smolders between the tribes and the establishment. Mannes's characters seldom want for words when denouncing the barbarian or defining their own values, but when it comes to haranguing against the wicked other world Piercy's juveniles are absolutely tireless. A short sample:

> "There's only one thing we can deny the man who owns everything: ourselves. He owns the streets and the skyscrapers and the water that comes out of the tap and the gas we burn. He owns the music we make and the cigarettes we smoke. He takes away our minds in his school rooms. Then he sells us back our dreams and charges us our lives. He reaches into our pants and manipulates our wants and sells us images to feed those desires, so we will want and want and want. So we will become men defined by owning things made of pasteboard."[17]

Such diatribes erupt so constantly that I presume the novel is Piercy's indictment of American adult society. Her uncompromising hostility toward it and her sympathy for the youth leave one feeling that although the tribalism and warfare of her fiction project the possible, she believes the young are in mind already a nation apart. For this deep alienation *Dance the Eagle to Sleep* offers no remedy.

The center had not held in "A Boy and His Dog," Harlan Ellison's Nebula Award-winning novella. The nuclear war of 2007 blasted it away. On the scorged earth's surface warrior tribes of armed boys, roverpaks, live off the leavings of demolished cities. And miles below in the skyless, insulated "downunders," other survivors yawn away placid, hollow lives of boring respectability. Vic, Ellison's fifteen-year-old hero-narrator, picks his way through the surface jungle as cautiously and daringly as a sapper in a mine field. A "solo," unattached, his survival depends on his .45 automatic, his rifle, and his loyal, sagacious talking dog, Blood, friend, dependent, advisor, comrade in battle, and expert sniffer of danger and the human female. Blood's nose leads his sex-hungry master to Quilla June Holmes, a downunder girl who had come up the access dropshaft disguised as a boy. Quilla proves a most appreciative and demanding rape victim and Vic's capable ally too when a roverpak, led by its dogs, surprise their hideout.

After the firefight Quilla escapes to the downunders, and Vic follows her, drawn by the thought of her willing body.

But Quilla had been bait and the downunders capture Vic. They need him for stud, many of the women being sterile and the rest having mostly girls. While Ellison doesn't explain the cause of their reproductive problem, he infers through Vic that their preoccupation with niceness and order gelded the sexual vitality of both women and men. The downunders are mush.

> They rocked in rockers on front porches, they raked
> their lawns, they hung around the gas station, they
> stuck pennies in gumball machines, they painted
> white stripes down the middle of the road, they sold
> newspapers on the corners, they listened to oom-
> pah bands on a shell in the park, they played hop-
> scotch and pussy-in-the-corner, they polished fire
> engines, they sat on benches reading, they washed
> windows and pruned bushes, they tipped their hats
> to ladies. . . . they walked hand-in-hand with some of
> the ugliest chicks I've ever seen, and they bored the
> ass off me. . . . Polite? Christ, you could puke from
> all the lying hypocritical crap they called civility.
> Hello Mr. This and Mrs. That. And how are you? . . .
> And how is business? . . . And I started gibbering in
> my room. . . . That clean, sweet, neat, lovely way
> they lived was enough to kill a guy. No wonder the
> men couldn't get it up and make babies that had balls
> instead of slots.[18]

Vic escapes to the surface with Quilla. The girl loves him and she picks off their downunder pursuers with his .45. They find Blood at the access dropshaft, weak from the wounds of the previous fight and dying of starvation, and they have no food. With another roverpak assault imminent Quilla urges Vic to abandon the dog. "She got a pouty look on her face. 'If you love me, you'll come *on*.' " — After Blood had eaten, Vic treats his wounds. The two strike out across the wasteland for another city. Thoughts of Quilla fade slowly, and "it took a long time before I stopped hearing her calling in my head. Asking me, asking me: *do you know what love is?*

"Sure I know.

"A boy loves his dog."[19]

It would be a mistake to cast Ellison's story among those depicting the mosaic of social disintegration after a nuclear war. The

war is a framework within which Ellison dramatizes varieties of
alienation, especially of youth, and despite the setting the alienation looks familiar. Like many of today's rebellious young, Vic
prefers his hard but free life to the contemptibly vapid existence
of the buried "squares." And to the squares he is an animal.
Quilla too revolts against her background, but she can not throw
off all its values. Her ending up as a dog's meal is, in retrospect,
less a shock than an expectable consequence of the dog's indis-
pensability and her burdensome downunder romantic notions.
The cuddling tentacles of love had to be cut away. To Vic a bind-
ing relationship based on little more than sentiment and archaic
traditions, the barnacles of obligation, love — what many-splen-
dored thing?[20] If a dog talks sense (and Blood does) a talking dog
is better than a lying song.

Clearly, *Dance the Eagle to Sleep* and "A Boy and His Dog"
do not represent the larger body of youth-revolt science fiction.
Both stand with the young. In Piercy the swooping, screaming,
clawing eagle, the predatory elder, is the persecutor of the child.
Barbarian may well describe Ellison's gun-weighted, priapic hero,
but at least he plies a healthy and honest barbarism and he is not
without sparkle and charm. Such can not be said of the embalmed
gentlefolk downunder. Still whatever the justification of youth's
disdain for the old order, Piercy and Ellison have written a minority report. Dystopian fiction is by nature invasion shy. The *new*
order, not the old, threatens. The new tyranny.

The conservatism of dystopian science fiction must be self-
evident from the works discussed in this chapter — indeed, from
the works of the entire study. In the dystopian there dwells a
sense of the finite and intractable. Nature, society, and man being
what they are, all three have only limited room for maneuver without inflicting injury upon the entire organism. (Yes, *organism*,
circumscribed by its anatomy and physiology and pulsing to a
mysterious logic; not *mechanism*, with limitlessly diverse and
arrangeable combinations.) For the dystopian the inelasticity of
things and the dubious gifts of progress prescribe now a time of
caution, a time for contemplating the organism. Americans especially have found this an age of unpredictable and vexing
paradoxes: We end a great war with a nuclear bomb; and our
cleverness condemns man to live in its shadow evermore. We dis-

patch food-laden armadas to hungry peoples; and our generosity swells our national debt and the number of hungry. We grant women their "rights" and sweep away age-old sexual taboos; and our liberalism blurs our sexual identities and roles and begets a spate of books informing men how to be men and women how to be women. We make schooling compulsory and education a science; and we ask "why Johnny can't read." And so on. The dystopian's conservatism is founded in the paradoxes of our time.

To be sure, none of the "new tyrannies" has come to pass in a form close to fiction's nightmares. However, the matter of this chapter, if not literally prophetic, certainly reflects the possibilities inherent in existing conditions. The closed totalitarian state has proven its ability to regiment and indoctrinate. The mind has never been more vulnerable to the invasion of its privacy and to mechanical and chemical manipulation. The plundered earth approaches an ecological crisis. The youth clamor for new systems, new life styles, new laws, new leaders. New tyrannies, new tryants? the dystopian asks.

If one were to distill from the works of this chapter some essence, some governing principle, he might press from their pages the voiceless sigh: Let there be, for a while, an end to new things.

CATASTROPHE

Nuclear War

The atomic bomb that leveled Hiroshima fertilized the soil from which science fiction grows. The genre's eschatological vision had long been traditional but it had always evolved from the raw material of sheerest fancy: the crazed scientist or dictator whose hands held some deadly devil-knows-what; the man-killing alien; the planet on a collision course with earth; some invincibly progressive plague, ice age, genetic mutation, etc., stamping *hic jacet* over man and his works. Now the deadly devil-knows-what has a name, a reality, and a history. The hands holding it are those of known world figures. And the causes of its possible use are reported to all in the daily outpourings of press, radio, and television. No wonder it has triggered an explosion in fiction.

Three million copies and a Hollywood production probably make Nevil Shute's *On the Beach*[1] the best known nuclear catastrophe story. In it, all life in the northern hemisphere has been destroyed by a nuclear war between several powers and now, two years later, radiation has drifted down over the equator. Over South America, Africa, and Australia the slow but inexorable southward shroud of radiation sickness puts out the light, land by land, city by city, life by life. Into Melbourne harbor Commander

147

Dwight Towers brings the submarine *Scorpion*, one of the few surviving ships of the U. S. Navy. Melbourne, the last to be extinguished of the great southern cities, has six months to live, and there Towers finds friendship and the love of a young woman. As for action, there is little. Shute's interest lies in the emotions of doomed people determined to live out their last days with civility and courage and to die with calm. He shows, on an earth drenched with poison, the morale of its last inhabitants withstanding panic, self-pity, and vice.

Much of the impact of the story comes from Shute's understating the emotions of his characters. The nobility of their last days is marked by the steady, taciturn fortitude characteristic of British Commonwealth people. Despite occasional lapses into the maudlin or absurd Shute kindles many touching moments, especially at the end — the parting words, the quick-death tablets, and night. He even manages an occasional stroke of humor, as when an old aristocrat, finding his club stocked with three thousand bottles of vintage port as time is running out, blames the Wine Committee, which "should have seen this coming." In all, the last generation consists of people, people too gentle, too uncomprehending and unprepared, too innocent, too strong, too meshed in the rhythm of existence, to be the last generation.

While *On the Beach* avoids overt philosophizing, the catastrophe, the total and permanent snuffing-out, compels one to ask: If this can happen, what is the human race all about? Shute symbolically raises that question in a curious episode — the *Scorpion's* trans-Pacific cruise to investigate unintelligible telegraphic signals from Puget Sound. But the answer to the riddle is only a mocking happenstance. A blown-out window frame, resting on an overturned bottle and rocking in the breeze, taps a babble on a live key. Is the human adventure too but a babble loosed by a cosmic wreckage as it, randomly poised, teeters in the winds of chance?

In Philip Wylie's *Triumph* only fourteen Americans survive in the U. S. after a sneak nuclear attack by Russia triggers a war killing most people in the northern hemisphere. The fourteen, the family and guests of a millionaire who had built a shelter-complex deep in a limestone mountain on the Connecticut coast, meet the crises of their two-year confinement until their rescue by New

Zealanders. Concurrent with their triumph over death is their country's military triumph (hollow though it may be), when the few remaining American nuclear-armed submarines, long secretly awaiting the day of revenge, exterminate the corps of Soviet butchers, who had started the war, as they emerge from their underground lairs.

One of many "nuclear ordeal" novels, *Triumph* concentrates on the physical action and psychological tension of its characters. Though Wylie's story does not arouse deep sympathy and a sense of futility, as does Shute's, its shivering descriptions are master-pieces of the gruesome. For example:

> Many [who escaped immediate incineration] were naked and of the naked, many were burned scarlet or, in places, black, from head to foot, or on arms and head.
> The ears of thousands were gone. Their eyes had "melted" and lay on their cheeks in phlegm-like gobbets. Their noses were not there, and they breathed through holes in crisp, black faces. Their hair was gone. It was impossible to tell of thousands (unless they walked) which was the front, which the back of their horrible heads.[2]

In view of such horrors, Wylie's title is, of course, ironic.

Mordecai Roshwald's *Level 7* is the diary of X-127, a name-less soldier of a nameless country. Once he had a name and walked the earth. But orders have sent him 4400 feet below the earth to Level 7, where he joins several hundred other men and women. None will ever see the earth's surface again. Level 7 is a secret, self-contained and insulated nuclear missile control center with life-support systems to last five hundred years. But the center's con-struction, while insuring the safety of its personnel, makes their exit physically impossible. Only their progeny, whom they will reproduce to replace them, may emerge centuries later to re-establish, if need be, human life *on* earth. Such must be the sacrifice of "the defenders of truth and justice." As one of those defenders, X-127 functions as one of a crew manning the missile-control console, people who, on order, will push buttons, destroy-ing the enemy and making the earth's surface uninhabitable for generations.

The possibility that he might be one of the "hangmen of

mankind" does not trouble X-127. He, like the others, was chosen because psychological tests had shown him emotionally cool and socially indifferent. But the thought of never again seeing a green field, a town, or the sun depresses him. To relieve that depression he begins to write a diary, "for this is the only way in which I can feel the sun."

The diary relates the regimen of Level 7, X-127's anxiety and self-questioning, and the world-destroying nuclear war. Though the diarist's reason for being is the enemy's extermination, it becomes clear from his narrative that his *personal* enemy is Level 7 and the mentality that conceived it and turned its human beings into pushbutton gods. Similarly, the personal enemy of Level 7, as one finds in so many dystopias, is the sense and sensation of the self. Code names replace personal names, which "have nostalgic association with life on the surface." Unflavored food blunts the appetite. Sex is therapeutic and procreative, but conditions do not allow fuller relationships. Yet despite the dehumanizing conditions and despite the fact that X-127 follows orders and presses the buttons of death, the diary reveals his yet warm embers of sympathy, repugnance, and life-yearning. Gladly would he barter his existence for a butterfly's but knows the butterfly would refuse the bargain. That he has been found suitable for his post troubles him: "I do not want to be a monster, and a man without emotions *is* a monster." And then he wonders, "Can a man become neurotic through worrying about his inability to be neurotic?" When his friend develops a hysterical paralysis of his right hand, revolted by what that hand may do, the diarist notes, "To care that much must be a wonderful sensation. . . . I envy him his abnormality." After the taste of an unbearably delicious piece of chocolate hospitalizes him, X-127 records that he enjoyed the pain. "It made me feel that I was still alive, alive to sensations which were felt by people up there on the surface." He wonders, a few days after obediently pressing the deadly buttons, why the military had given him a long, intensive, technical training in order to perform "this imbecile function." And he concludes that his training was a calculated deception "to camouflage the simplicity of my basic task." The deception had worked too well. Psychologists had "studied monkeys to learn about men, and then turned men into monkeys."[3]

While Roshwald's novel chronicles the death of the world, it also chronicles the rebirth of a man, X-127. When a married couple from an upper level rejects the underground life and decides to die in the sun, a strange feeling comes over him.

> A feeling of tenderness for those two up there . . . I wish I could have comforted them and helped them. . . . Is this compassion? Love? Sociability? Are other human beings able to arouse in me feelings like those? Was there a green spot hidden in my soul which they, the doves, have discovered? . . . I love that pair of doves, dying out there on the bare planet. I love them. . . . They have pushed the hidden button in my soul. The lost, forgotten, decayed button. . . . Why is it so difficult to push that button of humanity, and so easy to push the ones which launch deadly rockets? And why did nobody discover my good button earlier, before it was all too late?[4]

But what can this new feeling avail? Fired rockets can not be unfired. The killed can not be unkilled. His conscience awakened — too late! Futility runs the world. Stupidity is god.

And death is victor. Level 1, expectedly, perishes, but later relatively secure Level 2 reports radiation sickness and expires. In three months the sickness breaches the barriers of Level 3. Quickly then Levels 4 and 5 get it: vomiting, nausea, diarrhea; and recriminations, rioting, panic, and the execution of war criminals by war criminals. Level 6 falls silent. Only Level 7 lives, fearfully clinging (as others had) to assurances that it is invulnerable. But the unforeseen happens. In two days Level 7 is a mausoleum, the dead everywhere, and X-127, dying, knows he is the world's last man. Feebly he switches on the nuclear-powered tape and, comforted by the music of Beethoven, waits his turn. Faint though he is, he writes his diary, his contact "with what was," musing that for eternity, in the cave of the button-pushers, shall sound the "Eroica."

Shute, Wylie, and Roshwald cry the horror, torment, and imbecility of nuclear war. Walter M. Miller's *A Canticle for Leibowitz* adds to these curses a special dreadfulness: the idea that the insanity of war is chronic, that man will return to ashes what he raises up from past ashes, until he is no more. Beginning six hundred years after the "Flame Deluge," Miller's episodic narrative carries the reader through twelve centuries of recovery to the beginning of another Deluge, one which, if not the last, will teach men nothing, but will only rewind the clockwork of futility.

The Flame Deluge had left the world primitive and de-populated. Only isolated Catholic monasteries, maintaining for centuries a tenuous foothold in a heathen fastness, preserved scraps of the past culture — the Memorabilia and the germ of learning. Leibowitz Abbey in the Utah dessert is one such glim-mering candle, founded by a scientist who survived the Deluge, be-came a Catholic, dedicated his life to collecting and preserving the Memorabilia, and was martyred during the "Simplification" — when enraged mobs put to death the world's rulers and those who served them, the men of learning. Yet almost all the Memorabilia, its subject matter long since destroyed, remains inscrutable to its keepers, who for centuries have awaited the Integrator, who should fit the great puzzle together again.

Another six centuries unfold. Not one but many Integrators probe the Church's Memorabilia, and their findings usher in a renaissance which moves the hand of history toward its next midnight: increasingly centralized and aggressive nation-states, firearms, printing, electric power. The second Enlightenment and Age of Science gradually challenge the reigning king, Ignorance. The gulf between church and state, and conscience and know-ledge, widens. A scientist, servant to an ambitious despot, prophe-sies to the Abbot of St. Leibowitz' the triumph of Truth over Ignorance and the "many [who] enrich themselves by means of his dark monarchy":

> "Tomorrow, a new prince shall rule. Men of under-standing, men of science shall stand behind his throne, and the universe will come to know his might. His name is Truth. His empire shall encompass the Earth. And the mastery of Man over the Earth shall be renewed. . . . It will come to pass by violence and upheaval, by flame and by fury, for no change comes calmly over the world."[5]

Thus speaks the scholar-scientist, Thon Taddeo. In the intel-lectual conflict between him and Abbot Dom Paulo one sees the assumptions and expediencies which will nurture the second Deluge and, ominously, which exist today. The scientist declines to oppose a prince, regardless of his policies, who subsidizes his work. Besides, mankind profits from science's discoveries. The

Abbot rejoins:

> "Twelve centuries ago, not even the survivors profit-
> ed. Must we start down that road again? . . . You
> promise to begin restoring Man's control over Nature.
> But who will govern the use of the power to control
> natural forces? Who will use it? To what end? How
> will you hold him in check? . . . Mankind will profit,
> you say. By whose sufferance? The sufferance of a
> prince who signs his letters X? Or do you really be-
> lieve that your collegium can stay aloof from his
> ambitions when he begins to find out that you're
> valuable to him?"[6]

In his mind the scientist had long ago refuted this argument. To
him the Abbot's appeal meant, "Keep science cloistered, don't try
to apply it, don't try to do anything about it until men are holy."
Thon Taddeo closes the issue: "If you try to save wisdom until
the world is wise, Father, the world will never have it."[7]

The centuries pass. It is the thirty-eighth century, an age of
television, computers, and nuclear weapons, and one facing catastrophic war. Abbot Dom Zerchi of St. Leibowitz' anguishes
silently, "Are we doomed to do it again and again and again?
Have we no choice but to play the Phoenix in an unending sequence of rise and fall? . . . *Are we doomed to it, Lord, chained
to the pendulum of our own mad clockwork, helpless to halt its
swing?*"[8] Helpless, so it seems. Mass euthanasia centers had been
established for those who might be fatally exposed to radiation.
Helpless. Instead of bending all their efforts to make war impossible, the nations had sought in advance only to mitigate its
consequences. In the twentieth century each great prince believed he could smite the enemy first and overwhelmingly and not
suffer reprisal. But now nations knew safety to be unachievable,
and yet they prepared to kill and, painlessly if possible, be killed.
Man's *willingness* to be a victim answers Dom Zerchi's question:
helpless.

Miller's abbot contemplates the paradox of his time — the
paradox, too, of the twentieth century. The marvels of which
dreamers dreamed, now realized, spawned complication, frustra-
tion, and fear. The age for taking hope became an age of anxiety.

> The closer men came to perfecting for themselves a
> paradise, the more impatient they seemed to become
> with it, and with themselves as well. . . . When the

world was in darkness and wretchedness, it could believe in perfection and yearn for it. But when the
world became bright with reason and riches, it began
to sense the narrowness of the needle's eye. . . . Well,
they were going to destroy it again, were they — this
garden Earth, civilized and knowing, to be torn apart
again that Man might hope again in wretched darkness.[9]

Dom Zerchi had resolved that some fragment of mankind would
be spared this cycle of Deluges. When the expected nuclear holocaust engulfs the earth, a space ship carrying Leibowitzian clerics,
laymen, and the Memorabilia lifts off for a distant planet. Dom
Zerchi had bidden them farewell: "Be for Man the memory of
Earth and Origin. Remember this Earth. Never forget her, but —
never come back. . . . God bless you, and pray for us."[10]

No doubt Miller's novel would have seemed most illiberal in
less troubled times. Not only does he despair of man (not an
exceptional attitude in any age), but he displays a strongly pro-
clerical feeling vis-a-vis science. Huxley, on the other hand, never
combines the anti-scientism of *Ape and Essence* and *Brave New
World* with the idea that existing religions offer any remedies in
the nuclear age. Yet *if* one accepts the premise about man's in-
corrigibility with dangerous toys, Miller's gentle static clericalism
has its virtues. The clerical mentality and temperament is hardly
disposed towards inventing world-blasting armaments. In all,
however, Miller seems to be less assured by his faith in faith than
his faith in scientific ignorance to halt the deadly cycle. Here again
science fiction steps backward from the precipice, waiting for the
instinct for racial survival — should that ever come — to overtake
madness and the machines.

And the step backward is Miller's too. In 1952, eight years
before *Canticle*, he wrote "Dumb Waiter," a preachy story whose
optimism now leaves one with a feeling of sadness. I read it after
Canticle — an ironic postscript which only darkened the gloom.

Of course machines go wrong and men go wrong, but that's
no reason for giving up on either: This is the message of "Dumb
Waiter." The war was over, but bombless bombers keep "bomb-
ing" and robot cops keep giving war-withered survivors summonses
for jaywalking, all the doings of Central, the computer, which no
one knows how to reprogram. Miller's hero forestalls mobs of

angry computer wreckers and reprograms the machine to meet the realities of peace and reconstruction. He believes that the loss of the computer will set civilization back ages. He debates with the machine haters and brands them "the machine age's spoiled children," who thoughtlessly take from the machine and crack up with the machine because, like the politicians, they haven't the will to understand the machine:

"Politicians were given powerful tools, they failed to understand the tools. They wrecked our culture with them."

"You'd have a scientist in the White House?"

"If all men were given a broad technical education, there could be nothing else there, could there?"

"Technocracy − − "

"No. Simply a matter of education."

"People aren't smart enough."

"You mean they don't care enough. . . . If the common man were trained in scientific reasoning methods, we'd solve our problems in a hurry."[11]

But the author of *Canticle* no longer believed that. No longer did he see machines as servants waiting to be used wisely by knowledgeable masters. On the contrary, anything that could happen would happen. One falls down the dumb waiter shaft sooner or later. Sooner or later one drops the bomb. Sooner probably. What effect has knowledge on madness and the machines?

The Population Explosion

It is curious indeed that before the mid-1960's the population explosion had received such small attention in science fiction. The genre, so bulging with invasions from outer space, had virtually ignored the invasion of earth by her own kind. While the not-inevitable nuclear holocaust continued to be a dominant theme, the inevitable[1] population catastrophe remained all but unnoticed in fiction, despite a half century of scholarship on the coming crisis. One is hard put to account for the previous dearth of science fiction on this subject: Perhaps the genre's traditional reticence about sex[2] deterred writers from the overpopulation story. At any rate, while scientific scholarship on the population problem is profuse and continuous, its treatment in science fiction has been until recently inexplicably thin.

In James Blish and Norman L. Knight's *A Torrent of Faces* a character complains, "As soon as you start talking about human reproduction, everything turns out to be sacred."[3] He might just as truly have said, "As soon as you start talking about human reproduction, many people will start talking nonsense." The authors have chosen a striking piece of nonsense from Henry George's *Progress and Poverty* (1879) for their epigraph and have then proceeded to fabricate a world based on its assumptions. George writes:

> For that man cannot exhaust or lessen the powers of nature follows from the indestructibility of matter and the persistence of force. . . . That the Earth could maintain a thousand billions as easily as a thousand millions is a necessary deduction from the manifest truth that, at least as far as our agency is concerned, matter is eternal and force must forever continue to act. . . .[4]

Thus Blish and Knight reveal the world of 2794 groaning under a population of one trillion. The inefficient national states of the Age of Waste have long been swept away and rule of the world state has passed to Prime Center, a managerial elite. Planned cities cover almost all the land — from modest communities of five million to sprawling, largely subterranean labyrinths of three billion like Chicago, a city spilling and burrowing north toward Canada and south toward the Ohio, and growing by ten thousand daily. London covers half of England and extends into the sea, supported by pillars and arches. The Union of Occupied Classes, one-tenth of one percent of the race, operates the automated world machine, while the multitude contentedly vegetates in cubicles, living on the dole, watching 3-V, eating synthetic food from auto-servers, and making love. While "the leaching-out of the gene pool" through irresponsible breeding has left man "with a high majority of pure thumpheads," tectogeneticists have produced a gilled human, the Triton, to exploit marine resources. And though half-hearted birth control programs have repeatedly failed, engineers have nearly perfected an "interstellar drive," which will transport to other planets the soon-unmanageable glut of bodies. In short, *A Torrent of Faces* presents one of the classic conditions of dystopian fiction: the triumph of ingenuity over common sense.

As in many other "world machine" novels, one feels here the influence of E. M. Forster's "The Machine Stops." The clever contrivance that man has made of earth is on the verge of cracking. A two-million-guest floating resort sinks owing to short-circuited computers; a colossal supply pipeline bursts; the "torrent of faces" is unending; a small asteroid slams into the earth. The novel's thematic core, however, lies in the conflict between world leaders over population policy. One critic terms Chicago "this frightful human termitary of vitrolith and glastic and metal, of pipes and cables and computers, of myriads of escalators and elevators and moving floors. . . . It's an ugly tumor on the face of the earth."[5] Viewing a shattered earth at the novel's close, one, who had opposed the population torrent bitterly remarks:

> "If there was ever any hope of solving the population problem, it should have been tackled no later than the twenty-first century — even if it had to involve something mildly oppressive. . . . We let ourselves be sold on the notion that we could never have too many people, not even if they were standing on each other's feet. And we threw everything we had into just one effort — to accommodate *everybody*. . . . We've had it. From now on, it's going to be guns, starvation, and tyranny — and we brought it on ourselves."[6]

The majority of Prime Center obviously had not shared this opinion, holding that population control was unworkable and demeaning to human dignity. One of the advocates of unrestricted propagation, believing that human fertility, far from being a menace, constitutes the driving force behind man's destiny — the seeding of the universe — had cried out in debate: "Help increase the population pressure on this planet to the explosion point. Nothing else will serve. . . . Sooner or later the human race is going to burst out of this little egg, and spread. . . . Are we fertile for nothing? The sky is full of stars — does nobody here want them but me?"[7] Ironically instead of seeding the universe, upstart man finds his own planet "seeded" by a fragment of it — an asteroid, which makes earth a shambles. Again, the machine stops. The cosmic disaster, so it appears, had but preceded the inevitable demographic one.

Blish and Knight have issued more than a warning against overpopulation. The real villain of their story is not fertility but pompous ingenuity — the erector-set mentality, whose nature is *not* to avoid problems by exercising common sense, discipline, respect, and humility, but to allow problems, to welcome them as invitations to human resourcefulness or the spurs to some grand destiny. The novel assumes that given certain problems man would rather pave, tunnel, and wall the planet from pole to pole than sanely employ existing remedies. I do not quarrel with this assumption. Rather, I fear its validity, as the breach between *homo sapiens* and *homo faber* widens in this century.

Harry Harrison's *Make Room! Make Room!*,[8] an expansion of his fine short story "Roommates," balloons 1999's New York City out to a thirty-five million miserable people fleshball. Cubicle housing, barely palatable food, rationed drinking water, social breakdown. Three people, lovers Andy and Shirl and old wise Sol, share a small partitioned room, live amicably together, and manage to inject a little savor into their people-smothered, resource-poor existence. Sol grows herbs in a window box and the pathetic lovers love. When Sol dies the hideous Belichers, ugly, moronic overbreeders with seven obstreperous brats, arrive with a legal "squat order" and lay claim to the few square feet on Sol's side of the partition. The unstoppable brats tear open Sol's herb packets and spill them on the floor. Shirl can not bear the nine invaders and leaves Andy for someone who can offer her a better life.

Harrison's is an angry book: Yes, man has blundered into a crisis, but worse, few have the sense to acknowledge its cause and most who do lack the courage to do something about it. The book's very title mocks the prevailing delusion about overpopulation. Make room! As though room could be *made* in a finite area! As though the finite planet could be subdivided endlessly to house our redoubling breed! Amidst the national suffering and chaos of 1999 the timid Congress considers an emergency bill for increasing food production and hides the essential legalizing of birth control clinics in a rider. Even this belated move inflames the Save Our Babies fanatics, who equate birth control with child murder, and

they riot against the bill. Harrison's novel gives one a vision of
lunatics, on a roiling sea, bailing *into* the lifeboat.

In Robert Bloch's *This Crowded Earth* Harry Collins looks
down over Chicago's thirty-eight million and suffers a nervous
breakdown.

> The buildings below, black and sooty, their jagged
> outlines like the stumps of rotten teeth. And they
> stretched off in all directions, as far as the eye could
> attain; row after row of rotten teeth grinning up from
> the smog-choked throat of the streets. From the maw
> of the city far below came this faint but endless
> howling, this screaming of traffic and toil. And you
> couldn't help it, you breathed *that* in too . . . and it
> poisoned you and it did more than make your head
> ache. It made your heart ache and it made your soul
> sick, and it made you close your eyes and your lungs
> and your brain against it.[9]

Collins is not alone. "Moiling megalopolitanism" is driving millions
to insanity, suicide, and crimes of violence. Clearly the country is
going under. Yet despite this, a birth control program is unthinkable: the government would never dare, the people would riot, the
churches would cry out. Finally the government attacks the crisis
with a secret genetic mutation process which creates space-saving
"Yardsticks," humans who will grow no taller than three feet.
However, after a few generations the new breed proves inviable,
and humanity must be rescued from extinction by the few remaining normals.

The most harrowing pages of Bloch's novel describe oppressive crowding, forced bodily contact, the smell, throb, heat,
and trample of people, everywhere. Paradoxically the crush of
humanity also has humorous features. In Richard Wilson's story,
"The Eight Billion," an involuntary gesture by the King of New
York dislodges the Queen's crown, which falls, in the packed
throne room, no farther than the shoulder of her first lady in
waiting. As the King's thousand courtiers inch from the throne
room to their dinner of essence of plankton, ceiling nozzles spray
a mist of oxygen to facilitate their labors, while odd and even
numbers inhale and exhale alternately so as not to break the walls.
Even the compulsory birth control lectures for the city's eight
billion fail to check population growth because of "I. I.," illegal

impregnation: all those people standing pressed together – they're only human. Only Project Mohole, a frantic excavation gamble to discover a huge legendary cavern, can save millions from being edged into Manhattan's surrounding rivers. Finally, breakthrough and wild jubilation – the cavern is discovered. But the joy of the eight billion is short lived. Suddenly from the cavern stream hundreds of thousands of ugly, thin, livid, sunken-eyed people into the light. Speaking a strange tongue similar to English, they relate that their prayers have been answered by the "dimly-remembered topside god." They had long been boring upward, hoping to find "the surface for their teeming, expanding population . . . all eight billion of them."[10]

J. G. Ballard's "Billenium"[11] depicts another comic, sardine-can dystopia: a city of thirty million plagued by days-long pedestrian jams at street intersections, family separations owing to the rigors of a cross-town journey, exhausting queues for bathrooms and other necessary facilities, and a housing shortage so severe that a cot-sized cubicle is all the shelter one can expect. When Ward and Rossiter, two young men renting a double cubicle in a run-down house, accidentally break their partition and discover an unknown room-sized space, the find seems like a continent. Generous to a fault, the men take into their domain two evicted ladies, Judith and Helen, and build more partitions. Shortly they admit Judith's aunt to chaperone these proper ladies – and later Helen's sickly mother, who is then joined by her husband. With each immigrant's arrival the young men stealthily partition their secret America, their imaginations still held by that first view of near-boundless space. Soon the newcomers grow crotchety and demanding, dropping hints that Ward move out, complaining that the place is just as crowded as other places. And Ward awakens and sees – it is!

Science fiction and whimsy fuse in Earl Conrad's *The Da Vinci Machine: Tales of the Population Explosion*. With his first words Conrad begins his portrait of a zany disasterland and maintains his delightful irreverence till the last stroke – with the demise of sex. The first of his sixteen tales deals with a "nasty habit," cannibalism:

> Drinkwater had come by a rather nasty habit.

He was going around eating people.

Mostly people he didn't know, anybody that would make a good meal. Anybody that looked like a tasty morsel. . . .

The police called him in one day and said, "Drinkwater, we've been getting complaints about you and want you to stop it. . . . "

He told them to go to the devil and let him be. . . .

Well, you know the world we live in. So they gave him a good stiff warning and let him go about his nasty habit.

Since the world "we" live in, in *The Da Vinci Machine*, is committing suicide by overpopulation, on what moral ground can it forbid Drinkwater's nasty habit? The world doesn't care about itself and Drinkwater wants to prove it. "I want to prove you can go around eating a hundred and fifty people and get away with it," he says. "Columbus proved the world was round. I want to prove it doesn't give a damn." In time the press gives Drinkwater's habit two paragraphs. The one-column, two-line head discloses:

Drinkwater Has Eaten 148
Proves Nobody Really Cares[12]

That is Conrad's point. Mankind will suffer anything rather than bridle its procreative power.

The spell of romance and man's self-duplicating mania — these are the major targets of Conrad's satire. When the message center on Planet QB Millionth N picks up a voice caterwauling, "Love me baby till the day I die, Love me, love me, love little old I," the operators understand the signal is an appeal for help from another of those primitive planets with population trouble. After dismissing the idea of putting the insects out of their misery with a meteor, the operators try to establish communication with earth. But the tiny spheroid continues to bawl, "I wanna go where you go I wanna do what you do I wanna love when you love I wanna be happy." The operators, having wasted enough time, sign off after a final transmission: "Coming in, Earth, get this message. Your future hangs on it":

O O O O O O O O O O O O O O O O O[13]

In Conrad's closing tale, not man, but a Genesis-in-reverse miracle solves the population problem. Adam and Evelyn Worchester lie beside each other a mile high in their Manhattan cubicle saying goodbye. Two feet to the right and two feet to the left and below and across the world couples lie saying their farewells. What is happening no one knows, except that it is the end.

> For years they had known that this hour would ar-
> rive: the final asphyxiation of Man by himself, by his
> own body, by his insatiable quality of procreation,
> his impossibility of self-discipline, by the failure of
> the mechanisms, and by the ancestral need for lone
> and small Man to make himself endure and to im-
> mortalize himself in new human life. It had gone on
> since the 1970s at an impossible rate, and all the talk
> of controlling population had been for naught.[14]

A darkness envelops Adam and Evelyn, and in their touching exchange of I-love-you's she vanishes in the mystic and awesome moment. They call to each other for a time until she ceases to respond. For she has ceased to be. Alone, Adam realizes what has happened. Evelyn has returned to his chest. He feels the new rib but it is not Evelyn. That instant the population problem and most problems are solved. Yet Adam runs through the streets screaming, "Eveyln! Evelyn! Evelyn, where are you?" and the streets of the world are filled with men crying the names of their wives.

> So made He a rib as once before made He a
> woman out of a rib.
> Here ends the sad story of Man.
> There is no fig leaf. There is no Garden of Eden.
> There is no serpent.
> There is only Adam Worchester, alone, undying,
> screaming forever in the streets of Manhattan.[15]

The above fiction on the population explosion assumes that through inaction or extravagant evasions man will invite catastrophe. Max Ehrlich's *The Edict*[16] and Anthony Burgess's *The Wanting Seed*, on the other hand, present dystopias which have met the population problem head-on by stringently regulating reproduction and reshaping mores, politics, and economy to hold the tenuous balance between people and food. If the wretchedness of a fictional overpopulated world were reckoned in "dystopia points," Ehrlich's story of squashed humanity would be a leading contender for the wretchedness prize. *The Edict* layers more atrocities against a tolerable life than I have ever read, from drinking sterilized sewer juice to queuing up for a rentable privacy booth. With mass starvation looming in the twenty-first century, WorldGov issues the edict: No more babies for thirty years. Death for violators. To satisfy their maternal instinct, women, after a program of "persuasive psychonarcosynthesis," may have mechanical babies. But Carole Evans wants a real child, fakes contraception with the electronic aborter, and presents her "partner" Russ with a *fait accompli* — her pregnancy and their probable discovery and execution. After the child's birth, the fugitive family escapes to a radioactive island, a cemetery for the last century's atomic weapons. Though they can expect only a short life in this lethal sanctuary, they vow to live it without regrets, free and fully human.

The thematic schizophrenia of Ehrlich's novel should be apparent from even this brief synopsis. "ZERO POPULATION GROWTH — IT MUST BE ACHIEVED — OR THE POPULATION BOMB WILL DESTROY EARTH!" Ehrlich's cover warns. He dedicates the book "to our children . . . and their children . . . and their children's children. If any." But before the story's midpoint, the action and the author's sympathies are sharply focused on Carole's quite natural yearning for true motherhood. But this yearning is a basic part of the population bomb! Ehrlich, it seems, has not decided whether he wants to cry the horrors of overpopulation more than he wants to praise natural instincts and heroic defiance. Admittedly, the dilemma is a trying one, but a choice should have been made.

Anthony Burgess's *The Wanting Seed* avoids such a dilemma. The book is a satire, not a warning, and a spirit of the ridiculous often mitigates the mere vexing and the utterly abominable. The world is not to be saved or destroyed (unless some almighty power takes it seriously); and the best one can do is dodge its pendulums as they swing from the old follies to the new. And stay human.

In an overpopulated future England the Ministry of Infertility allows couples only one child. The government openly favors bachelors, castrates, and sexual inverts. *"It's Sapiens to be Homo"* and *"Love your Fellow-Men"*[17] proclaim the government posters. God, now Mr. Livedog, is a children's cartoon villain who mischievously pollutes the world with unwanted life. And the

Bible is an "old religious book full of smut," a product of primitive minds. In it "the big sin is to waste your seed, and if God
loves you He fills your house with kids. . . . They kept appealing
to this all the time, talking about fertility and barren fig trees
getting cursed and so on." "Waste not, want not" is carried to
coldly gruesome extremes: "Another dollop of phosphorous
pentoxide for dear old Mother Earth," says a physician as he
hands an infant's corpse to men from the Ministry of Agriculture.
Addressing the grieving mother, he counsels, "Think of this in
national terms, in global terms. One mouth less to feed. One
more half-kilo of phosphorous pentoxide to nourish the earth. In
a sense . . . you'll be getting your son back again. . . . Do try to
see all this rationally."[18]

But pent-up feelings finally explode after years of heartless
rationality. Open revolt topples the government and England is
caught up in an orgy of Bacchic release — bonfires, ebullient
dancing around Priapean poles, and wild love making in the warm
fields. The new regime abolishes the hated Population Police and
changes the Ministry of Infertility to the Ministry of Fertility.
Soon, however, the regime calls millions of men and women to
arms to fight a nameless enemy for an unstated cause. Unknown
to the troops, they themselves are the enemy and the cause is
their elimination. In the lines men and women massacre each other
in rigged "Extermination Sessions," and after they have "served
their country" they are served *to* their country — gathered up and
sent to packers to be processed into food. When Burgess's hero,
Tristram Foxe, threatens to expose the murderous fraud, a War
Department official defends the policy:

> "They died gloriously, believing they were dying in a
> great cause. And, you know, they really were. . . .
> We're better off without the morons and the enthusi-
> asts. Which means also the corner-boys and the
> criminals. And, as far as the women are concerned,
> the cretinous over-producers. That's genetically very
> sound you know. . . . What other way is there of
> keeping the population down?"[19]

The army has cleansed England of less desirable sorts, relieved it of
the odious anti-fertility apparatus, and solved the population
problem. The military has brought into being, the official contends, "a safe and spacious community. A clean house full of

happy people. But every house, of course, has to have a drainage system. We're that."

"It's all wrong . . . all, all wrong," says Tristram.

"Yes?" replies his adversary. "Well, when you can think out something better come and tell us all about it."[20]

Thus Burgess brings his dystopia to the solution that, by humanitarian standards, is no solution — copulation, carnage, and cannibalism. Yet these, one should assume, considering the author's tone and logic and his *A Clockwork Orange* (Chapters I and II), violate the human spirit less than the former life-denying, oppressive police state. Denaturalization is the ultimate evil. As Burgess asserts, (in *A Clockwork Orange*, that it is better to be a murderer than a dehumanized neuter) so he suggests, in *The Wanting Seed*, that it is better to be murdered than surrender one's primitive, orgiastic sensuality. Several things point to this: the celebration of wanting and the wanton; the heroic treatment of Foxe's wife, Beatrice-Joanna, a "handsome woman of twenty-nine, handsome in the old way . . . the moving opulence of her haunches . . . the splendid curve of her bosom . . . [who] seemed to glow and flame with health and, what was to be disapproved strongly, the threat of fecundity";[21] the savage satire of the infertility cult and creed; and statements associating sexuality with beauty and divinity.[22]

Although Burgess closes with the hint that in time man will find a middle ground on which to live the good life, the reader may feel that the author — in fact, all the authors of population fiction treated here — deal with a false dilemma: Either man resigns himself to inevitable strangulation through overbreeding or substitutes a different disaster by some frightful circumvention. The writers have established literally or implicitly that in their dystopias presently known and effective methods of population control are either unthinkable or unworkable. However, the dilemma is only *theoretically* false. Report after report on world population indicates that the catastrophe man need not suffer becomes increasingly probable. The world's three billion of 1965 will become six billion in 2000, though arable land will increase only five percent. The brothers Paddock, in *Famine — 1975!*, claim that even now — beginning agronomic advances and birth control programs will not save millions from death by famine in the coming decades; and in many lands apathy and technological backwardness hinder agronomic progress, and social and religious hostility proscribes birth control.[23]

This study is not the place to trumpet the alarming population statistics of which for years there has been no dearth. I wish to return, though, to the paradox which population fiction presents. While the reader will accept alien invasions of earth, world dictatorships, and fantastic mechanisms as *les données* of story, he may feel that population fiction proceeds from a false dilemma. But men will never allow these dystopias to come about, he may protest. These, mankind need never suffer. They are so avoidable; the remedies already exist and have existed. Then later he will read in his newspaper the latest dismal prognosis on the population explosion. Why is it that what is so immediate in reality may appear too contrived in fiction?

Race War in America

It is impossible at this time to predict with any assurance the outcome of the American sickness. No day passes without reports on the condition. The media, the scholars, the leaders, the followers, and we, all recite the latest findings: Blacks are advancing. Whites are resisting. Whites are conceding. Blacks are regressing. Tensions are subsiding. Discrimination is more subtle. Tensions are rising. Racism is waning. Polls, studies, statistics, pronouncements, the eyes and ears, and a feeling in the bones "prove" it.

Maybe there are some books in which black Horatio Algers — steady, enterprising, upright, skilled — enter the mainstream of American society, respected and fully accepted human beings. But I know of none. There *should* be such books because they would mirror the real lives of millions of people. And why should not science fiction project a future in which "We shall overcome" shall have become a peacefully achieved reality celebrated by black man and white? But it has not. Why? Perhaps race war in America offers a better or easier story line than racial harmony. Perhaps race war seems the more likely prospect. Perhaps some writers themselves feel angry and violent. Whatever the reason, science fiction finds the American sickness incurable.

In Warren Miller's tale of a black nation's birth, *The Siege of Harlem*, anger and violence are subdued. Grandpa gathers the children around him and tells the story they have heard many times, of the wonderful, terrible war for independence seventy-five years ago, which brought forth the country of Harlem. Grandpa's history has the mellowness of a cherished reminiscence. The children settle back into the glorious past and let the story flow, breaking it only seldom with brief ritualistic questions and remarks.

As a young man Grandpa and most American blacks got their leader's "call" to flock to Harlem. The black ghetto then proclaims its independence, seals itself off from the rest of Manhattan, and prepares to defend itself. But cold and hunger are its cruelest enemies. White America feebly reacts by attacking Harlem with a white-organized black invasion army, which the patriots soundly thrash. The whites lose heart and accept the inevitable – a proud, free, and now thriving black nation. Thusly from the mists of memory Miller raises the land of Harlem, unobliged (and rightly) to explain why the whites proved so impotent, how some twenty million people can survive and flourish on a chip of land, and how this resourceless chip could evolve into a viable state. Irrelevant here. Grandpa's "call" is the *yearning* for dignity and justice, against which all enemies are impotent and which survives in whatever space a yearning requires.

A soft, not bitter, remembrance, *The Siege of Harlem* is not a typical black-revolt novel. Nevertheless it bears the trademarks one finds in other books boiling with black rage: 1. Miller's novel rejects racial integration as unworkable. Miller's whites are the morally dulled "Privileged People," who could never ever understand blacks and would always be chafed and befuddled by what's gotten into "you people." 2. The power of these moral dullards rests in their ability to cunningly create a social environment which turns blacks into tools, into "Plastic Men," who "weren't men at all, no; they were products! Products is what they were and they had been made sick to their souls by their mechanical condition. They were wind-up men and they were the last of their kind for we don't breed them like that anymore and the Majority do not have the power to manufacture them anymore."[1] 3. If, in their exodus from such an Egypt, blacks take land and property not legally theirs, yet they are taking what is *rightfully* theirs through sweat and suffering. Thus Miller's gentle imaginary history speaks of the unbreachable racial gulf, the fragility of white power when manfully challenged, and the justice of compensation.

No black secession, no bristling barricades rend America in D. Keith Mano's *Horn*. But black Harlem might as well be another country. It is America only because no one thinks it worth the trouble to formalize the divorce. And if one does not *literally* find racial war between the covers of Mano's book it is because the ballistics of hatred remains to be discovered.

Calvin Beecher Pratt, forty, Episcopal minister, white, decides to "get out." He leaves the genteel rhythms of life in Greensprings, his sedentary scholarly dabblings, his comfortable WASP parishioners. To Harlem he goes. There, crumbling St. Bart's is his church and from its pulpit he faces a congregation numbering exactly zero. The blacks are at St. Catherine's, where the half-deranged white Rev. Meeker specializes in verbal self-abuse for the real and imagined crimes of the white race against the black — black bodies commanded there by the white-loathing ruler of Harlem, George Horn Smith.

In leaving his protected niche Pratt does not find the "real" world he expected. He goes from the mundane to the mad. Blacks twisted with fury and masochistic whites shamelessly flagellating themselves surpass his understanding. And the Horn Power Movement's hysterical hate-white carnivals bloody his body and endanger his very life. To gain the trust of the blacks Pratt attends a Movement rally and to his surprise is led on a stage with Meeker and other white dung eaters, dutiful veterans of such affairs, to face blacks soon whipped to a froth by black oratory. The white confessors send the fever of wrath higher: "I am ashamed — ashamed to be a white man. . . . To a man — to a man we are despicable in our hypocrisy. . . . We are the scum of the earth." In the ensuing tumult Meeker goes wilder than the blacks and beats Pratt, his fellow clergyman, to a pulp. Still undaunted, Pratt accepts Smith's invitation to a party at his headquarters. There he is shunted through a maze of encounters twining slapstick with terror, which culminate in his being overpowered and undressed by a young black whore. A frame-up of course. Then enters the

black lynch mob feigning outrage. Given the choice of saving
either his eyes or his genitals, Pratt luckily gets off with a mere
tarring of his mightily abused body. Enough. Pratt gives up his
post. "I've learned one thing here – in all this time. That I do not,
cannot, understand the Negro people. That's what I've learned."[2]

The above synopsis does little justice to *Horn*. For the sake
of brevity, vital action, thematic points, the character of George
Horn Smith, the soul of the book and the science fiction in it
have been passed over. Mano's *Horn* is an accomplished work of
art, a novel that can stand beside Ralph Ellison's *Invisible Man*. In
one sense, the protagonists of Mano and Ellison are counterparts:
Both, one white, one black, try to become accepted by the other's
race, and both fail. In Ellison the black man is "invisible" – that
is, not perceived as being a person. In Mano the white man is all
too visible, indelibly white, the agent of numberless, indelible
hurts; and he is unforgivable, not because he does not deserve
forgiveness, but because the hurts are too well remembered. Both
novels portray racism as so endemic that they make faultfinding
and kindly suggestions irrelevant. Ellison's whites *can* not see and
Mano's blacks *can* not forgive. Both suffer a disability, an im-
potency of command over themselves.

Mano's blacks are convinced that whatever interracial harmony there may be does not represent genuine goodwill but
rather mere motions for avoiding inconvenient unpleasantness.
They believe as an article of faith that an impenetrable chromatic
and genetic curtain forever shuts out understanding, friendship,
and cooperation. "Then you hate me?" Pratt asks his black sex-
ton, Nicholas, and the Negro's initial reluctance to get personal
soon turns to anger. The answer is essentially *Yes*. "All whites
are alike. . . . Enemies. . . . Plenty white men hate me – because
of this, because of my skin." And –

> "You whites are different from us. You all are, the
> good guys and the bad guys. You'll never know
> what's goin' on in here – inside me – even if you
> cared. You're different. We're different. I don't
> understand you and you don't understand me. Sure,
> you pee like me, you eat like me, you bleed just
> like me. So what? That don't mean nothin'. . . .
> Look, Mr. Pratt, you're a good guy – far as I can
> tell. Fine. I sit here with you an' it looks like we're

> real buddy-buddy, real friends. But it ain't so. I ain't
> never gonna feel free, feel comfortable talkin' to a
> white man."[3]

Mano expands upon this feeling in an electric confrontation between George Horn Smith and Pratt. Smith goes to the heart of the matter: fear. Get rid of the stupid words, he says — love, hate, prejudice. Why the surprise when all the appeals to love the black man fail? How can there be love with fear? Why the talk about white racism, as if its prejudice and hate come parentless into the world? They come from fear. And the fears are not irrational. A black on your street *will* lower property values. A black in your union *does* mean one less job for a white. A new black ghetto *does* threaten the physical safety of whites left behind. And the black man's fears are not irrational either.

> "Fear will always be with us — as long as men are
> different. And they will always be different. It won't
> be cured by saying, 'Let us love our fellow man.'
> Never by that." "When someone says to you, 'We are
> all equal. We eat and we sleep. We bleed. We die. We
> are all the same.' Spit in his eye, Mr. Pratt. He is an
> idiot."[4]

Not the brotherhood of man, but the differences between men — this is the sad doctrine that dominates the book. Against the differences that breed fear and the fear that breeds hate the Calvin Beecher Pratts and their good intentions don't stand a chance. As in the immemorial and everlasting wars — between the nations, between rich and poor, between male and female, between father and son — between white and black Mano foresees only truces, never peace. "Well . . . Don't take it so bad. . . . It's only life," Smith assures Pratt. But if true, to America it's death. The genius of this country lies in embracing differences and forging them into a mighty bond. *E pluribus unum.* Out of many, one. How this happens must be a mystery even to ourselves, as genius is a mystery even to itself. Perhaps, like so much science fiction, *Horn* is a warning, not a prediction. Yet however intended, its everlasting *Never* declares the American genius dead.

If *The Siege of Harlem* and *Horn* are enough to disturb a white New Yorker, he will find Edwin Corley's *Siege* and John A. Williams' *Sons of Darkness, Sons of Light* downright menacing. In both books black insurgents capture Manhattan and hold it hostage to their demands. It seems that New York, in the fiction of black revolution, represents the white jugular.

Siege. A note and murder: "WHITE MEN WAS NEVER MEANT TO TAKE ORDERS FROM NO NIGGER GENERAL."[5] Murdered, apparently by white racists, the wife and children of black Marine Major General Shawcross, a celebrated war hero. The shock radicalizes Shawcross and by stages he is drawn into a fanatic black movement as commander of its military arm. The blacks' objective: the capture of Manhattan and, in return for the lives of millions of white hostages, the ceding of New Jersey as a sovereign black nation. After infiltrating Manhattan the black guerrilla army, twelve thousand strong, strikes. It quickly isolates the island, destroying most of its bridge and tunnel links with the outside and controlling those yet intact. One force mans the perimeter and easily repels inept assaults of white police and military. Another occupies Harlem and drafts blacks into the defense force. And another controls and terrorizes the white hostages.

Yet despite these tactical successes, Shawcross's faith in the cause fades. A moderate unwarped by bloodlust or ideology, he is stunned by the movement's soon revealed vicious and corrupt senior leadership. Carpenter, chief of the Special Forces, responsible for discipline, internal security, and ideological purity, ruthlessly kills hostages, blows out the mayor's brains on T. V., and finally seizes command from Gray, the head. Gray, no less criminal, had murdered rival Malcolm X and had even ordered the murder of Shawcross's family to enlist the General in the movement. With bitterness and humility Shawcross surrenders the black army. The flames of the city consume Carpenter. And with two grenades rolled unflinchingly between them, Shawcross settles with Gray and with himself.

The fast-paced action of *Siege* does not obscure its evident racial points. Again the doctrine of immutable incompatibility, so constant in race-war fiction. Gray: "You [whites] think of us as white people with a skin problem. That's crap. We're as different from white people as our skin is different from their skin. We're black inside, too, and that makes it impossible for any white to ever understand us. I wish they wouldn't even try. I don't want to be understood."[6] Consequently the inevitability of the act of last resort — secession, either political or social. The vulnerability of America's cities. The brittle loyalty of the integrated black when forced by an extremity to choose between his color and his country. And lastly, the cheerless possibility that time sides with the violent, that integration in slow stages incubates not harmony but divorce. Indeed, one can only guess whether we have waited too long already.

The assertions of John A. Williams' *Sons of Darkness, Sons of Light*[7] closely parallel those of *Siege*, with Williams stressing that our present precarious racial truce is virtually in the hands of chance. In Eugene Browning, Williams gives us another Shawcross. Browning, a Negro, former professor of political science and now an officer of the Institute for Racial Justice, had always believed that blacks could succeed within the system. Like Shawcross he is radicalized by a single incident: five bullets pumped into the chest of a black youth by Police Sergeant Carrigan. *Five* bullets, the absence of the alleged attack knife, and Carrigan's record for disarming toughs convince Browning and the black community that the boy was executed. His own fury and the prospect of black riots transform Browning into a self-appointed "institute for racial justice." He has the Mafia kill Carrigan, a notice to the police that each would be held personally responsible for such outrages.

However, Browning's one-for-one stroke sets a civil war in motion. Throughout the country blacks begin killing dozens of police, and white gangs and off-duty police invade the ghettoes to retaliate. Adding to the scattered violence, a fanatical black organization commanded by Morris Greene blows Manhattan's bridges and tunnels, isolating the island, and issues a list of demands. Greene, who had taken credit for Carrigan's murder, wants ten acres, a car, and five thousand dollars for every needful black family head, the resignation of every senator, congressman, and legislator from states where blacks did not have "full enfranchisement," withdrawal of U. S. investments from South Africa, Mozambique, Angola, and Rhodesia, — and more. With the flames spreading, the book ends.

The hostage family rather than the hostage city is the key to black demands in Fletcher Knebel's *Trespass*. One night the wealthy Tim Crawford family finds itself the prisoner of four armed blacks. The "trespassers," members of the BOF (Blacks of February 21st, the date of Malcolm X's murder), demand that Crawford give them his gracious Fairhill estate. The reason: Much of Crawford's inherited fortune has come from his father's exploitation of blacks. Frightened but unyielding, the Crawfords soon learn that they are not alone in terror. Five other prominent and wealthy households, each allegedly bearing the taint of a racial offense, have been occupied, and for them too it's racial atonement or – – .

The plight of the six becomes a national drama covered by the media, while the government tries to negotiate the matter with black militants. However, the BOF itself is split. Daniel Smith, leader of the extremist faction, has targeted tens of thousands of white households for occupation and wants to strike immediately for "Gamal," the code name for the ultimate objective: Georgia, Alabama, Mississippi, and Louisiana. Once these states are ceded as an independent black nation, Smith's BOF would free its captive multitudes. But the BOF moderates understand that Gamal *now* will mean a black bloodbath. Furthermore there are not enough trained blacks to run such a nation. Smith's dream of "Gamal now" dies with him as federal agents wipe out his headquarters. Negotiating with the U. S. president the moderates win many concessions, among them the promise of a first-rate black university (to train the leaders of tomorrow's Gamal). Crawford agrees to donate a half million dollars to a black educational foundation, a gesture reflecting the prevailing white opinion that black militancy can be bought off with the tokens of compromise. But for the moderates an independent black nation carved out of the federal union is a matter of when, not if – an act of political surgery hardly moderate at all.

While rich in physical action the most lively moments in *Trespass* come in the point-blank verbal exchanges between black and white. These reveal the almost total segregation of their thinking processes once the racial issue arise. For example, the BOF wants blacks on Empire Motors' board of directors "to represent the hundreds of thousands of blacks who drive Empire cars." But directors represent stockholders, not drivers, Empire's head protests. Even here, on the subject of corporate management, the races speak a different language. One of Knebel's blacks calls the ceding of Gamal a "trade" for "the broken bodies of two hundred years of slavery"; and in this idea of compensation one can perhaps gain some understanding of black demands. Since the worth of broken bodies is unmeasurable, only whim decides the proper compensation, not tradition, logic, or law. This puts whites in an untenable position, and obviously they can not accept it. The blacks too are in a bind. Since *hurt*, past and present, is the trump card in their power play, how can they ever know when the white debt is fully paid? Does it not serve them, albeit perversely, to keep hurt alive — to keep hate alive? Knebel's militant blacks hate the "white niggers" working for integration and the white liberal as well as the white racist. Why? One of Crawford's captors tells him: "I found I disliked some of the white students [on freedom marches] almost as much as I hated the sheriff and his deputies. Some of those kids thought they were doing *me* a favor, for Cri-sakes. I gave up on honkies a long time ago. The good ones are so messed up with racism, they can insult me without knowing it. The bad ones are a bunch of nothin'."[8] Such blanket condemnations, the constant note of militant black rhetoric, make the reader wonder whether it is white racism — irremediably blind and habitual — or black racism — intransigently self-indulgent — which most feeds the fires.

When Nicholas, in Mano's *Horn*, says all whites are enemies, we have a character's perception. But when all whites *are* enemies, as in Sam Greenlee's *The Spook Who Sat by the Door*, we probably have a writer's perception. "Will cause many readers great annoyance — and what more can a writer ask than that?" writes Len Deighton. *Spook* . . . will annoy, I agree, but I can think of many things a writer might prefer to annoying — and one is that his perceptions do not fall too short of reality.

Greenlee's hero, Dan Freeman, sets out to get whitey off the back of his people by training the black ghetto youth in the tactics of guerrilla warfare. For this he needs training himself. White hypocrisy helps him here: Senator Hennington, courting the black vote, pressures the CIA to recruit blacks. Reluctantly the CIA succumbs to Hennington's self-serving benevolence, determined that black trainees need only be a temporary inconvenience. They are all predestined to be washed out. But Freeman's extraordinary competence in meeting the tests of mind and body prevents the

CIA from playing god with his destiny, and he alone completes the program. However, having learned all the CIA can teach, he resigns. When a white-run foundation enlists him as a contact with black youth gangs, Freeman begins the second stage of his plan: shaping the gangs into the elite shock troops of black freedom. Of course, the white foundation liberals are frauds. Their interest in the welfare of black youths goes no further than reducing crime, principally because it threatens whites. When the youths, at Freeman's direction, turn from crime and fake the torpor of their supposed new interest, heroin addiction, the foundation is pleased with Freeman's "success."[9] But Freeman's success also reduces police surveillance in the ghetto, his real motive, as he shapes rabble into a proud, disciplined, and deadly army of Freedom Fighters.

Just as Freeman has no illusions about white benevolence, he also has none about a military victory. His objective is strategic, not tactical. He will "force whitey to choose between the two things he seems to dig more than anything else: fucking with us and playing Big Daddy to the world."[10] Constant black insurrections would surely weaken the country as a world power and it is this fact that will turn Freeman's certain tactical armed defeats into a strategic victory. White America prefers playing Big Daddy and will finally leave black America alone. In the fiction of race war this is a unique objective. No new black republic, no concessions, no compensation. Freeman: "I don't want to change this system, just get it off my back. I'm no fucking integrationist. Integrate into what? Whitey's welcome to his chrome-plated shit pile. I dig being black and the only thing I don't dig about being black is white folks messing with me."[11]

At last the stage is set. Freeman sends his army into action, racking the major cities. Though wounded himself, he thrills to the rifle fire and explosions. He sips a stiff drink but "the pain didn't matter anymore. In fact, for the first time in many years, he hardly hurt at all."[12]

Such is the ending, such are the last words of *Spook . . .* , the most relentlessly bitter and depressing of these six novels. With a mess to end the "messing." With hurting to end the hurt.

I have been irritated by one aspect of this race-war fiction. Book reviewers have not mentioned it, but one book is not six.

Insofar as these books shed light on the intensity of racial feeling they serve the reader. Insofar as they *overstate* its intensity they misserve him. Much of science fiction is an extrapolation of what exists or what is possible. Though it has been prophetic, it is not prophecy but projection. Racism does exist and race war is possible. If a writer projects a *future* in which whites and blacks hate and butcher each other and tells in credible detail how such a catastrophe has come about, he should not be faulted for the gloom of his story. But the novels I have discussed set the racial catastrophe *in the present!* — and there's the rub. They declare that *now* virtually all whites and blacks, that people I know and work with, mistrust, despise, and fear each other, that friendship between them is impossible, their total political or social alienation is inevitable, and whatever appears to contradict this dismal opinion is mere sham. Do the writers of these books think they're "telling it like it is"? I think they're telling it like it isn't. If, on the other hand, they exaggerate in order to shock, only readers impressionable through temperament or ignorance will take the charge. No, "Time: Present" damages the credibility of books that otherwise speak truths worth knowing.

That matter aside — there is energy and muscle in these books; plots that bear down the track and won't let you off; straight-talk confrontations that cut like a rapier, smash like a baseball bat; authentic characters of passion and dimension; and there is always the impatient patient, sick with the American sickness, thrashing uncomfortably, now seen under the white light, now seen under the black; and warning, warning, warning.

The Obsessional Catastrophe

A sizable body of dystopian science fiction deals with catastrophes of obsession. Obeisance to the gods, the search for certainty, the relief from strain, the fear of death, the drive for knowledge, the will to dominate — these and other motives may grow so compelling that an entire society may abandon prudence and contort itself to pursue its obsession. The obsessional catastrophe need not be cataclysmic. More often it involves the perversion of the natural, the suffocation of compassion, the worship of folly, and the triumph of despair. It may manifest itself as a precipitate mania. On the other hand it may presently be so chronic and indwelling as to seem hardly a departure from the common state of things.

The chronic and indwelling obsession of war is the matter of Herman Wouk's *The "Lomokome" Papers*. The narrative, taken from the log of Lt. Butler, U. S. N., the first man on the moon,[1] describes the societies of Lomokome and Lomadine, the moon's two nations. The different ideological systems causing their historic enmity, Hydrogenism and Suggestionism, are to Butler and the reader as senseless as communism and democratic capitalism would seem to moonmen. Yet the slender but unmistakable similarities between Lomokome's Hydrogenism and communism and Lomadine's Suggestionism and democratic capitalism, together with each nation's intolerance of the other's system, subtly satirize the heated parochialism of these contending earthly ideologies. Wouk implies that the national doctrines for which millions of earthmen would (and perhaps *will*) give their lives are but the gibberish of massive delusional systems.

Butler devotes half his log to the moonmen's rules of war, the only point of agreement between Lomokome and Lomadine. He records that after the discovery of the "silicon reaction," the great thinker Ctuzelawis saw that the next war would destroy all moon life. To save his world he wrote the *Book of Ctuzelawis*, in the light of whose wisdom both nations agree to live. The Book, which Butler copies in its entirety, contends that neither treaties, nor disarmament, nor world government would keep peace, for suspicion and deception would foil all precautions against war. The reason:

> War is no evil. We love to say it is, but we do not believe it.
>
> War is necessary to us. . . .
>
> You need war as you need food.
>
> Until you understand this, there is no hope.
>
> If you say, "No, no, but war can be abolished by a world government," I swear to you that the silicon doom will destroy you. . . .
>
> War cannot be abolished.
>
> War *can* be controlled.
>
> I give you a law to control war.
>
> If you will take this law to your hearts, if you will

> make the Law of Reasonable War your law, you will
> avert destruction.[2]

Ctuzelawis proceeds to support these convictions and explain the Law of Reasonable War. "We must have enemies. We cannot be happy without them,"[3] he insists. Following quite the same logic as William James' "The Moral Equivalent of War," the sage declares that war inspires one's finest qualities — love, self-sacrifice, charity, loyalty, and ingenuity. During war nations throb with joy, zest, and productivity. The attending sorrows of war are small compared to its delights, for men never tire of beginning new wars. Even now that the silicon reaction makes it suicidal for all, men yet need not be denied its benefits, for the Law of Reasonable War will control war.

The Law provides for the creation of a College of Judges, which shall decide victor and vanquished according to an impartial and scientific calculus of power. When war is declared the College assigns the combatants a specific number of tasks related to the invention and manufacture of materiel. Upon the war's end the College evaluates the might of opposing war machines, the proficiency of the battle plans, and the valor of the citizenry (the latter being determined by the number volunteering to die on Death Day), and issues its verdict. All the while no battles have been fought, no cities destroyed, and no materiel used except that which was necessary to perform specific tasks. However, so that the economy and practicality of Reasonable War not tempt the nations to war constantly, the strict observance of Death Day "shall render victory painful and defeat disastrous." In their verdict the Judges calculate the number that shall die, and each nation is bound to slay that number of its own. *The Book of Ctuzelawis* counsels:

> Do not shrink at the seeming cruelty of this por-
> tion of the Law. It is the cornerstone of Reasonable
> War.
> And I say to you, is it really cruel?
> A government that declares war now, whether in
> aggression or self-defense, by that act sentences to
> death a certain part of its people. The stroke of the
> pen that signs the war document is a knife stroke,
> butchering thousands. We all know these things.
> Reasonable War brings clarity and order to what
> exists — to what must exist, until men change in

> spirit. It eliminates waste and chance. It reduces a
> foolishly chaotic arrangement, which threatens our
> total destruction, to a sane, safe, workable process.[4]

In the final pages of his log Butler describes the ceremony of
Death Day among the Lomokomians, who have recently lost a
war: "The worst horror of the whole business is that nobody
seems to think it horrible. It's like some huge college commence-
ment, except that instead of shaking hands and getting a diploma
when they come up, the boys get their throats cut." Yet, not the
Death Day spectacle, but the government documents appending
the log imparts the more penetrating shock. These consist of a
foreword by the Chief of Naval Operations, a preface by a scientist
corroborating, with data and argument, the navy's position, and an
excerpt from the report of the pilot, who had discovered Butler's
disabled craft and had recovered his log. (Wouk presents the
entire novel as an official U. S. Navy document: *EXTRA-
GRAVITATIONAL PROPULSION FOR MILITARY PUR-
POSES.*) In the prefatory material officialdom condemns the
disclosures about the substance of Butler's log in a St. Louis
newspaper, which had obtained a smuggled copy of it, as "sensational, fanciful and, in large measure, false" and "a breach of
ethics of American journalism, as well as a blow to the nation's
security." It is explained that the navy had not intended to
acknowledge Butler's landing in view of the army's previous public
report on the atomic bomb, which revealed technical details
thought to be common knowledge to world scientists, but which
possibly disclosed to potentially hostile nations, it was later
feared, information they did not yet possess. The substance of
Butler's log now having become public, the navy is moved to
refute its errors — particularly the "wildest of all, that a race of
beings has been discovered on the moon, hardly different from
humankind, but vastly ahead of us in scientific knowledge and
possessed of incredibly powerful military weapons." The prefatory material strains to discredit every facet of the log, at-
tributing its wondrous narrative to the intoxicating effect of
oxygen starvation and childhood readings about moonmen. The
public is cautioned to bear in mind that "few normal people can
be as persuasive as a man in the grip of a systematic delusion,"[5]
the words of such deranged persons often being more successful

in mirroring reality than the artistry of the professional writer. To further support the official position that Lomokome is the creation of a demented mind, the navy appends an excerpt from the second craft's flight log to Butler's closing lines, lines which *unaccountably* depart from script and cite, in unsteady block letters, the location of the crater leading to Lomokome and a large mushroom-shaped stone near it. But the second pilot has found no sign of these near Butler's craft. In all, Wouk's book as an official *document* supports the navy's case. But Wouk's book as *art* undermines it.

Butler's narrative, as adventure, as satire, and as food for thought, could well stand alone. What, then, is the function of Wouk's addenda? They provide satire in themselves to frame the satire of the narrative. One can see in them the marks of an official conspiracy. Is the unaccountable block printing about the crater and the stone a forgery? or is the report of the second pilot (name withheld for security reasons), denying the existence of these landmarks, an official fabrication? These certainly impugn Butler's sanity. Why should the press disclosures be deemed "a blow to the nation's security"? What significance can be attached to the navy's explanation that its decision to conceal Butler's crash landing on the moon and the recovery of his log stems from the army's injudicious publication of atomic data possibly useful to potential enemies?

The "Lomokome" Papers is a satire within a satire. Butler's narrative satirizes man's obsession with war. But the official addenda satirize *man's obsession to maintain his obsession*. They attempt to screen the fact that the navy, not absolutely convinced of Lomokome's nonexistence, will explore further. If there is such a thing as the deadly silicon reaction, the navy will get it from the Lomokomians. In *any* case and *above all*, the Law of Reasonable War must be shown as the product of a mind unhinged: the pomp and power of military status; the satisfying tension of constant preparedness — the maneuvers, the new-launched cruiser's proud slide to meet the sea, the swift fighters roaring above on guard; the test and thrill of real battle — what would become of these in Reasonable War?

Wouk never settles the matter of Butler's madness — that is, of Lomokome's existence, which is not relevant to his point. But of the cold, respectable madness of admirals, scientists, politicians, and plain people who refuse to think seriously about the realities of human survival, his novel leaves little doubt. In his preface to the 1968 edition Wouk writes that he is "sobered by the speed with which truth is overtaking my grim fiction [of 1949]. But at least we are still here, still seeking a way out, and — as I write this — still with a little time left."[6]

Like The "Lomokome" Papers, Bob Shaw's Ground Zero Man[7] concludes that man's love affair with his weapons will be almost impossible to dissolve. Convinced that the atom bomb will forever hold man hostage, Lucas Hutchman, Shaw's hero, decides to play God and free us. He secretly builds a device which will spontaneously explode all the world's nuclear bombs and then informs the N-powers of the day he will trigger their arsenals. The day comes and the bombs go, but not forever. Before long the nuclear arms race begins again, with bombs designed to foil the Hutchman Trigger. Hutchman realizes the he has only detoured the arms race, and unnecessarily. The restockpiling meant fewer schools and hospitals, less food and medicine. How many babies had he killed, he wonders, by vainly meddling with man's oldest obsession?

Bernard Wolfe's Limbo, Aldous Huxley's Ape and Essence, and John Wyndham's Re-Birth deal with obsessional catastrophes following the catastrophe of nuclear war. In Wolfe's decimated post-war world only two sizable population centers have survived: The Inland Strip and East Union — the American and Russian heartlands. The ideological differences that brought America and Russia to destroy most of the world have become irrelevancies, for Strippers and Unioneers have embraced "Immob" (See Chapter I), a program of psycho-political immobilization and evolutionary revitalization. According to the doctrine of Immob, the organs of grasping and marching, the limbs, being the foci and agents of aggression, must be severed, to be later replaced with atomic-powered, versatile, detachable, but dead prosthetics. Only by such truncation could man "dodge the steamroller" of war. Everywhere, from loud-speakers, on banners, buildings, and bandanas, the slogans of Immob proclaim, "HE WHO HAS ARMS IS ARMED," "WAR IS ON ITS LAST LEGS," "MAKE DISARMAMENT LAST," "TWO LEGS SHORTER, A HEAD

TALLER," "ARMS OR THE MAN," "NO DEMOBILIZATION
WITHOUT IMMOBILIZATION," "DODGE THE STEAM-
ROLLER!"[8] And in the hysteria of pacifism multitudes submit
their arms and legs to the knife.

Status in *Limbo* belongs to the "vol-amps" (voluntary
amputees), who have embraced the "cyber-cyto dialectic — the
dwindling distance between cybernetics and cytoarchitectonics.
The bridging of the gap between the mechanical and the human —
the discovery of the Hyphen between machine and man." Thus
Immob reaches beyond pacifism. It seeks to incorporate the
machine into man. Furthermore, Immob claims that the riddance
of limbs stimulates cortical enlargement, allowing the Immob
brain to surpass the efficiency of its machines. Subsequently
"it will invent still more fantastic machines to outstrip, for the
machine is eternally the brain's dream of fulfillment."[9]

The mania to damp man's grand and dangerous spirit by
mutilating his body, the mania to set in human stumps the
"dream of fulfillment," the obedient machine, Wolfe's hero
brands as "an aching need to recapture the uterine warmth," the
"thirst for oblivion," and the fear of "living with the impossible
anguished tension of humanness."[10] The fear of life on human
terms, which spawned the sacrificial lunacy of Immob, proves in
the end a hypocritical lunacy as well: The nations, yet suspicious
of each other, had been arming all the while and fall again under
the atomic clouds of World War IV.

In Aldous Huxley's *Ape and Essence* one finds another
penitential body of nuclear war survivors, this one in Southern
California. The Californians ascribe their misery to Belial, the
devil, whose pleasure is man's eternal perdition. To honor Belial
the penitents must dishonor themselves and cast joy from their
lives. Except for a brief yearly orgy, the cult forbids the sex act,
since it is the source of Belial's cursed pawns. Most newborn, deformed mutants, are destroyed in the ceremony of Purification.
Woman serves as scapegoat, being, according to the Catechism,
"the vessel of the Unholy Spirit, the source of all deformity,
. . . the enemy of the race,"[11] a creature demeaned, yet the
agent of Him who is worshipped. In brief, the obsessions of
Huxley's cult sustain a compound paradox: man hating himself
for being hated by that which he hates, and yet acknowledging

the deservedness of all the hatred.

While Wolfe's Immob arises from the need to avoid the next war, Huxley's Belial worship arises from the need to explain the last one. The belief in His existence and primacy imposes a logic upon the bewildering follies of history, especially the holocaust brought by the "Thing." The Arch-Vicar of the Belialists cites historical proofs that supernatural malevolence, working through the blunders of man, has gained victory over the Providence that had favored him: Three centuries ago the tide of battle between Belial and the "Other One" suddenly ran to Belial's advantage. The new machines that alleviated toil made mind the "slave of wheels," and the bounty of food from the New World swelled the population. Inevitably came the "New Hunger, the Higher Hunger, the hunger of enormous industrialized proletariats," who are the children of modern conveniences and gadgets — "the hunger that is the cause of total wars and the total wars that are the cause of yet more hunger."[12] The genius of Belial provided the groundwork for the machines and population, the hunger and war; for He had put into men's heads the baneful ideas of Nationalism and Progress.

> "Nationalism — the theory that the state you happen to be subject to is the only true god; . . . and that every conflict over prestige, power or money is a crusade for the Good, the True and the Beautiful."

> "Progress — the theory that you can get something for nothing; the theory that you can gain in one field without paying for your gain in another."[13]

Belial knew that, in their fatuous vanity about technology, men would erode the topsoil, slash down the forests, squander the minerals, and then imagine themselves Conquerors of Nature, when actually, in upsetting Nature's vital balances, they stood to *be conquered* themselves.

The ideas of Nationalism and Progress were too perniciously fiendish for men to come by without Outside Help, the Arch-Vicar maintains. Each is absurd and fatal. Yet men, despite their vaunted rationality, accept them as part of the rightful order of things. Why? Only the fact of diabolic possession can account for this. Hence, hail to the "Lord of the Flies, who is also the Blowfly in every individual heart."[14] If man has nothing else, he shall have the truth and know whose power rules the world.

Almost the entirety of *Ape and Essence* is the screenplay of
William Tallis. Huxley introduces the play with a brief chapter,
"Tallis," narrated by a Hollywood executive, who relates that on
the day "we" assassinated Ghandi ("this man who believed only
in people [but] had got himself involved in the sub-human mass-
madness of nationalism"),[15] he came upon "Ape and Essence." It
had fallen off a truck laden with manuscripts for the incinerator.
Curious as to why fate had chosen some words to be saved from
the flames, he picked up the volume and began to read. A few
days later he drove to a small California town to find the author,
but six weeks before Tallis had died. And that is all. But the
chapter's ironies intensify the impact of the screenplay: Murder
stills a voice of peace on the day fate allows a voice to prophesy
murder. The words warning of fire are consigned to fire. And a
city built on celluloid happy endings and just deserts dreams
on, never dreaming that in the end, for it and for man, just deserts
might wait in hell.

John Wyndham's *Re-Birth* presents yet another colony of
penitential survivors of nuclear devastation. Again the primary
catastrophe sows the seeds of a secondary one — the obsession
to regain God's favor by purging every thought, act, and form
deemed an aberration of holy will and design. In the settlement
of Waknuk, Labrador, several hundred years after the "Tribulation," Wyndham's characters persevere in a manner comparable
to that of Colonial America. Most of humanity has been destroyed
and the survivors are either Norms or Mutants. The Norms control
Waknuk, having driven out the Mutants into the "Fringes," a wild
badland region. Ignorant of the atomic war and the conditions
that caused it, they attribute mutation, which still occurs among
their offspring, cattle, and crops, to the Tribulation, a world
disaster sent by God upon the "Old People" for their wickedness.
Their overriding religious and social passion is to keep their genetic
stock pure by killing off mutants. The *Repentances*, a hallowed
work born of the Tribulation, urges fidelity to the divine pattern,
and although the people still respect the Bible, it is the precepts of
the *Repentances*, with its stringent injunctions about purity and
conformity, that dominate their religious temperament: "ONLY
THE IMAGE OF GOD IS MAN." "KEEP PURE THE STOCK
OF THE LORD." "BLESSED IS THE NORM." "IN PURITY

OUR SALVATION." "THE NORM IS THE WILL OF GOD."
"THE DEVIL IS THE FATHER OF DEVIATION." "WATCH
THOU FOR THE MUTANT."[16]

Wyndham's story, which concerns the perils of nine Norm
youths who discover that they have become telepathic mutants,
not only indicts the sterile conformity of the Norms but even
manages to find a silver lining in the atomic cloud by suggesting
that the holocaust had accorded man a re-birth. In their obsession
with purity the Norms had tried "to strangle the life out of Life,"
had tried to strangle change and growth. The youths, ultimately
rescued by another society of telepaths, are assured by their new
comrades that telepaths, far from being abominations, are a
"superior variant, and we are only just beginning":

> "We are able to think-together and understand one
> another as they never could. . . . We could never
> commit the enormity of imagining that we could
> mint ourselves into equality and identity, like stamp-
> ed coins; . . . we are not dogmatists teaching God
> how he should have ordered the world. The essential
> quality of life is living; the essential quality of living
> is change; change is evolution; and we are part of
> it."[17]

Like so many other dystopians, Wyndham allows a saving remnant
— the seed of hope as a world goes down.

The obsessions dominating the post-nuclear-war societies of
Wolfe, Huxley, and Wyndham — avoiding another catastrophe,
founding a rationale for the past catastrophe, regaining the divine
grace enjoyed before the catastrophe — lie well within the boundaries of the possible. Even if one regards the exotica of their
novels as the *outré* fare of science fiction, he must acknowledge
the likelihood that these obsessions could seem to offer a post-
war society a means of accommodating itself to the exploded
past, precarious present, and darkened future — though *as obsessions* they are catastrophes in themselves. Thus *Limbo, Ape
and Essence,* and *Re-Birth* stress what is too seldom considered:
that after a third World War the human psyche, as well as the torn
earth, will bear scars, incalculable, extravagant, and cruel.

In Clifford D. Simak's *Why Call Them Back From Heaven?*
and Anders Bodelsen's *Freezing Down* the quest for physical
immortality poisons the living present. In Simak's world of 2148

not the bliss of heavenly immortality but the search for *worldly*
resurrection after death has obsessed mankind for over a century.
The instrument of this search, Forever Center, an organization of
scientists, administrators, and financiers, has become the capital
of world power. It is the focus of man's hopes, having made
religion frivolous. It is an economic colossus, having drawn enormous revenues from the faithfully fearful. And it is the real
government, having puppetized formal government into a tool for
reaching its own goals. For generations people have been invest-
ing in its stock so that they may be frozen after death and, once
the secret of immortality has been discovered, revived to resume
life again, wealthy and immortal. Since failure to make the costly
investment in eternal life means eternal death, parsimonious
billions endure a drab, puritanical, rigid existence. That which
made life vibrant two centuries earlier — art, travel, sport,
romance, luxury — has been choked off by the single resolve to
live forever, and only science prospers. Simak reverses the former
roles of science and religion in his dystopia. Now science ushers in
a new dark age. Now science bans books and wrings bogus confes-
sions from heretics at "narco-trials," while the powerless, underground "Holies," representing the spirit of religion, chalk on walls
by night, "WHY CALL THEM BACK FROM HEAVEN?"[18]

Anders Bodelsen's *Freezing Down*[19] deals with the same condition raised by Simak: the flattening of life by the promise of
immortality in the flesh. Advances in cryonic and transplant
technology have virtually freed man from death's inescapable fiat
and replaced it with a hardly less cruel election. In young adult-
hood one must choose between "now-life" and "all-life." Now-
lifers die natural deaths when the first vital organ gives out, but
they live in luxury on the fortune from their eventually trans-
planted organs. All-lifers drudge joylessly for thousands of years
to pay their organ donors and surgeons. One thing only matters —
to exact the most from his hard choice. For some, frantic self-
stuffing with pleasure before their bodies lie on the chopping
block. For others, the greedy unraveling of heavy days "as though
to breathe were life." Again, a scientific advance and the compulsion to exploit it strips living of its infinite dimensions.

Obsessive, self-defeating humanitarianism furnishes the
satirist with a shooting gallery of targets. Evelyn Waugh's "Love

Among the Ruins"[20] and Damon Knight's "The Country of the Kind" riddle the softer penology with controlled, withering derision. Waugh's protagonist, Miles Plastic, a psychopathic arsonist, is being discharged as cured from Mountjoy Castle. Even though he had not received the finer accommodations that Mountjoy reserved for murderers and sexual offenders, he knew he would miss its palatial furnishings, its flowered walks, and his solicitous attendants. The New Law maintained that since no one could be held responsible for his acts, the "crimes" of old were merely the anti-social doings of the "martyrs of maladjustment." Having adjusted Plastic the state assigns him to a job in the Department of Euthanasia, where his duties are to channel the push of impatient, life-weary citizens when the department's doors opened and keep the clients orderly until their turn in the cyanide chamber. A disappointing love affair ignites his not-quite-extinguished "anti-sociality," and Plastic incinerates his old alma mater, Mountjoy, and most of its patients. His deed undiscovered, Plastic is sent by the Minister of Welfare on a lecture tour to defend the new penology and to personify its success.

Waugh's mordant satire perhaps inspired Damon Knight's "The Country of the Kind."[21] (1955) Knight's psychopathic narrator is condemned to live in a "humane, permissive" society in which he may freely go about smashing, annoying, intruding, and threatening. But, he may not be touched, spoken to, or acknowledged willingly; he has been programmed to get violently sick before he commits personal violence; he exudes a strongly offensive odor. In effect, he is in permanent social solitary confinement. Obviously, neither Knight's country nor Waugh's is "of the kind." Not kind to miscreants, not kind to itself.

On the most literal level these stories of Waugh and Knight may be considered satires on humanitarianism gone silly. Seen more broadly they appear as indictments of an increasingly fashionable faintheartedness disguising itself as magnanimity or practical morality. The dissolving ethical absolutes of our time encourage a breakdown of personal and social discipline which can not be faced for what it is — a breakdown — but must be transvalued into new dogmas, which are "modern," "scientific," "liberal," "people oriented." However, a yet more comprehensive view of these stories takes one beyond the satire and social criticism and into the writers' intuitive fear that something, not necessarily *that* thing of the story, but *something* unexpected, unprecedented, and massively perverse looms not too distantly ahead. It will not be something unwittingly or halfwittedly blundered into, like war or an ecological disaster. Rather, something sought, heralded, and embraced and so compelling and deviant as to all but repeal the past. Some writers suggest its coming. Others give it shape.

Robert Silverberg's novella, *How It Was When the Past Went Away*, closes with an ominous postscript. After San Francisco recovers from the chaos caused by an amnesia-inducing drug in the water supply, one character founds the Church of Oblivion in a public park. Passing bowls of drugging water among his followers, he cries out to onlookers, "Brothers and sisters . . . the joy, the sweetness of forgetting . . . come up here with us, take communion with us . . . oblivion . . . redemption . . . even for the most wicked . . . forget . . . forget. . . . " Mueller, another character, watching this, "felt a chill. He suspected that what had been born in this park during this week would endure, somehow . . . and it seemed to him that something new and frightening had been loosed upon the land." The cult will spread the drug, Mueller fears, and their appeal to unreason and their offer of psychological emancipation will make them unstoppable. And "after a while, no one will *want* to stop them. . . . We'll give up all the griefs we carry around, and we'll give up everything else, identity, soul, self, mind. We will drink sweet oblivion. Mueller shivered."[22]

Three years later, Silverberg gives shape to a "something new and frightening" in *The World Inside*.[23] Twenty-fourth century — world population seventy-five billion and going up. Crisis? Not with the vertical "urbmon" (urban monad). Each thousand-floor urbmon holds almost a million people, with the eventual overflow going to new urbmons in the constellation, and there are many constellations. Unlike the hives in Asimov's *The Caves of Steel*, Blish and Knight's *A Torrent of Faces*, and other "world machine" novels, the world of urbmons is not collapsing. Its cry is not "Make room!" but "Make babies!"

The single religious tenet of *Homo urbmonensis* is to please God by reproducing. People marry in their early teens and begin

to pour out babies, pleasing God and urbmon; and to insure the
steady flow the social rule requires that everyone be sexually accessible to everyone else. Silverberg offers no practical reason for
the breeding mania. Parents do not show their children much
affection, and their concept of God embraces nothing more subtle
than His being a Being who wants them to have babies. Silverberg
seems to be saying what dystopian fiction says so constantly: that
if man has the capacity to do something preposterous but not
immediately or obviously hurtful to him, he will likely exploit
that capacity.

While most urbmonites adapt happily to the generally permissive "world inside," some can not bear it and its few prohibitions. The greatest crime is opposition to its baby-making
obsession; another — going outside the urbmon to experience
primitive horizontal living; another — feeling, like some of
Huxley's brave-new-worlders, unfulfilled. Only "flippos" would
commit such crimes, and the punishment for "going flippo" is to
be summarily thrown "down the chute." One of Silverberg's major
characters, Jason the historian, theorizes that urbmon life could
only have evolved by selective breeding: Centuries of tossing
flippos down the chute had stripped the race of the gene pool
which had borne men with the urge for adventure, power, and
knowledge, the hunger for land and property, and the qualities
that make for nonconformity. *Homo urbmonensis* was virtually
a new race.

The ramifications of Silverberg's fiction should not be over-
looked. True, we know that society's needs can alter the genetic
constitution of the race, but such changes have been insignificant
in recorded history. Silverberg speculates that a profound extremity may effect significant changes, a possibility that Charles L.
Fontenay's fresh and controversial *Epistle to the Babylonians*
strongly supports. Fontenay maintains that *Homo sapiens* consists
of two *genetic* types, *Homo socialis* and *Homo individualis*. Traits
of sociality dominate in the former, while traits of individualism
dominate in the latter. *Homo individualis* is the mutant, creative
minority inclined to initiate and advance higher levels of thought
and activity, which *Homo socialis* adopts and utilizes. A society
with a high concentration of *Homo individualis* genes will be an
advancing one, and a society with a low concentration will be

stagnant or decaying. Civilization therefore is not a creation of general humanity but rather of the creative minority.

However, Fontenay continues, *Homo individualis* often sets in motion a chain of events which frustrates his energies and reduces his representation in the gene pool. Firstly, when a society develops beyond a certain point, *Homo socialis* is unable to deal with problems resulting from creativity, and *Homo individualis* finds himself in an inhospitable world. The establishment of libertarian democracy leads, in most cases, to egalitarian democracy (*e.g.,* ancient Greece and modern U. S.), which stifles the creative minority. Secondly, the improved physical environment forged by creative genes increases urbanization, which, if rampant, requires excessive social adaptation and a "protectionism" allowing "survival without the individual responsibility required under more stringent conditions." Obviously these situations favor *Homo socialis*. Yet, asserts Fontenay, the trait that has led man from the jungle to civilization is not his social trait but "the intangible conviction of the individual that he is born free, that he has the inherent right to converse one-to-one with the universe without paying undue tribute to the opinions of his society." The denial of this "in the interest of better social adjustment, however well intentioned, has not led to social perfection, but to regression."[24] Fontenay fears that the forces adverse to *Homo individualis* today may seriously diminish his representation in the human gene pool — to the detriment or collapse of our civilization. And if his thesis is valid, that "something new and frightening," which has become such a dominant motif in science fiction, might be diminished man, half man, should some future obsession or the natural course of events thrust *Homo individualis* "down the chute."

Gore Vidal, in *Messiah*, portrays a dystopia in which the oblivion of death becomes the passion and religion of the western world. A first-person narrative by Eugene Luther, now an ailing old man in his last days, who has been hiding in Egypt from the assassin's bullet for twenty years, the novel is a memoir of the early history of the Cavite Movement in whose founding Luther was instrumental.

He recalls his involvement in the movement. One evening in a mortuary he and a friend, Iris Mortimer, with a small group of people listened to a talk by John Cave, a young man unlettered and unpretentious yet possessing some almost hypnotic power to move, to captivate an audience. Though left, with the others, electrified, chilled, and weak, he later asks Iris, "What *did* he say?" Her answer: "That it is good to die." Later other hands were to fashion a moral and ethical system upon the foundation of Cave's single vision. But that one vision, repeated and embellished in the quiet conviction of Cave's simple rhetoric and strangely compelling presence, draws converts by the hundreds of millions to the Cavite Movement and its doctrine, "Cavesword," which echoes Lucretius:

> Death is nothing; literally no thing; and since, demonstrably, absence of things is a good; death which is no thing is good.

> Death is neither hard nor bad. Only the dying hurts.

> It was the dead man who was right, who was part of the whole. . . . The living were the sufferers from whom, temporarily, the beautiful darkness of non-being had been withdrawn.

> "Death brings us back to the whole. . . . How dark, how fine the grave must be! Only sleep and an end of days, an end of fear. The end of fear in the grave as the 'I' goes back to nothing. . . . Neither revenge nor reward, only the not-knowing in the grave which is the same for all."[25]

From the doctrine of death, "Cavite, Inc." is born. Among its directors: Iris Mortimer, fascinated by Cave and in love with him; Paul Himmell, a public-relations expert, sensing something big, pressing toward the center of power to increase his own; Ivan Stokharin, a psychologist, eager to establish his own scientific hegemony in the organization; Clarissa Lessing, a gay, witty, sophisticated mystic, wanting change because it is the law of life, believing Cave's doctrine wrong, but a *new* wrong and thus better than the old; and Eugene Luther. Luther joins out of curiosity and idealism. He sees Cave's message freeing man from fear of death; erasing the false hope of personal immortality; exposing the absurdity of the personal God, which has been the source of religious factionalism, superstition, cruel laws, and social disorganization; allowing the fusion of the ideas of Zoroaster, Plato, Christ — "the best ideas of the best men" — to form an

eclectic morality for a richer life. Embracing Cave's doctrine in
a spirited conversation, he proclaims:

> "Yes, Cave, life will be wonderful when men no
> longer fear dying. When the last superstitions are
> thrown out and we meet death with the same equa-
> nimity that we have met life. No longer will children's
> minds be twisted by evil gods whose fantastic origin
> is in those barbaric tribes who feared death and
> lightning, who feared life. That's it: life is the villain
> to those who preach reward in death, through grace
> and eternal bliss, or through dark revenge. . . . Life
> is all while death is only the irrelevant shadow at the
> end, the counterpart to that instant before the seed
> lives."[26]

Too late, however, did he realize that in their apparent concord
lay a vital conflict. For each time Luther spoke in terms of life,
Cave replied in terms of death.

With the machinery for marketing John Cave established,
Cavite, Inc. advances upon Western civilization like an invading
army. Himmell masterminds promotional and financial matters.
Iris directs the recruitment and training of Cavesword proselyt-
izers. Stokharin organizes counseling centers for the faithful,
uniting psychology with Cavesword. Luther serves as the Cavite
publicist, writing *An Introduction to John Cave*, editing *The
Cavite Journal*, and synthesizing his talks with Cave into *Dia-
logues*, treating of Cave's views on politics, marriage, morals, and
other issues. The smoothly functioning organization and especially
Cave's hypnotically persuasive T. V. appearances capture America,
submerging Christianity and dominating government. But the
success of the Cavites infects the leaders with the vices that come
with power. Cave, who at first wanted nothing but to voice his
single word, is drawn into affairs in which he has little interest
and knowledge. Though initially seeing no ideological conflict
between his truth and the Christian establishment, the growing
opposition of the churches provokes his first aggressive strike:
"There's no need for churches; . . . their power derives from
superstition and bloody deeds." On a national telecast he states,
"Our quarrel is not with Christ but with his keepers."[27] The push
of Himmell and Stokharin heads the movement towards dogma,
hierarchization, and cynical and lucrative commercialism. Iris'

love for Cave turns to a cold love for power as she waits for the
messiah's crown to fall to her hands. Luther performs his role,
fascinated by the tide of change, yet aware of the corrosive moral
deterioration of the Cavite juggernaut. Indeed, the action of the
novel is a chronicle of a spiritually exhausted civilization collapsing before a dupery that has nothing to sell but death and of a
leadership growing progressively corrupt and reckless with the
reins of power. Only Iris survives the fratricidal struggle for those
reins, holding them at last, while Cave must answer to the inexorable logic of his vision: "Cavesway."

It naturally follows that suicide would be the final sacrament
of the Cavite faithful. Cavesword openly accepts suicide in its
doctrine, Cavesway. But unorganized suicide is disruptive. Now
Cavesway will be systematized under the aegis of the Corporation,
which will provide, for those "taking the better way," comfortable
rooms for receiving last visits, legal assistance, and the means to
dignified, responsible death. "The deserving, those whose lives
have been devoted and orderly, may come to us and receive the
gift." Here finally, Luther breaks with Cave: "The meaning of
live, Cave, is more life, not death. . . . You've been able to dispel
our fear of the common adversary; that was your great work in
the world. Now you want to go further, to make love to this
enemy we no longer fear, to mate with death, and it is here that
you, all of you, become enemies of life." The appeal is fruitless
and Cavesway dooms Cave himself when the others demand that
the messiah proceed to his own golgotha. He consents, but when
he insists on a delay and seclusion, the heirs apparent suspect he
plans an escape; and he dies under Stokharin's gun. Whispered to
Iris are his last words: "Gene [Luther] was right."[28]

In the power struggle that follows Luther tries unsuccessfully
to rally an anti-Cavesway minority and then flees to Egypt, Stokharin fades, Himmell takes Cavesway in defeat, while Iris, supporting Cavesway, prevails as high priestess of the establishment,
falsifying Cave's life and death, sending the missionaries of Cavesway, now the heart of Cavite doctrine, across the oceans to other
continents. Two Cavite "Communicators," years later, meet
Luther in Egypt. His remaining hours are few and painful, but he
will not take the kindly offered, peppermint-flavored, pleasantly
hallucinogenic Cavesway pill. No, Anubis must wait and even in

his arms the old man shall resist. In the closing words of the memoir, at once heroic and pathetic, Luther sounds his defiance and revelation: "For I know now that life, *my* life, was more valuable than I knew, more significant and virtuous than the other's was in her bleak victory. . . . I was he whom the world awaited. I was that figure, that messiah whose work might have been the world's delight and liberation."[29]

As a fictional statement of the possible, Simak's dystopia neither has nor needs justification. Most people wish to preserve the vitality and life of their bodies. But if Vidal's story is to reach beyond a mere death-wish fantasy, it too must establish a rationale of the possible. And this it does in the opening three brilliantly narrated chapters describing the malaise of the mid-twentieth century. Blending pessimism and satire, Vidal presents a civilization adrift in a sea of fatuousness and fear, desperate for reassurance and relief. The years following the Second World War, the narrative relates, were marked by frightening marvels and omens. The "luminous crockery" that raced across the sky, Washington explained as atmospheric reflections or tricks-of-eye, implying the susceptibility of the citizenry to "delusions and mass hysteria," abberations not to be censured severely since the tenure of the government "was based, more or less solidly, on the franchise of those same hysterics and irresponsibles." The inevitability of space exploration raised the disquieting possibility that our own planet might be invaded by hostile neighbors. "Sightings" of strange creatures — in West Virginia one ten feet tall, green, and odoriferous — were almost daily news in the press. The disciples of Marx ("an ill-tempered social philosopher of the nineteenth century") and Freud ("an energetic, unreasonably confident mental therapist, a product of that century's decline"), confronted by the portents of the times, strove to outdo each other in quackery. The intellectuals, "a small militantly undistinguished minortity," followed in the spirit of Rousseau ("that rhetorical eighteenth-century Swiss whose romantic and mystical love for humanity was magically achieved through a somewhat obsessive preoccupation with himself").[30]

> Men of letters lugubriously described their own deviations (usually political or sexual, seldom aesthetic), while painters worked devotedly at depicting unique

inner worlds which were not accessible to others
except in a state of purest empathy hardly to be
achieved without a little fakery in a selfish world. It
was, finally, the accepted criterion that art's single
function was the fullest expression of a private
vision.[31]

At cocktail parties the intellectuals relieved their guilt feelings by
confessing to each other their nasty ways and foul fantasies, a
somewhat useful therapy; yet "once promiscuously shared, vice
becomes ordinary, no more troublesome than obvious dentures."
Romanticists, uncomfortable with social change and technology,
rejecting both reason and science to reveal the universal mysteries
and dispel their private boredom, turned to personal emotion to
sense meanings otherwise elusive. The granite truths of the past
wore away to sand. Promising political and social experiments
disappointed or failed. The disillusioned searched for some
absolute, wanting "above all else, to *feel*, to know without reasoning." And "since reason had been declared insufficient, only a
mystic could provide the answer, only he could mark the boundaries of life with a final authority, inscrutably revealed. It was
perfectly clear. All that was lacking was the man."[32]

The above summary captures little more than the trajectory
of Vidal's persiflage as he recounts, always with enough serious-
ness for his morbid story, the trials and lunacies of a dispirited
age. Though his gambol may not quite prepare one for the moment when Cave, seated beside a coffin in a mortuary, stuns all
with his dust-hole vision, Vidal's picture of the times does place
the subsequent action in the realm of the possible. Writer-critic
Damon Knight affirms that *Messiah* "has a quality so uniformly
absent from science fiction novels that it comes here as a shock:
conviction, the feeling that the story is in some deep sense true.
This means that Vidal's plot is almost beyond criticism — the story
does not impress you as plot, but as something that happened."[33]

I believe Vidal's *Messiah* to be a superb achievement. Vidal
has related what is all too rare in science fiction, the *genesis* of a
dystopian state. He has presented an incredible obsession as more
than an extrapolation of the possible or an allegory of modern
spiritual bankruptcy. He has infused it with a pulse, a presence,
and made it, in a sense, a character: which is to say, the *spell* of

the novel carries it closer to realistic fiction than science fiction.

In John Wyndham's haunting novella, *Consider Her Ways*, Jane Waterleigh, a young widow, finds herself in a home for fat, cheerful mothers, who address her as Mother Orchis and tell her that she has just given birth to her third set of quadruplets. Her surroundings and her own monstrously blubbered body are completely alien to her. After insisting on an explanation for this madhouse situation, she is eventually brought to an old historian, Laura, who explains that all men had succumbed to a virus bred by an obscure biochemist, Perrigan, to exterminate the brown rat. Some undetermined but fortunate accident had occurred. Men quickly perished, and women, immune, found themselves at last emancipated from bondage.

Since a rare experimental drug had restored Jane's memory of the distant past but obliterated the recent past, Laura proceeds to define and defend the unisexual society: Before their liberation, women, deluded by romantic nonsense, had been little more than sexual playthings. They believed that "to be owned by some man and set down in a little brick box to buy all the things that the manufacturers wanted them to buy would be the highest form of bliss that life could offer."[34] But seldom were their romantic expectations realized, and the "little brick box" proved to be a most uneconomic and wastefully consuming unit and a stifler of interests, talents, and ambitions. The virus had ended the fraud, and the male, the "painful and costly parasite," whose only useful function had been to impregnate, was extinct, his unruly vitality replaced by stability, his procreative function replaced by parthenogenesis. As for the social structure of the new world of their own, the liberated women drew upon the Biblical prescript, "Go to the ant, thou sluggard; consider her ways." To insure a smoothly functioning society, the ant-nest became their model, and each woman was bred to a special class: the Doctorate for ruling; the Mothers for bearing; the Servitors for semi-skilled jobs; the Workers for heavy labor.

Jane, appalled by the unisexual ant world described to her, defends the old world in earnest and conventionally romantic terms. But to the historian her romantic panegyrics are only the primitively animalistic cant of faulty conditioning. Love, she had previously explained, does not make the world go round. What

does? "It is the will to power. We have that as babies; we have it
still in old age. It occurs in men and women alike. It is more
fundamental, and more desirable, than sex." Even if the criminally
subversive Reactionists were right and the old bisexual system
could be restored, "you can scarcely expect us to surrender our
freedom, to connive at our own re-subjection by calling our op-
pressors into existence again."[35]

But it had been a hallucination − all of it − that Jane had
experienced after taking a drug in a medical experiment: the
elephantine Mothers, the historian, the plague, the unisexual ant-
nest − all trenchantly vivid fictions. Except Perrigan. He existed,
an obscure biochemist developing a virus to exterminate the
brown rat. Convinced that her vision had been prophetic (since
she could hardly have heard of the scientist and his work), she
tries to persuade Perrigan to abandon his work − fails − kills him
and burns his laboratory. As Wyndham's story closes, Jane's
solicitor and the doctor who had administered the drug discuss her
impending prosecution. A plea of temporary insanity will save
her, of course, they agree. Yet the solicitor confesses himself
foolish enough to find a few points "slightly disturbing": There
was no way that his client could have known of Perrigan. Secondly, the scientist's son, having saved some specimens of the virus
from the fire, has resolved that his father's work shall not be
wasted. "It does disturb me a little," he repeats, "to find that he,
also, happens to be . . . a biochemist; and that, very naturally, his
name, too, is Perrigan. . . . "[36]

Wyndham's plot transcends mere cleverness in an age of
Perrigans. Conrad's whimsy will lose its sparkle in the Age of
Famines. And where shall the yet unborn read Roshwald − in
the sunlight or in Level 8?

I am aware, reviewing the matter treated in this chapter, of
a strange dichotomy in my judgment. The words *unnecessary* and
preventable have constantly entered my thoughts. "It *was*, it *is* so
preventable" − and my uncertainty about the tense of my belief
betrays my uncertainty about its truth. If "it *was* preventable"
becomes the idiom with which one expresses the conjectural,
has he not unconsciously conceded that "it might be *un*preventable"? I confess a heavy pessimism about man's fate, not only
in the light of − in the gloom of − this chapter but of the entire

study. The great thematic aorta through which anti-utopian fiction flows is the postulate that this century is the hinge of history, that now is the time: Now is the time for all bad men, for all hubristically clever men, for all blind men, for all reckless men to cause the defilement of their species. And so many are the means. A "motion" seems to have caught the world, drawing it to some cruel penalty. Is it preventable? What meanings lie in the lines from Eliot's "The Hollow Men": "This is the way the world ends / Not with a bang but a whimper"? Is it — catastrophe, dystopia — preventable? If it *is* preventable and it is not prevented, even the bang is a whimper.

The preventable is not prevented in the last work of this study, Wyndham's *Consider Her Ways*, the quintessence of dystopian fiction, incorporating its most important motifs: the omen of catastrophe dismissed; tinkering, swollen-headed science damaging irreparably; the will to power subsuming the nobler passions; the truncation of the human spirit and potential rationalized as an advance toward freedom, order, and efficiency; humanity fusing itself into the automatic, untroubled machine, here the ant-machine; the traditions and values of the past lost; the pattern of the future unalterably set. And for what? The extermination of the brown rat.

I recall this study's first work of fiction, William Golding's *Envoy Extraordinary*. I hear again the Roman Emperor's words to the inventor of the steam engine, gunpowder, and the printing press: "Oh, you natural philosophers! Are there many of you, I wonder? Your single-minded and devoted selfishness, your royal preoccupation with the only thing that can interest you, could go near to wiping life off the earth as I wipe the bloom from this grape." And I wonder, with others, what "only thing" might wipe the bloom from this earth.

CONCLUSION

"A country that never existed has been completely destroy-ed. . . . Utopia is no more. Its disappearance is portentous enough, but an even more sinister phenomenon has been its replacement with a new kind of imaginative society which, instead of evolving the possibilities of earthly bliss, serves only as a lens through which every barbarity of our age is magnified."[1] Karl Meyer, whose observation I quote, calls the new society "Futopia" (future and futile); Lewis Mumford calls it "Cacotopia"; V. L. Parrington, "Dystopia"; Erich Fromm, "negative utopia"; many simply, "anti-utopia." But call it what one may, the nightmare world of the future is one of the facts of modern fiction. Anti-utopian science fiction, in a span of some forty years, has es-tablished itself as a literary genre.

The suddenness of its establishment, the speed of its growth, and the attraction it holds for writers of note and talent has made dystopian science fiction one of the literary phenomena of the century. That such a genre should emerge so soon after Bellamy's *Looking Backward* (1888) and the dozens of stories it inspired, so soon after Wells's *A Modern Utopia* (1905), *The World Set Free* (1914), and *Men Like Gods* (1923) is solidly founded in the events of history. Many survived the "war to end wars" (Wells's phrase) only to be sentenced to await the war to end men. Tech-nology drains the planet to offer luxury, speed, and convenience,

199

yet leaves its beneficiaries poorer and unfulfilled. The art of government moves ever closer to efficiently serving government and regimenting people. Science advances from discovery to discovery in probing the mystery of the psyche, but not swiftly enough to keep pace with those losing their minds. And in the laboratories and chancelleries of the world evolve the formulas, the instruments, the programs, and the will, one fears, to change man into something other than man. H. G. Wells, once this century's most ardent champion of the scientific utopia, eventually recognized that "these new powers, inventions, contrivances and methods are not the unqualified enrichment of normal life that we had expected. They are hurting, injuring and frustrating us increasingly. . . . We are only beginning to realize that the cornucopia of innovation may perhaps prove far more dangerous than benevolent." Later, in *Mind at the End of Its Tether* (1946), he bitterly declared, "The end of everything we call life is close at hand and cannot be evaded." Those words, written in Wells's last year of life, move one deeply with their personal melancholy and despair for humankind, for they issue from a man who earlier had written, "I saw a limitless universe throughout which the stars and nebulae were scattering like dust, and I saw life ascending, as it seemed, from nothingness toward the stars."

The spectacular achievements of science have begotten an age of anxiety about man's survival, man's integrity and wholeness, and man's compatibility with the natural universe. Dead is the dream of the scientific utopia. Few now believe that *faster, bigger, stronger, surer, more efficient, more intricate,* and *more amazing* will cure the spiritual malaise of the aging twentieth century. Still how hard the dream dies: When Americans landed on the moon in 1969, the President expressed the hope that the technological feat would instill in all men a sense of brotherhood and faith in man's capacity to transcend his limitations and animosities and prosper. But the success of mechanism has not induced these felicities. It would appear that a better world will not evolve from any number of blastings off, pluggings in, switchings on, and startings up.

Anti-utopian science fiction springs from man's disappointment in the promise of a scientific utopia and, most intensively, from his fear that "progress" will carry him into some absurd or hellish nightmare world in which the power of technique, directed by cold intellect, to debase value will be supreme. The dystopias depicted in such fiction often reflect both man's subconscious and conscious apprehensions regarding threats to his integrity and well-being, threats made all the more possible by the awesome physical and social instruments increasingly dominating his life.

However, "pure" anti-utopian fiction not only describes abhorrent and warped societies but ascribes their dystopian features to their utopian programs. Such societies usually achieve their specific utopian goals but at the cost of a dehumanized citizenry or a perverted natural order, or both. The word *anti-utopian* applied to fiction of this sort does not merely describe the imagined society; it also indicates the conviction of the writer: *He is* an anti-utopian. He believes that utopian success in one area opens a Pandora's box of dystopian reactions. He believes that even if a perfect world could be realized, such perfection would erode the moral qualities which make man man: creativity, courage, humility, repentance, righteous anger, charity, perseverance . . . for these root only in the imperfect man in the imperfect world. A perfect world of "unman" is not utopia. To the anti-utopian the more utopia becomes itself, the more it becomes its opposite. He senses that the organism comprising man, society, and nature is not infinitely plastic but fragile and is now exposed to severe and irreparable damage. He is more impressed by the organism's intractability than by man's ingenuity. And he believes that should the god of progress do battle with the god of intractability, the latter shall have the victory, even though man may not survive to know it.

Anti-utopian science fiction, more than any other literary genre, reflects the monumental problems of our age. Its dystopias will reveal to posterity, more incisively than historical texts, the crisis of confidence man now faces. It is the prophetic form of our times. If, as Oscar Wilde wrote, "a map of the world that does not include Utopia is not worth even glancing at, for it leaves out the one country at which Humanity is always landing," I submit that one that does not include Dystopia is dangerously misleading. In these times of precarious balances and doomsday technology, Dystopia is the more likely landing place. This study's maps of new hells should make one pause before the treacherous terrain and resolve which paths must *not* be taken, what deeds must *not* be done.

NOTES

CHAPTER I
THE THREAT OF SCIENCE

I. The Hostility to Science

[1] "Utopias You Wouldn't Like," *Harper's*, CCX (April 1955), 87.

[2] Richard E. Sullivan, "The End of the 'Long Run,' " *The Centennial Review of Arts and Sciences*, IV (Summer 1960), 391-392.

[3] Sullivan, pp. 392, 403.

[4] William Golding, *Envoy Extraordinary*, in *Sometime Never* (New York, 1957), pp. 48-49, 59, 55.

[5] Aldous Huxley, *Ape and Essence* (New York, 1948), p. 53.

[6] D. G. Compton, *The Steel Crocodile* (New York, 1970), p. 13.

[7] Here, as in other dystopias, the scientific elite has subtly unsurped the power of the politicians. Since almost all research is funded by government, Colindale, in its advisory capacity, determines what shall or shall not be discovered or undertaken. Strictly speaking, however, the real ruler is the Bohm 504. For an in-depth study of the enormous power scientists now wield in advising government see Ralph E. Lapp, *The New Priesthood: The Scientific Elite and the Uses of Power* (New York, 1965).

[8] Compton, pp. 243, 251, 252.

[9] Compton, p. 128.

[10] C. S. Lewis, *The Abolition of Man* (New York, 1965); *Mere Christianity* (New York, 1952); *The Screwtape Letters* (New York, 1968).

[11] C. S. Lewis, *Out of the Silent Planet* (New York, 1965), p. 153.

[12] *Out of the Silent Planet*, pp. 135, 136.

[13] *Out of the Silent Planet*, p. 138.

[14] *Out of the Silent Planet*, p. 154.

[15] C. S. Lewis, *Perelandra* (New York, 1965), pp. 81-82.

[16] *Perelandra*, pp. 115, 118.

[17] "In battle it is not syllogisms that will keep the reluctant nerves and muscles to their post in the third hour of the bombardment. The crudest sentimentalism . . . about a flag or a country or a regiment will be of more use. . . . The Chest—Magnanimity—Sentiment—these are the indispensible liaison officers between cerebral man and visceral man. It may even be said that it is by this middle element that man is man," (New York, 1965), p. 34.

[18] C. S. Lewis, *The Abolition of Man* (New York, 1965), pp. 43-44, 53.

[19] C. S. Lewis, *That Hideous Strength* (New York, 1965), pp. 37-38.

[20] *That Hideous Strength*, pp. 40-41.

[21] *That Hideous Strength*, pp. 42, 172-173.

[22] *That Hideous Strength*, p. 42.

[23] *That Hideous Strength*, pp. 178, 179.

[24] *That Hideous Strength*, pp. 203-204.

II. Man Versus Machine

[1] "The plain message physical science has for the world at large is this, that were our political and social and moral devices only as well contrived to their ends as a linotype machine, an aseptic operating plant, or an electric tram-car, there need now at the present moment be no appreciable toil in the world, and only the smallest fraction of the pain, the fear, and the anxiety that now makes human life so doubtful in its value. There is more than enough for everyone alive. Science stands, a too competent servant, behind her wrangling underbred masters, holding out resources, devices, and remedies they are too stupid to use." H. G. Wells, *A Modern Utopia* (Lincoln, Neb., 1967), p. 102.

[2] "The fundamental objection to Mr. Wells's god of progress is that it is too limited; it takes no cognisance of the human soul or the human mind, but only of mathematical ability and manual skill. Its idea of greatness is merely one of size, not one of quality. A journey to the moon, and not something like the composition of Beethoven's A minor quartet, is treated as the greatest achievement possible to man." Michael Roberts, "Mr. Wells' Sombre World," *The Spectator*, CLVII (December 11, 1936), p. 1033.

[3] Kurt Vonnegut, Jr., *Player Piano* (New York, 1966), p. 28.

[4] Vonnegut, pp. 260-261.

[5] Vonnegut, pp. 104, 277, 52.

[6] Frederik Pohl, *The Midas Plague*, in Pohl, *The Case Against Tomorrow* (New York, 1957), p. 5.

[7] Theodore Tyler, *The Man Whose Name Wouldn't Fit* (Garden City, N. Y., 1968), p. 44.

[8] Gordon R. Dickson, "Computers Don't Argue," in Damon Knight, ed., *Nebula Award Stories: 1965* (Garden City, N. Y., 1966), pp. 201-202.

[9] Arthur T. Hadley, *The Joy Wagon* (New York, 1958).

[10] Martin Caiden, *The God Machine* (New York, 1968), p. 223.

[11] Man's rescue from computer dominance leaves one issue unresolved. 79 had predicted the 99 percent probability of man's extinction in a thermonuclear war by 1982 and the 100 percent certainty of avoiding it if nuclear weapons were removed from human control. With 79 blasted what has man been saved for? Caiden totally ignores this question, unfortunately.

[12] Burt Cole, *The Funco File* (Garden City, N. Y., 1969), pp. 268, 270.

[13] Cole, p. 271.

[14] Cole, p. 282.

[15] H. G. Wells, *The Time Machine*, in E. F. Bleiler, ed., *Three Prophetic Novels of H. G. Wells* (New York, 1960), pp. 287, 288, 289.

[16] E. M. Forster, "The Machine Stops," in *Collected Short Stories of E. M. Forster* (London, 1965), pp. 134, 140-141.

[17] Quoted in Mark R. Hillegas, *The Future as Nightmare: H. G. Wells and the Anti-Utopians* (New York, 1967), p. 86. Forster was referring to Wells's *A Modern Utopia.*

[18] Paul W. Fairman, *I, The Machine* (New York, 1968), p. 14.

[19] Fairman, pp. 97-98.

[20] Fairman, p. 204.

[21] Antony Alban, *Catharsis Central* (New York, 1969), pp. 148-149.

[22] Edmund Cooper, *Deadly Image* (New York, 1958), p. 164.

[23] Jack Williamson, "With Folded Hands," in Sam Moskowitz, ed., *Modern Masterpieces of Science Fiction* (Cleveland, 1965), p. 126 *et passim*.

[24] Frederik Pohl and Cyril M. Kornbluth, *Search the Sky* (New York, 1954), pp. 163, 165.

[25] Isaac Asimov, *The Caves of Steel* (Garden City, N. Y., 1954), p. 113.

[26] Robert Sheckley, *The Status Civilization* (New York, 1968), p. 147.

[27] Arthur Koestler, *The Ghost in the Machine* (New York, 1968), pp. 267, 332-333.

[28] Koestler, p. 336.

[29] Koestler, pp. 338-339.

[30] John Brunner, *Stand on Zanzibar* (Garden City, N. Y., 1968), p. 502.

[31] Philip K. Dick, "The Defenders," in Roger Elwood, ed., *Invasion of the Robots* (New York, 1965).

[32] Jack Williamson, *The Humanoids*, (New York, 1948), p. 82.

[33] Williamson, pp. 226-227, 229.

[34] Williamson, p. 239.

[35] The Three Laws of Robotics: 1. A robot may not injure a human being, or, through inaction, allow a human being to come to harm. 2. A robot must obey the orders given it by human beings except where such orders would conflict with the First Law. 3. A robot must protect its own existence as long as such protection does not conflict with the First or Second Law. (Asimov)

[36] Isaac Asimov, "Evidence," in Asimov, *I, Robot* (Garden City, N. Y., 1963), pp. 181, 177.

[37] Asimov, "The Evitable Conflict," in *I, Robot*, p. 218.

[38] Asimov, "And It Will Serve Us Right," *Psychology Today*, II (April 1969), 64.

III. The Synthetic Experience

[1] "In *Brave New World* non-stop distractions of the most fascinating nature (the feelies, orgy-porgy, centrifugal bumblepuppy) are deliberately used as instruments of policy, for the purpose of preventing people from paying too much attention to the realities of the social and political situation. . . . A society, most of whose members spend a great part of their time, not on the spot, not here and now and in the calculable future, but somewhere else, in the irrelevant other worlds of sport and soap opera, of mythology and metaphysical fantasy, will find it hard to resist the encroachments of those who would manipulate and control it." Aldous Huxley, *Brave New World Revisited* (New York, 1958), pp. 45-46.

[2] Aldous Huxley, *Brave New World* (New York, 1946), pp. 82-83.

[3] Ray Bradbury, *Fahrenheit 451* (New York, 1967), pp. 62, 63, 65, 67.

[4] Robert Silverberg, *The World Inside* (Garden City, N. Y., 1971).

[5] Philip K. Dick, *The Three Stigmata of Palmer Eldritch* (Garden City, N. Y., 1965).

[6] Frederik Pohl, "What to Do Till the Analyst Comes," in Pohl, *Alternating Currents* (New York, 1956).

[7] Philip Wylie, *The End of the Dream* (Garden City, N. Y., 1972), pp. 210-211.

[8] Wylie, p. 213.

[9] Shepherd Mead, *The Big Ball of Wax* (New York, 1954), pp. 121-122, 235.

[10] Mead, pp. 71, 72.

[11] D. G. Compton, *Synthajoy* (New York, 1968), p. 63.

[12] Compton, pp. 23, 152.

[13] Nathaniel Hawthorne, "Ethan Brand," *Hawthorne: Selected Tales and Sketches* (New York, 1964), pp. 314, 306.

[14] Compton, pp. 74, 170-171.

[15] Dean R. Koontz, *The Fall of the Dream Machine* (New York, 1969), pp. 59-60.

[16] Marshall McLuhan, "Verbi-Voco-Visual," in Gerald Emanuel Stearn, ed., *McLuhan: Hot & Cool* (New York, 1967), pp. 108-109. McLuhan reasons that literacy demands content; content demands thought; and thought proves an undependable bridge between man and nature, man and feeling.

[17] McLuham, *Understanding Media: The Extensions of Man* (New York, 1964), pp. 171-172.

[18] McLuhan, *Understanding Media*, p. 80.

IV. Ignoble Utopias

[1] B. F. Skinner, "Utopia and Human Behavior," *The Humanist* (July/August 1967), p. 120.

[2] "The Newest Utopia is a Slander on Some Old Notions of the Good Life," *Life*, XXIV (June 28, 1948), p. 38.

[3] Glenn Negley and J. Max Patrick, *The Quest for Utopia* (New York, 1952), pp. 589-590.

[4] B. F. Skinner, *Walden Two* (New York, 1948), pp. 213, 262.

[5] Joseph Wood Krutch, *The Measure of Man* (Indianapolis, 1954). Donald C. Williams, "The Social Scientist as Philosopher and King," *The Philosophical Review*, LVIII (1949), 345-359. Andrew Hacker, "The Specter of Predictable Man," *The Antioch Review*, XIV (1954), 195-207; "Dostoyevsky's Disciples: Men and Sheep in Political Theory," *The Journal of Politics*, XVII (1955), 590-608. Carl R. Rogers in Carl R. Rogers and B. F. Skinner, "Some Issues Concerning the Control of Human Behavior," *Science*, CXXIV (1956), 1057-1066. George Kateb, *Utopia and Its Enemies* (New York, 1963). Karl Popper, *The Open Society and Its Enemies* (Princeton,

N. J., 1963). Arthur Koestler, *The Ghost in the Machine* (New York, 1968).

[6] Robert L. Schwitzgebel, "A Belt From Big Brother," *Psychology Today*, II (April 1969), 65.

[7] Skinner, p. 247. *Cf.* Feverstone's statement, p. 15.

[8] Chad Walsh, *From Utopia to Nightmare* (New York, 1962), p. 26.

[9] Arthur Koestler, *The Ghost in the Machine* (New York, 1968), p. 17.

[10] Ludwig von Bertalanffy, Heinz Werner Memorial Lectures, 1967. This view is restated in Bertalanffy, *Robots, Men and Minds: Psychology in the Modern World* (New York, 1967), pp. 15-16.

[11] Joseph Wood Krutch, *The Measure of Man* (Indianapolis, 1954), pp. 42, 54.

[12] Krutch, pp. 154-156.

[13] Krutch, p. 148.

[14] Skinner, p. 210.

[15] George Orwell, *Nineteen Eighty-Four* (New York, 1949), pp. 272-273.

[16] Krutch, pp. 76, 261.

[17] Krutch, pp. 107-108, quoting Skinner, p. 214.

[18] Krutch, p. 108.

[19] Skinner, pp. 163, 145, 161, 225, 174.

[20] Skinner, p. 218.

[21] Skinner, pp. 243, 244.

[22] Skinner, pp. 249-250.

[23] Skinner, pp. 217ff. Specifically Frazier is referring to the principle of loving one's enemies, which, he insists, was hit upon by *accident*. For Jesus "had none of the experimental evidence which is available to us today, and I can't conceive that it was possible, no matter what the man's genius, to have discovered the principle from casual observation."

[24] Skinner, "Freedom and the Control of Men," *The American Scholar*, XXV (Winter 1955-1956), 61, quoting T. H. Huxley, *Method and Results* (New York, 1896), pp. 192-193. Huxley's following sentence: "The only freedom I care about is the freedom to do right; the freedom to do wrong I am ready to part with on the cheapest terms to anyone who will take it of me."

[25] Krutch, p. 172.

[26] Krutch, p. 101, quoting Skinner, p. 260.

[27] Krutch, pp. 101, 170.

[28] George Kateb, *Utopia and Its Enemies* (New York, 1963), p. 155.

[29] Kateb, p. 159.

[30] Kateb, pp. 227, 217, 164, 214, 215.

[31] Kateb, p. 179.

[32] Kurt Vonnegut, Jr., *Player Piano* (New York, 1966), p. 262.

[33] Bernard Wolfe, *Limbo* (New York, 1952), pp. 385, 381, 399-400.

[34] William Hjortsberg, *Gray Matters* (New York, 1971), p. 160.

[35] John Wyndham, *Trouble With Lichen* (New York, 1969).

[36] In Bob Shaw's *One Million Tomorrows* (New York, 1970) the sole

drawback of an immortality drug is that it makes males impotent. At about 40 they must choose either a sexless forever or a natural life — and death. Other works on longevity treated in this study are Bodelsen's *Freezing Down*, Jones' *The Cybernetic Brains*, Laumer's *The Day Before Forever*, Silverberg's *To Live Again*, and Simak's *Why Call Them Back From Heaven?*

[37] Anthony Burgess, *A Clockwork Orange* (New York, 1963), pp. 21-22.

[38] Burgess, p. 40. Alex speaks the argot of the young, Nadsat, a composite of common English, gypsy talk, rhyming slang, amputations, and ingeniously Anglicized Russian. Some examples: *eggiweg* (egg); *pee* and *em* (pop and mom); *horrorshow* (good; Rus. "khorosho"); *millicents* (police; Rus. "militsia").

[39] Based on Pavlovian principles, this technique is described in Chapter II.

[40] Burgess, p. 95.

[41] Burgess, p. 179.

[42] Rex Gordon, *Utopia Minus X* (New York, 1966), p. 32.

[43] Gordon, pp. 48 ff.

[44] Gordon, pp. 56 ff.

[45] Gordon, pp. 172-173.

[46] R. A. Lafferty, *Past Master* (New York, 1968).

[47] Colin Anderson, *Magellan* (New York, 1970), p. 125.

[48] Anderson, pp. 162-163.

[49] Leonard C. Lewin, *Triage* (New York, 1972), pp. 99, 93.

[50] Lewin, pp. 166-167.

[51] Lewin, pp. 11, 12.

[52] Lewin, p. 53.

[53] Lewin, p. 26.

[54] Lewin, pp. 67-70.

[55] In William and Paul Paddock's *Famine — 1975!* (1967), a work cited later in this study, the authors advocate that the U. S. practice triage in allocating food to starving nations. The severity of the coming population-food crisis in India and Egypt, the Paddocks claim, condemns those nations to the "can't be saved" list; our aiding them further only makes the position of others more precarious.

[56] Michael Young, *The Rise of the Meritocracy: 1870-2033* (London, 1958), pp. 135-136.

[57] Young, p. 152.

CHAPTER II
THE NEW TYRANNIES

I. The Totalitarian State of The Future

[1] Hannah Arendt, *The Origins of Totalitarianism* (Cleveland, 1958), pp. 473-474.

[2] Quoted by Irving Howe, *"1984*: History as Nightmare," in Irving Howe, ed., *Orwell's "Nineteen Eighty-Four": Text, Sources, Criticism* (New York, 1963), p. 109n.

[3] Erich Fromm, "Afterword on *1984*," in Irving Howe, ed., *op. cit.*, p. 206.

[4] Irving Howe, "The Fiction of Anti-Utopia," in Irving Howe, ed., *op. cit.*, p. 178.

[5] George Orwell, *Nineteen Eighty-Four* (New York, 1949), p. 173.

[6] Orwell, p. 127.

[7] Orwell, p. 177.

[8] Orwell, p. 53.

[9] Orwell, p. 81.

[10] Orwell, pp. 167, 284, 272.

[11] Fromm, in Irving Howe, ed., *op. cit.*, p. 209.

[12] From Valerius Bruzov, *The Republic of the Southern Cross*, a novel depicting a benevolent, efficient, but overly regulated society, which is torn asunder by an epidemic of incurable *Mania Contradiceus*. The disease drives its victims to do the opposite of what is logical or expected. (An irresistible impulse compels conductors to pay their passengers, etc.) People crack under the tension, and the formerly well-ordered republic soon becomes a madhouse.

[13] L. P. Hartley, *Facial Justice* (Garden City, N. Y., 1960), pp. 207-208.

[14] *Facial Justice* gives an excellent example of what Chad Walsh has called "the Law of Reverse Effect" (*From Utopia to Nightmare*, New York, 1962, p. 151): The inordinate pursuit or achievement of a desirable goal — such as equality — produces a grievous condition. From the "law" both Greek tragedy and anti-utopianism have drawn significant inspiration. And, of course, the "law" is one of the keystones of anti-utopian science fiction.

[15] Ayn Rand, *Anthem* (Caldwell, Idaho, 1964), pp. 19, 93-94, 21, 30, 74, 61-62.

[16] Rand, pp. 96-97.

[17] David Karp, *One* (New York, 1953), pp. 57-58.

[18] Karp, pp. 68, 172-173.

[19] Karp, p. 109.

[20] Karp, pp. 299, 256.

[21] Ira Levin, *This Perfect Day* (New York, 1970).

[22] "Marvelously entertaining." *Look;* "Absorbing from start to finish." *Book-of-the-Month Club News*; "Another extraordinary reading experience." *Los Angeles Herald-Examiner.*

[23] Douglas R. Mason, *From Carthage Then I Came* (New York, 1966).

[24] Peter Wahlöö, *The Thirty-First Floor* (New York, 1967), pp. 36-37.

[25] Wahlöö, p. 183.

[26] Wahlöö, p. 109.

[27] His early enthusiasm for the Russian Revolution soon turning to alarm as he sensed the regime's drift toward dogma and repression, Zamiatin wrote *We* as a warning against the excesses he feared might be perpetrated. The book was never published in Russia, and the regime's hostility toward him led to his self-exile in 1931.

[28] Eugene Zamiatin, *We*, trans. Gregory Zilboorg (New York, 1952), pp. 129, 38.

[29] Zamiatin, pp. 3, 6, 24, 166.

[30] Zamiatin, pp. 22, 13. Like *Anthem, Facial Justice,* and *One, We* exhibits the totalitarian state's linguistic assault against the sense of identity and possession. D-503 muses that if an ancestor were writing the journal, a paramour would probably be called "by that funny word, *mine.*" (p. 7.) Hartley's Jael is advised, *"Mine* is not a word you ought to use. . . . 'In my charge,' you ought to say, or 'in my care.' " (*Facial Justice,* pp. 89-90.) Karp's Church of State families "spoke of themselves in the third person as if they did not exist by themselves but only as part of a third group. *Me, my, I, mine* did not exist in [their] language." (*One,* p. 18.)

[31] Zamiatin, pp. 166-167.

[32] Huxley's dystopia and the totalitarian state of Ray Bradbury's *Fahrenheit 451* have been treated in Chapter I.

[33] Chad Walsh, *From Utopia to Nightmare* (New York, 1962), p. 135.

II. The Mind Invasion

[1] Robert Sheckley, "The Academy," *If: Worlds of Science Fiction* (August 1954). In Hartley's *Facial Justice* the Dictator employs a "discontentometer," which registers the degree of public hostility to his rule.

[2] Robert Sheckley, *The Status Civilization* (New York, 1968).

[3] Alfred Bester, *The Demolished Man* (Chicago, 1953).

[4] Kenneth Bulmer, *The Doomsday Men* (Garden City, N. Y., 1968).

[5] Philip K. Dick, *Ubik* (Garden City, N. Y., 1969).

[6] Robert Silverberg, *To Live Again* (Garden City, N. Y., 1969).

[7] In some science fiction novels psionic talent has beneficial effects. In John Wyndham's *Re-Birth* (New York, 1955) and Theodore Sturgeon's *More Than Human* (New York, 1953) it promotes mutual understanding and fulfillment.

[8] Ralph Blum, *The Simultaneous Man* (Boston, 1970).

[9] Anthony Burgess, *A Clockwork Orange* (New York, 1963), pp. 102-103.

[10] Burgess, p. 128.

[11] Burgess, p. 129. Two British psychiatrists have successfully employed

a similar associative technique — "aversion therapy" — in treating gamblers and homosexuals. Describing their practice in the medical journal *Pulse*, they cite the case of an adulterer, who is now completely indifferent to his former paramour. In six half-hour sessions the doctors alternately flashed on a screen pictures of the patient's wife and his lover, jolting him with a seventy-volt shock upon each projection of the lover's photograph. The doctors reported: "Immediately after the first session, he developed a deep sense of guilt and broke down completely. Subsequent sessions appeared less traumatic, but nevertheless left a deep impression on him." *The Hartford* [Connecticut] *Courant*, December 4, 1966, p. 28.

[12] Piers Anthony and Robert E. Margroff, *The Ring* (New York, 1968), pp. 62-63.

[13] Raymond F. Jones, *The Cybernetic Brains* (New York, 1962).

[14] Robert A. Heinlein, *The Puppet Masters* (Garden City, N. Y., 1951), p. 214.

[15] Robert Silverberg, "Passengers," in Damon Knight, ed., *Orbit 4* (New York, 1968), p. 177.

[16] Silverberg, pp. 165, 168.

[17] Robert A. Heinlein, "They," in Damon Knight, ed., *The Dark Side* (Garden City, N. Y., 1965), p. 34.

[18] Colin Wilson, *The Mind Parasites* (New York, 1968), pp. 57, 59.

[19] Wilson, p. 67.

[20] Samuel Johnson, "A Review of Soame Jenyns' *A Free Inquiry into the Nature and Origin of Evil*," in Bertrand H. Bronson, ed., *Rasselas, Poems, and Selected Prose* (New York, 1958), pp. 204, 206.

[21] Frank Herbert, *The Heaven Makers* (New York, 1968), p. 19.

[22] Isaac Asimov, "Breeds There a Man . . . ?" in Asimov, *Nightfall and Other Stories* (Garden City, N. Y., 1969), p. 113.

[23] Herbert, p. 22.

III. Commerce and Exploitation

[1] To cite a few: Mark Twain, *The Gilded Age*; William Dean Howells, *A Hazard of New Fortunes*; Frank Norris, *The Octopus*; Theodore Dreiser, *The Titan*; Upton Sinclair, *The Jungle*; Sinclair Lewis, *Babbitt*; John Dos Passos, *U. S. A.*; Frederic Wakeman, *The Hucksters*. In nonfiction: Henry George, *Progress and Poverty*; William H. Whyte, *The Organization Man*; Vance Packard, *The Hidden Persuaders*.

[2] Frederik Pohl, "The Tunnel Under the World," in Pohl, *Alternating Currents* (New York, 1956), p. 119. Robert Sheckley's "Cost of Living" reveals a society so coerced by salesmen that people commonly mortgage the future earnings of their children and even grandchildren to purchase the extravagant and often ludicrous "necessities" of civilized living. In Sheckley, *Untouched by Human Hands* (New York, 1954).

[3] Frederik Pohl, "The Wizards of Pung's Corners," *Galaxy* (October 1958).

[4] Frederik Pohl and C. M. Kornbluth, *The Space Merchants* (New York, 1953), pp. 5 ff.

[5] Pohl and Kornbluth, p. 8.

[6] Pohl and Kornbluth, p. 76.

[7] Pohl and Kornbluth, pp. 83, 78.

[8] Pohl and Kornbluth, p. 127.

[9] Pohl and Kornbluth, *Gladiator-at-Law* (New York, 1955), p. 41.

[10] Pohl and Kornbluth, p. 171.

[11] Damon Knight, *Hell's Pavement* (Greenwich, Conn., 1955), pp. 36, 94-95.

[12] In J. G. Ballard's "The Subliminal Man" (1964) a mercantile tyranny is making people compulsive consumers. Finally zombiized by secret subliminal catchwords, the country turns into a consuming madhouse. (In Robert Silverberg, ed., *The Mirror of Infinity*, New York, 1970.)

[13] Robert Silverberg, *Invaders From Earth* (New York, 1968), p. 40.

[14] Shepherd Mead, *The Big Ball of Wax* (New York, 1954), pp. 216, 48-49.

[15] Kurt Vonnegut, Jr., *Player Piano* (New York, 1966), pp. 55, 79, 260.

[16] Keith Laumer, *The Day Before Forever* (Garden City, N. Y., 1968), p. 29.

[17] Robert Silverberg, *Tower of Glass* (New York, 1970), p. 6.

[18] Silverberg, pp. 35, 36, 228.

[19] Ira Levin, *The Stepford Wives* (New York, 1972).

[20] Norman Mailer, *The Prisoner of Sex* (Boston, 1971).

[21] George Gilder, *Sexual Suicide* (New York, 1973).

[22] Isaac Asimov, *The Gods Themselves* (Garden City, N. Y., 1972), p. 69. In view of the novel's title and the quotation from which it is drawn, one would expect to see the end of man. However, the world is rescued by another discovery and some last-minute twists in the plot. But since *men*, at least, successfully contend with stupidity, Asimov's title seems inappropriate. Furthermore, since virtually the whole drift of the book argues the impotence of reason against entrenched stupidity, the happy resolution in the final pages comes as a clumsy *deus ex machina*.

[23] James Blish, *A Case of Conscience* (New York, 1958), pp. 37-38, 71.

[24] The priest cites the heretical premises to his fellow scientists. "*One*: Reason is always a sufficient guide. *Two*: The self-evident is always the real. *Three*: Good works are an end in themselves. *Four*: Faith is irrelevant to right action. *Five*: Right action can exist without love. *Six*: Peace need not pass understanding. *Seven*: Ethics can exist without evil alternatives. *Eight*: Morals can exist without conscience. *Nine*: Goodness can exist without God. *Ten* — but do I really need to go on? We have heard all these propositions before, and we know What proposes them." Blish, p. 78.

[25] Blish, p. 79.

IV. The Revolt of Youth

[1] Josephine Lawrence, *Not a Cloud in the Sky* (New York, 1964).

[2] John Christopher, *Pendulum* (New York, 1968), p. 108.

[3] Christopher, p. 93.

[4] Robert Thom, *Wild in the Streets* (New York, 1968), pp. 32-33.

[5] Thom, pp. 58-59.

[6] Thom, pp. 98, 112-113.

[7] Thom, pp. 117-118.

[8] Thom, p. 127.

[9] Wm. F. Nolan and George Clayton Johnson's *Logan's Run* (New York, 1969) also employs peremptory death as the controlling circumstance of its plot. In the overpopulated world of 2116, one lives twenty-one years of un-limited sensuality and then submits to a painless death on "Lastday" or becomes a "runner," hunted by the brutal death squad.

[10] Marya Mannes, *They* (Garden City, N. Y., 1968), p. 31.

[11] Mannes, p. 32.

[12] Mannes, pp. 23, 34, 86-87, 94.

[13] Mannes, pp. 27-28.

[14] Mannes, pp. 94, 24, 96.

[15] Mannes, pp. 14, 13.

[16] Mannes, p. 96.

[17] Marge Piercy, *Dance the Eagle to Sleep* (Garden City, N. Y., 1970), pp. 110-111.

[18] Harlan Ellison, "A Boy and His Dog," in James Blish, ed., *Nebula Award Stories Five* (Garden City, N. Y., 1970), pp. 53-54.

[19] Ellison, p. 63.

[20] See Ellison, *Love Ain't Nothing But Sex Misspelled* (New York, 1968).

CHAPTER III
CATASTROPHE

I. Nuclear War

[1] Nevile Shute, *On the Beach* (New York, 1957).

[2] Philip Wylie, *Triumph* (Garden City, N. Y., 1963), p. 260.

[3] Mordecai Roshwald, *Level 7* (New York, 1959), pp. 16, 58, 61, 91, 131.

[4] Roshwald, pp. 158-160. Later, meditating on the moral numbness with which he and others had pushed deadly buttons, X-127 concludes that he belonged to that breed of men required by dehumanized war. He writes, "I do not think I could be a swordsman. I could not kill with a club or a bayonet or a knife, let alone with my bare hands. But pushing a button — that was a different matter. It has become so easy to destroy and kill. . . . The head-hunter might have made a bad button-pusher, and the button-pusher a poor infantryman." (pp. 168-169).

[5] Walter M. Miller, Jr., *A Canticle for Leibowitz* (Philadelphia, 1960), p. 206.

[6] Miller, p. 215.

[7] Miller, pp. 215-216.

[8] Miller, p. 255.

[9] Miller, p. 274.

[10] Miller, p. 277.

[11] Miller, "Dumb Waiter," in Damon Knight, ed., *Cities of Wonder* (Garden City, N. Y., 1966), pp. 37-38.

II. The Population Explosion

[1] William and Paul Paddock, *Famine — 1975!* (Boston, 1967). In this most frightening and persuasive study of the population and food crisis, the authors contend that the time to brake world population and increase food production has long passed and that no measures taken now can avert the coming age of famines. The famines "will last for years, perhaps several decades, and they are, for a surety, inevitable. Ten years from now parts of the undeveloped world will be suffering from famine. In fifteen years the famines will be catastrophic and revolutions and social turmoil and economic upheavals will sweep areas of Asia, Africa, and Latin America." (p. 8.)

[2] Although citing several exceptions, such as Aldous Huxley's *Brave New World* and Olaf Stapledon's *Last and First Men*, science fiction historian Sam Moskowitz acknowledges that "science fiction is surpassed in prudery only by the Frank Merriwell stories." (*Seekers of Tomorrow: Masters of Modern Science Fiction*, Cleveland, 1966, p. 395.) G. Legman (*The Horn Book: Studies in Erotic Folklore and Bibliography*, 1964), whom Moskowitz quotes, theorizes that science fiction is largely indifferent to sex because

the majority of its readers "is composed of adolescent boys (who continue reading it even after they are grown up), who are terrified of women, sex, and pubic hair." (p. 398.) Moskowitz rejects Legman's derision of science fiction's audience and offers his own explanation: "The answer most probably is that science fiction is a literature of ideas. The people who read it are entertained and even find escape through mental stimulation. Sex, vulgar or artistic, is available to them in countless forms if they wish it, but the type of intellectual speculation they enjoy is presented only in science fiction." (p. 398.) Whatever the merits of these scholars' arguments, the modesty about which both agree may become a thing of the past if Norman Spinrad's blazingly erotic tour de force, *Bug Jack Barron* (New York, 1969), sets a trend in science fiction.

[3] James Blish and Norman L. Knight, *A Torrent of Faces* (Garden City, N. Y., 1967), p. 268.

[4] Blish and Knight. Though one may forgive George for his fatuous theorizing of 1879, it is shocking to find otherwise responsible contemporary public figures ignorant of the magnitude of the population crisis. Demographers expect world population to reach an *unsupportable* six billion by 2000. Yet in 1965 the late Senator Robert F. Kennedy (at that time the father of nine) shouted to a crowd of Peruvians, "I challenge any of you to produce more children than I have." (Drew Pearson, *The Washington Post*, November 30, 1965.) The Peruvians, as yet, have declined his invitation to mass suicide.

[5] Blish and Knight, pp. 45-46. Isaac Asimov's *The Caves of Steel* (mentioned in Chapter I) depicts a world notably similar to that of *A Torrent of Faces*, one of some eight hundred, emotionally stifling, underground-hive machines of ten million people. The "caves of steel" are doomed by the strain on their complex life-support systems.

[6] Blish and Knight, pp. 268-269.

[7] Blish and Knight, p. 28.

[8] Harry Harrison, *Make Room! Make Room!* (Garden City, N. Y., 1966).

[9] Robert Bloch, *This Crowded Earth* (New York, 1968), p. 19.

[10] Richard Wilson, "The Eight Billion," in Edward L. Ferman, ed., *The Best From "Fantasy and Science Fiction,"* 15th Series (Garden City, N. Y., 1966), p. 156.

[11] J. G. Ballard, "Billenium," in Damon Knight, ed., *Cities of Wonder* (Garden City, N. Y., 1966). Kurt Vonnegut's "Tomorrow and Tomorrow and Tomorrow" also treats the overpopulated dystopia humorously. Some members of the nose-to-nose Schwartz family get slapped in jail for disorderly conduct. The cells: four-by-eight foot desert island paradises, with modern conveniences — private cots, washbasins, and lights. A good lawyer might get them a year. In Vonnegut, *Welcome to the Monkey House* (New York, 1968).

[12] Earl Conrad, *The Da Vinci Machine: Tales of the Population Explosion* (New York, 1968), pp. 11-12, 13, 16.

[13] Conrad, pp. 50, 54.

[14] Conrad, p. 184.

[15] Conrad, p. 189.

[16] Max Ehrlich, *The Edict* (New York, 1972).

[17] Anthony Burgess, *The Wanting Seed* (New York, 1964), pp. 8, 9. Isaac Asimov, foreseeing changes in American social mores in the 1990's, when the U. S. population passes three hundred million, predicts: "Practices, previously considered perverse, because they do not lead to conception, will become tolerable and even praiseworthy for exactly the same reason." Asimov expects homosexuality, masturbation, and oral-genital contacts to gain general acceptance. *The Hartford* [Connecticut] *Times*, April 5, 1970, pp. 1C, 4C.

[18] Burgess, pp. 37-38, 5, 6.

[19] Burgess, pp. 216 f.

[20] Burgess, p. 218.

[21] Burgess, p. 7.

[22] "All art is an aspect of sexuality" and a product of *"paternity lust."* (p. 55.) "All dirty words are fundamentally religious. They are all concerned with fertility and the processes of fertility and the organs of fertility. God, we are taught, is love." (p. 95.)

[23] Former Director of the U. N. World Health Organization, Brock Chisholm, has written that despite the Population Commission's alarming yearly reports, it does not make any recommendations because "every committee . . . is under the influence of the Roman Catholic Church." When the Norwegian delegate once proposed that the WHO "set up a medical committee to study the medical aspects of population problems, representatives of six governments, chiefs of delegations, immediately got up and said that if this question were even discussed their governments might have to withdraw from the World Health Organization." (William and Paul Paddock, p. 35, quoting Brock Chisholm.)

III.   Race War In America

[1] Warren Miller, *The Siege of Harlem* (New York, 1964), p. 130.

[2] D. Keith Mano, *Horn* (Boston, 1969), pp. 153, 337.

[3] Mano, pp. 170-171.

[4] Mano, pp. 324, 325.

[5] Edwin Corley, *Siege* (New York, 1969), p. 85.

[6] Corley, p. 134.

[7] John A. Williams, *Sons of Darkness, Sons of Light* (Boston, 1969).

[8] Fletcher Knebel, *Trespass* (Garden City, N. Y., 1969), p. 81.

[9] Pleasure not without reservations, Freeman knows: "They can forgive a nigger almost anything other than competence. . . . They want me to fumble, stumble, turn to them for help. . . . Part of them wants me to vindicate their choice of a spade for the position, but another part wants me to prove once again that it is spade incompetence, not white racism, which

is responsible for the scene. They'll use me, but they'll never like me."
(p. 90.)

[10] Sam Greenlee, *The Spook Who Sat by the Door* (New York, 1969),
p. 112.

[11] Greenlee, p. 243.

[12] Greenlee, p. 248.

IV. The Obsessional Catastrophe

[1] Butler had crashed in Lomokome. Five months later a second U. S.
spaceship discovered his wrecked craft and the log. Butler was not found and
is presumed dead.

[2] Herman Wouk, *The "Lomokome" Papers* (New York, 1968), p. 67.
Lomokome in Hebrew means utopia or nowhere.

[3] Wouk, p. 69.

[4] Wouk, pp. 90-91.

[5] Wouk, pp. 104, 4, 12.

[6] Wouk, p. viii.

[7] Bob Shaw, *Ground Zero Man* (New York, 1971).

[8] Bernard Wolfe, *Limbo* (New York, 1952), p. 119.

[9] Wolfe, pp. 147, 148.

[10] Wolfe, pp. 413-414.

[11] Aldous Huxley, *Ape and Essence* (New York, 1948), p. 98.

[12] Huxley, p. 123.

[13] Huxley, pp. 126, 125.

[14] Huxley, p. 120. Compare this view of malignant possession with that
in Colin Wilson's *The Mind Parasites* (Chapter II).

[15] Huxley, p. 8.

[16] John Wyndham, *Re-Birth* (New York, 1955), p. 15.

[17] Wyndham, p. 181.

[18] Clifford D. Simak, *Why Call Them Back From Heaven?* (Garden City,
N. Y., 1967), p. 111. In the end earthly "forever" is doomed — impossible.
But even if achieved, Simak asks, "What kind of world could there be, or
would there be, when all of humankind lived eternally and in the flesh and
guise of youth? Would wisdom come without gray hair and wrinkled brow?
. . . Would the gentleness and the tolerance and the long reflective thought no
longer be with mankind? . . . Might youth itself be no more than a trapping
and a coloration? Would mankind finally sink into an atmosphere of futility,
impatient with the endless days, disillusioned and disappointed with eternity?
After the millionth mating, after the billionth piece of pumpkin pie . . . what
would there be left?" (pp. 107-108.)

[19] Anders Bodelsen, *Freezing Down* (New York, 1971).

[20] Evelyn Waugh, "Love Among the Ruins," in Waugh, *Tactical Exercise* (Boston, 1954).

[21] Damon Knight, "The Country of the Kind," in Robert Silverberg,

ed., *Science Fiction Hall of Fame*, I (Garden City, N. Y., 1970).

[22] Robert Silverberg, *How It Was When the Past Went Away*, in *Three for Tomorrow* (New York, 1969), pp. 78, 79, 80.

[23] Robert Silverberg, *The World Inside* (Garden City, N. Y., 1971).

[24] Charles L. Fontenay, *Epistle to the Babylonians: An Essay on the Natural Inequality of Man* (Knoxville, Tenn., 1969), pp. 161, viii.

[25] Gore Vidal, *Messiah*, rev. ed. (Boston, 1965), pp. 64, 69-70, 72, 109-110.

[26] Vidal, p. 110.

[27] Vidal, pp. 139, 145.

[28] Vidal, pp. 210, 211, 244.

[29] Vidal, p. 244.

[30] Vidal, pp. 5, 7, 9.

[31] Vidal, p. 9.

[32] Vidal, pp. 11-12.

[33] Damon Knight, *In Search of Wonder*, 2nd ed. (Chicago, 1967), pp. 175-176. So assured in tone is the narrative "as something that happened" that the schemework of traditional dystopian oppressions and perversions which impart so much to the shock of other novels, here, is only ancillary. Yet the schemework is there and should be cited. After Luther's defection the apparatus of totalitarianism emerges and grows. "Squads of the word," masters of brainwashing, demoralization, and autohypnosis purge the heresy of life. The establishment controls the "sacred" records and sources so that it may fabricate new texts to meet any moral or political problem which previous texts pass over, and it also controls the communication media; such dominance assures the successful falsifying of records and expunging of names — in short, the rewriting of history. Another Orwellian feature is the establishment's twisted reasonings, advanced as truths, but nourished by a transparent casuistry and the denial of objective truth: "Nothing is good. Nothing is right. . . . Mother love exists because we believe it exists. Believe it does not exist and it won't." (p. 175.) The Cavite Testament states, "A truth known to only half the world is but half a truth." (p. 91.) Though Iris died of pneumonia, the Cavite Council shall establish "that intent and fact are the same. . . . She *intended* to take Cavesway and, therefore, took Cavesway in spirit and therefore in fact. . . . It is beautifully clear, though perhaps difficult for an untrained mind." (p. 242.)

[34] John Wyndham, *Consider Her Ways*, in *Sometime, Never* (New York, 1957), pp. 103-104.

[35] Wyndham, pp. 107-108, 111.

[36] Wyndham, p. 125.

CONCLUSION

[1] Karl Meyer, "O Scared Old World, That Has Such Robots In't!" *The Reporter*, July 6, 1954, p. 35.

BIBLIOGRAPHY

Alban, Antony. *Catharsis Central.* New York: Berkley Medallion Books, 1969.

Aldiss, Brian W. *Billion Year Spree: The True History of Science Fiction.* Garden City, N. Y.: Doubleday, 1973.

Amis, Kingsley. *New Maps of Hell: A Survey of Science Fiction.* New York: Harcourt, Brace & World, 1960.

Anderson, Colin. *Magellan.* New York: Walker, 1970.

Anthony, Piers, and Robert E. Margroff. *The Ring.* New York: Ace Books, 1968.

Arendt, Hannah. *The Origins of Totalitarianism.* Cleveland: World, 1958.

Asimov, Isaac. "And It Will Serve Us Right," *Psychology Today,* II (April 1969), 38-41, 64.

Asimov, Isaac. "Breeds There a Man . . . ?" In Asimov, *Nightfall and Other Stories.* Garden City, N. Y.: Doubleday, 1969.

Asimov, Isaac. *The Caves of Steel.* Garden City, N. Y.: Doubleday, 1954.

Asimov, Isaac. "Evidence." In Asimov, *I, Robot.* Garden City, N. Y.: Doubleday, 1963.

Asimov, Isaac. "The Evitable Conflict." In Asimov, *I, Robot.* Garden City, N. Y.: Doubleday, 1963.

Asimov, Isaac. *The Gods Themselves.* Garden City, N. Y.: Doubleday, 1972.

Asimov, Isaac. "You've Come a Long Way, Baby . . . ," *The Hartford* [Connecticut] *Times,* April 5, 1970, pp. 1C, 4C.

Ballard, J. G. "Billenium." In Damon Knight, ed., *Cities of Wonder.* Garden City, N. Y.: Doubleday, 1966.

Ballard, J. G. "The Subliminal Man." In Robert Silverberg, ed., *The Mirror of Infinity.* New York: Harper & Row, 1970.

Bellamy, Edward. *Looking Backward: 2000-1887.* Ed. John L. Thomas. Cambridge, Mass.: Harvard University Press, 1967.

Bertalanffy, Ludwig von. *Robots, Men and Minds: Psychology in the Modern World.* New York: George Braziller, 1967.

Bester, Alfred. *The Demolished Man.* Chicago: Shasta, 1953.

Blish, James. *A Case of Conscience.* New York: Ballantine Books, 1958.

Blish, James, and Norman L. Knight. *A Torrent of Faces.* Garden City, N. Y.: Doubleday, 1967.

Bloch, Robert. *This Crowded Earth.* New York: Belmont Books, 1968.

Blum, Ralph. *The Simultaneous Man.* Boston: Little, Brown, 1970.

Bodelsen, Anders. *Freezing Down.* Trans. Joan Tate. New York: Harper & Row, 1971.

Bradbury, Ray. *Fahrenheit 451.* New York: Simon and Schuster, 1967.

Brunner, John. *Stand on Zanzibar.* Garden City, N. Y.: Doubleday, 1968.

Bruzov, Valerius. *The Republic of the Southern Cross.* New York: McBride, 1919.

Bulmer, Kenneth. *The Doomsday Men.* Garden City, N. Y.: Doubleday, 1968.

Burgess, Anthony. *A Clockwork Orange*. New York: W. W. Norton, 1963.

Burgess, Anthony. *The Wanting Seed*. New York: Ballantine Books, 1964.

Caiden, Martin. *The God Machine*. New York: E. P. Dutton, 1968.

Christopher, John. *Pendulum*. New York: Simon and Schuster, 1968.

Clareson, Thomas. *Science Fiction Criticism: An Annotated Checklist*. n.p.: Kent State University Press, 1972.

Cole, Burt. *The Funco File*. Garden City, N. Y.: Doubleday, 1969.

Compton, D. G. *The Steel Crocodile*. New York: Ace Books, 1970.

Compton, D. G. *Synthajoy*. New York: Ace Books, 1968.

Conrad, Earl. *The Da Vinci Machine: Tales of the Population Explosion*. New York: Fleet Press, 1968.

Cooper, Edmund. *Deadly Image*. New York: Ballantine Books, 1958.

Corley, Edwin. *Siege*. New York: Stein and Day, 1969.

Davenport, Basil, and others. *The Science Fiction Novel: Imagination and Social Criticism*. 2nd. ed., rev. Chicago: Advent, 1964.

Dick, Philip K. "The Defenders." In Roger Elwood, ed., *Invasion of the Robots*. New York: Paperback Library, 1965.

Dick, Philip K. *The Three Stigmata of Palmer Eldritch*. Garden City, N. Y.: Doubleday, 1965.

Dick, Philip K. *Ubik*. Garden City, N. Y.: Doubleday, 1969.

Dickson, Gorden R. "Computers Don't Argue." In Damon Knight, ed., *Nebula Award Stories: 1965*. Garden City, N. Y.: Doubleday, 1966.

Ehrlich, Max. *The Edict*. New York: Bantam Books, 1972.

Ellison, Harlan. "A Boy and His Dog." In James Blish, ed., *Nebula Award Stories Five*. Garden City, N. Y.: Doubleday, 1970.

Fairman, Paul W. *I, The Machine*. New York: Lancer Books, 1968.

Fontenay, Charles L. *Epistle to the Babylonians: An Essay on the Natural Inequality of Man*. Knoxville, Tenn.: University of Tennessee Press, 1969.

Forster, E. M. "The Machine Stops." In *Collected Short Stories of E. M. Forster*. London: Sidgwick and Jackson, 1965.

Fromm, Erich. "Afterword on *1984*." In Irving Howe, ed., *Orwell's "Nineteen Eighty-Four": Text, Sources, Criticism*. New York: Harcourt, Brace & World, 1963.

George, Henry. *Progress and Poverty*. New York: Robert Schalkenbach Foundation, 1958.

Gilder, George. *Sexual Suicide*. New York: Quadrangle, 1973.

Golding, William. *Envoy Extraordinary*. In *Sometime, Never: Three Tales of Imagination*. New York: Ballantine Books, 1957.

Gordon, Rex. *Utopia Minus X*. New York: Ace Books, 1966.

Greenlee, Sam. *The Spook Who Sat by the Door*. New York: Richard W. Baron, 1969.

Hacker, Andrew. "Dostoyevsky's Disciples: Men and Sheep in Political Theory," *The Journal of Politics*, XVII (1955), 590-608.

Hacker, Andrew. "The Specter of Predictable Man," *The Antioch Review*, XIV (1954), 195-207.

Hadley, Arthur T. *The Joy Wagon*. New York: Viking Press, 1958.

Harrison, Harry. *Make Room! Make Room!* Garden City, N. Y.: Doubleday, 1966.

Hartford [Connecticut] *Courant*, December 4, 1966, p. 28.

Hartley, L. P. *Facial Justice*. Garden City, N. Y.: Doubleday, 1960.

Hawthorne, Nathaniel. "Ethan Brand." In *Nathaniel Hawthorne: Selected Tales and Sketches*. New York: Holt, Rinehart and Winston, 1964.

Heinlein, Robert A. *The Puppet Masters*. Garden City, N. Y.: Doubleday, 1951.

Heinlein, Robert A. "They." In Damon Knight, ed., *The Dark Side*. Garden City, N. Y.: Doubleday, 1965.

Herbert, Frank. *The Heaven Makers*. New York: Avon Books, 1968.

Hillegas, Mark R. *The Future as Nightmare: H. G. Wells and the Anti-Utopians*. New York: Oxford University Press, 1967.

Hjortsberg, William. *Gray Matters*. New York: Simon & Schuster, 1971.

Howe, Irving. "The Fiction of Anti-Utopia" and "*1984*: History as Nightmare." In Irving Howe, ed., *Orwell's "Nineteen Eighty-Four": Text, Sources, Cirticism*. New York: Harcourt, Brace & World, 1963.

Huxley, Aldous. *Ape and Essence*. New York: Harper, 1948.

Huxley, Aldous. *Brave New World*. New York: Harper & Row, 1946.

Huxley, Aldous. *Brave New World Revisited*. New York: Harper, 1958.

Huxley, Thomas Henry. *Method and Results*. New York: Appleton, 1896.

Johnson, Samuel. "A Review of Soame Jenyns' *A Free Inquiry into the Nature and Origin of Evil*." In Bertrand H. Bronson, ed., *Rasselas, Poems, and Selected Prose*. New York: Rinehart, 1958.

Jones, Raymond F. *The Cybernetic Brains*. New York: Avalon Books, 1962.

Karp, David. *One*. New York: Vanguard Press, 1953.

Kateb, George. *Utopia and Its Enemies*. New York: Free Press of Glencoe, 1963.

Knebel, Fletcher. *Trespass*. Garden City, N. Y.: Doubleday, 1969.

Knight, Damon. "The Country of the Kind." In Robert Silverberg, ed., *Science Fiction Hall of Fame*. Vol. I. Garden City, N. Y.: Doubleday, 1970.

Knight, Damon. *Hell's Pavement*. Greenwich, Conn.: Fawcett, 1955.

Knight, Damon. *In Search of Wonder*. 2nd. ed., rev. and enl. Chicago: Advent, 1967.

Koestler, Arthur. *The Ghost in the Machine*. New York: Macmillan, 1968.

Koontz, Dean R. *The Fall of the Dream Machine*. New York: Ace Books, 1969.

Krutch, Joseph Wood. *The Measure of Man: On Freedom, Human Values, Survival and the Modern Temper*. Indianapolis: Bobbs-Merrill, 1954.

Lafferty, R. A. *Past Master*. New York: Ace Books, 1968.

Lapp, Ralph E. *The New Priesthood: The Scientific Elite and the Uses of Power*. New York: Harper & Row, 1965.

Laumer, Keith. *The Day Before Forever*. Garden City, N. Y.: Doubleday, 1968.

Lawrence, Josephine. *Not a Cloud in the Sky*. New York: Harcourt, Brace & World, 1964.

Legman, Gershon. *The Horn Book: Studies in Erotic Folklore and Bibliography*. New Hyde Park, N. Y.: University Books, 1964.

Levin, Ira. *The Stepford Wives*. New York: Random House, 1972.

Levin, Ira. *This Perfect Day*. New York: Random House, 1970.

Lewin, Leonard C. *Triage*. New York: Dial Press, 1972.

Lewis, C. S. *The Abolition of Man*. New York: Macmillan, 1965.

Lewis, C. S. *Out of the Silent Planet*. New York: Macmillan, 1965.

Lewis, C. S. *Perelandra*. New York: Macmillan, 1965.

Lewis, C. S. *That Hideous Strength*. New York: Macmillan, 1965.

McLuhan, Marshall. *Understanding Media: The Extensions of Man*. New York: McGraw-Hill, 1964.

McLuhan, Marshall. "Verbi-Voco-Visual." In Gerald Emanuel Stearn, ed., *McLuhan: Hot & Cool*. New York: Dial Press, 1967.

Mailer, Norman. *The Prisoner of Sex*. Boston: Little, Brown, 1971.

Mannes, Marya. *They*. Garden City, N. Y.: Doubleday, 1968.

Mano, D. Keith. *Horn*. Boston: Houghton Mifflin, 1969.

Mason, Douglas R. *From Carthage Then I Came*. Garden City, N. Y.: Doubleday, 1966.

Mead, Shepherd. *The Big Ball of Wax: A Story of Tomorrow's Happy World*. New York: Simon and Schuster, 1954.

Meyer, Karl. "O Scared Old World, That Has Such Robots In't!" *The Reporter*, July 6, 1954, pp. 35-37.

Miller, Walter M., Jr. *A Canticle for Leibowitz*. Philadelphia: J. B. Lippencott, 1960.

Miller, Walter M., Jr. "Dumb Waiter." In Damon Knight, ed., *Cities of Wonder*. Garden City, N. Y.: Doubleday, 1966.

Miller, Warren. *The Siege of Harlem*. New York: McGraw-Hill, 1964.

Moskowitz, Sam. *Seekers of Tomorrow: Masters of Modern Science Fiction*. Cleveland: World, 1966.

Negley, Glenn, and J. Max Patrick. *The Quest for Utopia: An Anthology of Imaginary Societies*. New York: Henry Schuman, 1952.

Newest Utopia is a Slander on Some Old Notions of the Good Life, The," *Life*, XXIV (June 28, 1948), 38.

Nolan, William F., and George Clayton Johnson. *Logan's Run*. New York: Dell Books, 1969.

Orwell, George. *Nineteen Eighty-Four*. New York: Harcourt, Brace, 1949.

Paddock, William, and Paul Paddock. *Famine — 1975!* Boston: Little, Brown, 1967.

Pearson, Drew. *The Washington Post*, November 30, 1965.

Piercy, Marge. *Dance the Eagle to Sleep*. Garden City, N. Y.: Doubleday, 1970.

Pohl, Frederik. *The Midas Plague*. In Pohl, *The Case Against Tomorrow*. New York: Ballantine Books, 1957.

Pohl, Frederik. "The Tunnel Under the World." In Pohl, *Alternating*

Currents. New York: Ballantine Books, 1956.

Pohl, Frederik. "What to Do Till the Analyst Comes." In Pohl, *Alternating Currents.* New York: Ballantine Books, 1956.

Pohl, Frederik. "The Wizards of Pung's Corners," *Galaxy* (October 1958), pp. 64-93.

Pohl, Frederik, and C. M. Kornbluth. *Gladiator-at-Law.* New York: Ballantine Books, 1955.

Pohl, Frederik, and C. M. Kornbluth. *Search the Sky.* New York: Ballantine Books, 1954.

Pohl, Frederik, and C. M. Kornbluth. *The Space Merchants.* New York: Ballantine Books, 1953.

Popper, Karl. *The Open Society and Its Enemies.* 2 vols. 4th ed., rev. Princeton, N. J.: Princeton University Press, 1963.

Rand, Ayn. *Anthem.* Caldwell, Idaho: Caxton Printers, 1964.

Roberts, Michael. "Mr. Wells' Sombre World," *The Spectator*, CLVII (December 11, 1936), 1032-1033.

Rogers, Carl R. In Carl R. Rogers and B. F. Skinner, "Some Issues Concerning the Control of Human Behavior," *Science*, CXXIV (1956), 1057-1066.

Roshwald, Mordecai. *Level 7.* New York: McGraw-Hill, 1959.

Schwitzgebel, Robert L. "A Belt From Big Brother," *Psychology Today*, II (April 1969), 45-47, 65.

Shaw, Bob. *Ground Zero Man.* New York: Avon Books, 1971.

Shaw, Bob. *One Million Tomorrows.* New York: Ace Books, 1970.

Sheckley, Robert. "The Acadamy," *If: Worlds of Science Fiction* (August 1954), pp. 45-62.

Sheckley, Robert. "Cost of Living." In Sheckley, *Untouched by Human Hands.* New York: Ballantine Books, 1954.

Sheckley, Robert. *The Status Civilization.* New York: Dell Books, 1968.

Shute, Nevil. *On the Beach.* New York: William Morrow, 1957.

Silverberg, Robert. *How It Was When the Past Went Away.* In *Three For Tomorrow.* New York: Meredith Press, 1969.

Silverberg, Robert. *Invaders From Earth.* New York: Avon Books, 1968.

Silverberg, Robert. "Passengers." In Damon Knight, ed., *Orbit 4.* New York: G. P. Putnam's Sons, 1968.

Silverberg, Robert. *To Live Again.* Garden City, N. Y.: Doubleday, 1969.

Silverberg, Robert. *Tower of Glass.* New York: Charles Scribner's Sons, 1970.

Silverberg, Robert. *The World Inside.* Garden City, N. Y.: Doubleday, 1971.

Simak, Clifford D. *Why Call Them Back From Heaven?* Garden City, N. Y.: Doubleday, 1967.

Skinner, B. F. *Beyond Freedom and Dignity.* New York: Alfred A. Knoph, 1971.

Skinner, B. F. "Freedom and the Control of Men," *The American Scholar*, XXV (Winter 1955-1956), 47-65.

Skinner, B. F. *Science and Human Behavior.* New York: Macmillan, 1953.

Skinner, B. F. "Utopia and Human Behavior," *The Humanist* (July/August

1967), pp. 120-122, 136-137.

Skinner, B. F. *Walden Two*. New York: Macmillan, 1948.

Spinrad, Norman. *Bug Jack Barron*. New York: Avon Books, 1969.

Sturgeon, Theodore. *More Than Human*. New York: Ballantine Books, 1953.

Sullivan, Richard E. "The End of the 'Long Run,'" *The Centennial Review of Arts and Sciences*, IV (Summer 1960), 391-408.

Thom, Robert. *Wild in the Streets*. New York: Pyramid Books, 1968.

Tyler, Theodore. *The Man Whose Name Wouldn't Fit*. Garden City, N. Y.: Doubleday, 1968.

"Utopias You Wouldn't Like," *Harper's*, CCX (April 1955), 87-88.

Vidal, Gore. *Messiah*. Rev. ed. Boston: Little, Brown, 1965.

Vonnegut, Kurt, Jr. *Player Piano*. New York: Holt, Rinehart and Winston, 1966.

Vonnegut, Kurt, Jr. "Tomorrow and Tomorrow and Tomorrow." In Vonnegut, *Welcome to the Monkey House*. New York: Delacorte, 1968.

Wahlöö, Peter. *The Thirty-First Floor*. Trans. Joan Tate. New York: Alfred A. Knopf, 1967.

Walsh, Chad. *From Utopia to Nightmare*. New York: Harper & Row, 1962.

Waugh, Evelyn. "Love Among the Ruins." In Waugh, *Tactical Exercise*. Boston: Little, Brown, 1954.

Wells, H. G. *Men Like Gods*. New York: Macmillan, 1923.

Wells, H. G. *Mind at the End of Its Tether*. New York: Didier, 1946.

Wells, H. G. *A Modern Utopia*. Lincoln, Nebraska: University of Nebraska Press, 1967.

Wells, H. G. *The Time Machine*. In E. F. Bleiler, ed., *Three Prophetic Novels of H. G. Wells*. New York: Dover, 1960.

Wells, H. G. *The World Set Free: A Story of Mankind*. New York: E. P. Dutton, 1914.

Williams, Donald C. "The Social Scientist as Philosopher and King," *The Philosophical Review*, LVIII (1949), 345-359.

Williams, John A. *Sons of Darkness, Sons of Light*. Boston: Little, Brown, 1969.

Williamson, Jack. *The Humanoids*. New York: Grosset & Dunlap, 1948.

Williamson, Jack. "With Folded Hands." In Sam Moskowitz, ed., *Modern Masterpieces of Science Fiction*. Cleveland: World, 1965.

Wilson, Colin. *The Mind Parasites*. New York: Bantam Books, 1968.

Wilson, Richard. "The Eight Billion." In Edward L. Ferman, ed., *The Best From "Fantasy and Science Fiction."* 15th Series. Garden City, N. Y.: Doubleday, 1966.

Wolfe, Bernard. *Limbo*. New York: Random House, 1952.

Wollheim, Donald A. *The Universe Makers: Science Fiction Today*. New York: Harper & Row, 1971.

Wouk, Herman. *The "Lomokome" Papers*. New York: Pocket Books, 1968.

Wylie, Philip. *The End of the Dream*. Garden City, N. Y.: Doubleday, 1972.

Wylie, Philip. *Triumph*. Garden City, N. Y.: Doubleday, 1963.

Wyndham, John. *Consider Her Ways*. In *Sometime, Never: Three Tales of Imagination*. New York: Ballantine Books, 1957.

Wyndham, John. *Re-Birth*. New York: Ballantine Books, 1955.

Wyndham, John. *Trouble With Lichen*. New York: Walker, 1969.

Young, Michael. *The Rise of the Meritocracy: 1870-2033*. London: Thames and Hudson, 1958.

Zamiatin, Eugene. *We*. Trans. Gregory Zilboorg. New York: E. P. Dutton, 1952.

INDEX